BUG OUT

BUG OUT

The Complete Plan for Escaping a Catastrophic Disaster Before It's Too Late

SCOTT B. WILLIAMS

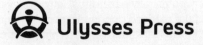

Published in the United States by
Ulysses Press
P.O. Box 3440
Berkeley, CA 94703
www.ulyssespress.com

ISBN 978-1-56975-781-9
Library of Congress Control Number 2009940327

Acquisitions Editor: Keith Riegert
Managing Editor: Claire Chun
Editor: Bill Cassell
Proofreader: Lauren Harrison
Production: Abigail Reser
Index: Sayre Van Young
Cartographer: Pease Press
Cover design: what!design @ whatweb.com
Cover images: fire © istockphoto.com/schlol,
    truck © istockphoto.com/plasticsteak1
Interior photos: See page 301

Printed in the United States by Bang Printing

10 9 8 7 6 5 4 3 2 1

Distributed by Publishers Group West

NOTE TO READERS: This book has been written and published strictly for informational purposes, and in no way should be used as a substitute for actual instruction with qualified professionals. The author and publisher are providing you with information in this work so that you can have the knowledge and can choose, at your own risk, to act on that knowledge. The author and publisher also urge all readers to be aware of their health status, to consult local fish and game laws, and to consult health care and outdoor professionals before engaging in any potentially hazardous activity. Any use of the information in this book is made on the reader's good judgment. The author and publisher assume no liability for personal injury, property damage, consequential damage or loss, however caused, from using the information in this book.

For my father,
who taught me the things that matter most, took the time to take me hunting and fishing as a kid, and instilled in me a love and appreciation for the outdoors.

TABLE OF CONTENTS

ACKNOWLEDGMENTS

As always, I would first like to thank my best friend, Michelle, for her love, encouragement, and unwavering faith during the writing process. Without her, I may never have finished this or my other books.

Special thanks to my lifelong friend Mike Jones, an officer with the Mississippi Department of Wildlife, Fisheries, and Parks, as well as a recent graduate of the Air Force SERE school, for his input on bug-out bag gear. I'm grateful to my big brother, Frank—the most knowledge-able motor vehicle enthusiast I know—for all his insight into off-road vehicles and motorcycles that was so helpful in writing Chapter Four. And without Ernest Herndon, my adventurous canoeing partner and fellow Mississippi author, I probably would not have visited half the places that I've written about in this book.

Finally, I would like to thank Keith Riegert, acquisitions editor at Ulysses Press, for recognizing the potential of this project and for help-ing me shape it into the final product you are reading here.

INTRODUCTION

Think for a minute about where you live and where you spend most of your days, whether at work or school or just out and about. For most of us these places are in cities or suburbs, or other populated areas surrounded by lots of other people; such is the reality of modern life in the United States. We've spun a web of interconnected networks of communication and transportation, and rely on a vast and complex infrastructure to hold it all together. Getting around, staying sheltered, and finding nourishment are easy, requiring little effort on an individual level, so long as all of this is working as it should. But the price of this convenience for most people is a disconnection from the land and the basic resources that sustain us. With this disconnection comes a loss of knowledge of what to do and where to go in the event of a major disaster or other disruption of our interdependent lives, so insulated from the realities of nature.

Do you know where you would go if disaster struck near you? Have you studied the exit routes that will get you out of congested areas when they become gridlocked in the event of a major breakdown? What would you take with you if it all had to fit in a single bag or pack that you could carry on your back? More importantly, where will you go if you do survive a mass exodus and make it to the surrounding countryside? Are you familiar with the uninhabited areas of your region? Are you aware that no matter where you may be in the lower 48 states, there are still remote tracts of land within a reasonable distance that offer safe hideouts and everything you need to survive for the short term, and possibly longer? If you've thought about these things, you're far ahead of most people, who will be clueless if they are ever tested in times of real trouble.

Bug Out is not another "how-to" manual on the subject of survival or living off the land. A recent surge of interest in the subject has already resulted in many excellent and comprehensive books, as well as popular television documentaries such as *Man vs. Wild* and *Survivorman* and instructional DVDs where viewers can see survival techniques demonstrated and explained. Those who want to delve more deeply into survival can choose from a variety of qualified instructors offering hands-on courses at every level.

Rather than repeat the "how-to" information, my focus here will be the "where-to" of survival. First of all, I am not assuming the usual scenario of a lost hiker, downed pilot, or other unfortunate individual who is involuntarily thrust into the wild and must survive while awaiting rescue or attempting to find a way out. Instead, I will look at voluntarily getting away from other people and finding a place sufficiently isolated to provide the essentials for short- or long-term survival using the resources nature provides.

The first step in this sort of preparation and in gathering the knowledge you need in order to know where to go is to accept the possibility that such preparation and knowledge might be needed. What could possibly happen that would require you to abandon everything you know in your comfortable surroundings? What would it take to make you head off to the nearest swamp or mountain wilderness, reduced to trying to live off the resources of the land?

The reality is that our present way of life is more susceptible to disruption or total breakdown than most people care to acknowledge. Several events in recent years bear this out and show that nothing is certain, other than uncertainty itself. The unprecedented terrorist attacks of September 11, 2001, revealed that enemies who are creative enough can find a way to strike, despite our seemingly impregnable military defense systems. Natural disasters, while usually local in impact, can cause utter chaos, as was seen when Hurricane Katrina struck the Gulf Coast in 2005.

As a resident of southern Mississippi living in the impact zone of this huge storm, I witnessed first-hand the devastation it left in its wake. This was an event that completely shut down the infrastructure of a large part of two states (Louisiana and Mississippi). Thousands of miles of roads were washed away by the storm surge or rendered impassable by fallen trees. Phone lines and cell phone towers were destroyed, erasing all communications in the region except for the few agencies equipped with satellite phones. The power grid was shut down not only in the coastal areas, but hundreds of miles inland, and it stayed down for weeks.

For those with a preparedness mind-set, the real lesson of Katrina was the desperation it caused among those left with nothing in the days and weeks that ensued. The authorities were caught unprepared and unable to respond to an event of such magnitude, and the result was a good example of what can happen when all the comforts of modern life are stripped away in the midst of the suffocating heat and humidity of a Gulf Coast summer.

Many people recognized the need for self-reliance and cooperation with their neighbors and worked together to survive and improve their situation. Others waited on outside help that was slow in coming and did little to help themselves or those around them. Still others took advantage of the situation by hoarding what they had and reselling it at exorbitant prices to those less fortunate who were left with nothing. This included food, generators, tools, and especially gasoline. Gasoline was in short supply with all stations either sold out or unable to pump what they had because of the power outage. Lines stretching for miles formed at the few stations that did have fuel to sell, leading to impatience, arguments, fistfights, and even a few shootings.

In another category altogether, beyond the impatient and overstressed victims of the disaster, were those who deliberately took advantage of the situation to pillage, loot, and rob in the lawless and mostly abandoned communities left in the storm's wake. Most of the world saw some of what was happening in New Orleans on television, but many more incidents across the region went unreported. It was a dangerous time for anyone who had to travel in the area, and it remained that way until the streets were once again lit by electric lights and order was restored along with supplies of food, fuel, and drinking water. In some areas security was not reestablished until large numbers of armed National Guard soldiers were sent in to take control.

Hurricane Katrina had a tremendous impact in the limited geographical area it affected, but those who had the means to get out of its path or leave the area shortly afterward could simply travel far enough inland to avoid all the inconvenience and danger of the aftermath. Imagine a scenario, though, where this sort of breakdown is much farther-reaching—it could happen. History has proven time and time again that no society, no matter how advanced, is immune from failure or destruction. Living in a time when life is easy, surrounded by an incredible array of technology and presented with more lifestyle options than individuals have ever enjoyed in human history, it is easy to get complacent. It is easy to forget how thin is the veneer of civilization that separates us from our ancestors and how quickly many will revert to savagery if it is all stripped away.

Dedicated survivalists have been talking about such a breakdown for years, and although it hasn't happened, it's certainly within the realm of possibility. Recent failures of corporations and financial institutions, followed by government bailouts, as well as high unemployment and a dismal economic outlook in general, have added more cause to be concerned. Some fear that a worsening economy will lead to fundamental changes in government, loss of many freedoms, and a possible declaration of martial law. Such changes could lead to widespread civil disorder and even more chaos—in short, the kind of scenario frequently discussed on Internet forums as SHTF (when the Shit Hits The Fan). These forums are abuzz with discussions on what to do if the SHTF. In fact, the topic has so dominated many firearms and survival forums that the moderators have had to resort to banning any threads dealing with SHTF or TEOTWAWKI (The End Of The World As We Know It).

Such an event may never happen your lifetime, but if you acknowledge the possibility that it could and want to do something to prepare yourself to survive, what can you do? Although many survival and preparedness experts tout the idea of buying a remote parcel of private land somewhere and building a retreat—usually stocked with supplies, guns, and ammunition to last a year or more—this is not my focus in this book. While that kind of detailed planning and preparedness is fine for those who can pull it off, most people will not have the financial means, the time, or the desire to make such a big investment in preparing for some calamity that may not come to pass. Most of us have other interests and financial concerns that preclude purchasing second homes or parcels of land somewhere in the country. Even if you can afford it, putting all your resources into one fixed location may not be desirable in many scenarios, because of the difficulty of hiding and defending what you have so carefully built and stockpiled. And without such stockpiling, small land holdings are not viable as there will not be enough resources on the land to make it self-sustaining.

It is human nature to want to hunker down in the comfort of your own home and surround yourself with the familiar, including your everyday possessions as well as the gear and supplies you've stockpiled to get through bad times. But these very possessions and carefully planned "bug-in" preps can be your undoing if you are reluctant to leave them behind when the situation dictates that moving on would be wiser. History is full of examples of people who stayed behind and died because they were not willing to pack their bags and leave. This has happened both in natural disasters such as Katrina and in times of unrest and outright war.

Most of us would be better off to learn to survive on the move and to adapt as needed to changing circumstances. This is the strategy commonly referred to as "bugging out." To bug out is to get out of Dodge quickly, carrying with you only the survival essentials that fit in a "bug-out bag," hopefully one that you have carefully packed in advance. But bugging out is useless if you don't have at least some idea of where you will go—hence the need for a handy guide to bugging out in the lower 48 states.

Note that I am deliberately not including Alaska, because residents there will likely already know where to go in a state that has more wilderness than inhabited land. I've also omitted Hawaii, because as an island state so far removed from the mainland it will most likely not be involved in the same scenario affecting the rest of the nation. But residents of those states can still use the principles in this book for planning if they are concerned.

Even in the continental U.S., it is not my intention to attempt to cover every possible location in the 48 states where someone could go into the wild and survive. There are simply far too many such places. However, by presenting enough representative bug-out locations for each region, I can provide you with the knowledge of what to look for and what to avoid so that wherever you live, you can begin finding and exploring the best possibilities nearby.

The good news is that despite an ever-increasing population and all the concrete that seems to be spreading and covering everything in sight, vast tracts of land in the United States are still uninhabited. Many of these areas are designated parks or other public recreation areas, and many more are simply undeveloped, unused, or abandoned lands that are owned by federal or state governments, corporations, or private individuals. Some of the most remote and most inaccessible wilderness areas in this country have remained practically unchanged since the first frontier explorers penetrated them. The most outstanding of these, of course, are protected as sanctuaries by the National Park Service or the National Forest Service. But many lesser-known wilderness areas are equally wild, whether they enjoy federal protection or not. And a trend away from small family farms in recent decades has resulted in many agricultural areas reverting to woodlands or tree farms as populations move to cities and suburbs and away from the land.

Proponents of the "bug-in" strategy would have you believe that there is not nearly enough land to go around and that people flooding out into the countryside would quickly consume or scare away what game there is. While that would be true if everyone in America's large population centers actually attempted to bug out, you have to remember that most people will not even try, preferring instead to wait for outside assistance while remaining helpless in their inability to take responsibility for their own survival. As a result, there will be places to go, and certainly most of them will not be overcrowded. And no matter where you bug out to, you can always move on again if need be, unlike those who have based their entire plan on one fixed location.

While I can appreciate what our cities have to offer, I've spent a large part of my life seeking out and exploring as many of the above-mentioned places as possible. Maps fascinate me and hold my attention the way most people are swept up in the plot of a gripping novel. I can spend hours studying the details and intricacies of road maps, county and state maps, forest service maps, topographical maps, and nautical charts. Maps to me are possibilities, and I find myself drawn time and time again to the empty spots on them, interspersed as they are between the roads, towns, and cities of the present reality of civilization.

The empty spots on maps have seduced me into so many hiking, backpacking, canoeing, sea kayaking, and sailing adventures that my life has been reshaped by them. I've felt a need to go and find out what was in the blank spots since I was a small boy exploring the woods near my family home. Even then I looked for the deepest hidden hollows, forgotten streambeds, and overgrown ridges where I thought I could hide out and live in the wild by hunting and fishing.

I never quite got up the nerve back then to carry out my plan to run away from the rigid rules and suffocating confinement of school, but as soon as I became an adult, I ranged far and wide whenever I had the free time. In my mid-twenties, I "checked out" for a few years when I sold all my possessions and lived and traveled out of a sea kayak in the Caribbean, Canada, and many places in between. Later, I made countless road trips throughout the country, parking my truck on the edge of wilderness areas throughout the Appalachians, Rockies, and desert Southwest and taking off on foot for weeks of solo backpacking. I experimented with the principles outlined in this book, carrying what I needed to survive and supplementing my supplies by hunting small game and gathering edible plants. I practiced evading other hikers and hunters, and bushwhacked far off the established trails to find those hidden canyons and valleys that few ever visit.

In planning my journeys, I researched places and studied maps with the idea of specifically seeking out those locations where it might be feasible to "disappear" for a while and live a life in the wild as I had dreamed of doing as a boy. I looked for the most remote and inaccessible places I could find, and then set about figuring out how I could get there and how I would get around in the area once I did. I learned a lot in my years of such travels. I found some aspects of wilderness travel

and survival much more difficult than I could have imagined, while others things came quite naturally and proved easy to implement. Some
of my trips were exceedingly difficult and I would not want to repeat
them; I experienced frustrations with faulty gear that didn't last or work
as it should, as well as disappointments in places that promised to be
virtual paradises until I actually got there. Other experiences I think
about often and look forward to trying again if given the chance. Few
things in life can match the feeling of complete freedom that learning to
travel and make yourself at home in a wild place can impart, and I feel
that every moment I've spent in the wilderness was time well-spent
that has helped me in every aspect of my life. The logical result of all
this planning and backcountry travel was, of course, the book you hold
in your hands. Hopefully what I've learned will be of use to you, and
serve as an inspiration for you to do your own survival planning—and
better yet, to get out in the wild and see for yourself what it's like to live
there, if only for a few days at a time.

Part I
Bug-Out Basics

1

THE FANTASY
& THE REALITY
OF LIVING OFF THE LAND

Americans by nature have a propensity to turn to the wilderness and start over when things get bad. After all, this country was explored and settled by a steady stream of dreamers, individualists, fortune seekers, malcontents, and assorted outlaws striking out into the untamed frontier to escape the oppression of the overly restrictive societies they left behind them to the east. The need for wilderness is embedded in our national psyche, and for many, just the idea that it is there to provide a last resort is comforting. Never mind the fact that there are no more "new frontiers" and that there is certainly not enough wilderness left anywhere on Earth to accommodate a mass exodus from the cities and suburbs. It is enough that there is wilderness at all, and most people are content to know it still exists, even if they never set foot in it. The idea that they could escape to the nearest forest, mountain range, desert, or swamp is a popular fantasy, and many people who have read a survival book or own a few items of camping gear and a knife feel that they would be okay in the event of the SHTF.

It took a long time for modern humans to progress from Stone Age hunter-gatherers to the creators of an artificial environment almost completely insulated and protected from the uncertainties of nature. As a result, you cannot expect the transition in the other direction to

FANTASY VS. REALITY

If you get your survival how-to information from television shows, movies, or adventure novels, you too might think all you need to survive in the wilderness is a good knife. Everyone knows that fictional heroes from Tarzan to Crocodile Dundee can be cast out into jungles, deserts, and mountains with nothing but a knife and not only survive but dominate their surroundings. Similar powers are often attributed to real-life figures like legendary mountain men and other frontier explorers, Native American hunters and warriors, and elite Special Forces operatives such as the Navy SEALS. The knife is portrayed as the key element that gives an otherwise helpless human the ability to overcome the odds when pitted against nature in a life-or-death struggle.

While there is certainly some basis for truth in these stories, and there are indeed a few contemporary experts who can pull this off, it is hard for most people to separate the fantasy from the reality of survival in the wild—at least until they have tried it. It's one thing to read a detailed description in a how-to book about how to carve out a bow stave and make a set of arrows to hunt with, but it's quite another experience to actually try to do this when you're deep in the woods and hungry. Watching Bear Grylls on *Man vs. Wild* demonstrating how to build a fire without matches makes it appear that anyone can do it, but how many people have tried it in a rain-soaked forest while shivering from the onset of hypothermia?

be much easier. Knowledge has been lost, skills that are necessary to thrive in the wild are difficult to learn, and senses and instincts are dulled by lack of daily use in a world where survival of the fittest is no longer the rule.

Although many people today engage in outdoor pursuits like hunting, fishing, hiking, camping, and canoeing, they often do so with the help of expensive high-tech gear like satellite communication and navigation equipment, sophisticated ultra-lightweight stoves, freeze-dried foods, and clothing and shelter systems made of synthetic fabrics. Unfortunately, much of this equipment will eventually fail and may not be replaceable. This is not a problem in times of normalcy when re-supplying or returning to civilization are viable options, but in an SHTF situation, you will far better served by cultivating skills and knowledge. Our ancestors would be amused, to say the least, at the sight of a modern backpacker struggling along under the weight of a bulky pack almost as large as the bearer. They, like the few remaining bands of aboriginal people still living in isolated groups today in places like the Amazon Basin and New Guinea, could get by with practically nothing but what could be found in their environment.

To approach the prospect of bugging out into the wilderness from a realistic perspective, you have to strike a balance somewhere between the naked native adept and the overburdened recreational outdoorsman when it comes to equipping yourself for survival. It's also important to have realistic expectations about what life in the wild will be like, whether it is just for a few days or for a period of weeks or months. Most people, especially overconfident males who are outdoor-oriented and may already be competent sport hunters and experienced campers, tend to overestimate their abilities when it comes to wilderness skills. After all, according to writers of popular literature and screenplays, manly men are supposed to be able to survive in the wilderness. Admitting to inadequacies in this department will be hard for some, but unless you've actually tested your skills beforehand, you won't really know your limits and which areas of knowledge need improvement. It's much better to test your skills now, in a situation where your life is not in the balance if you fail, than to find yourself in for a rude awakening if the time ever comes for real-life bugging out.

If you are not already an outdoorsy sort of person but are now beginning to sense the need to acquire survival skills and knowledge, you will have an advantage at least in the fact that you don't have too many preconceived notions about your abilities. Successful students of survival courses frequently come from all walks of life and from environments far removed from contact with the natural world. Anyone with a desire to learn these skills can do so; after all, they are our common heritage if you simply go back far enough. But many urban and suburban residents are now so far removed from the process of actually procuring or producing their own food that the idea of getting it in any form other than plastic packaging at the supermarket is utterly foreign. Some of these people will have a hard time adapting to digging for edible roots, identifying and gathering wild greens, and especially hunting, killing, and butchering animals for meat.

This is not meant as a comment on vegetarianism, only a statement of the fact that your life in the wild will be easier if you are flexible enough to take advantage of whatever resources you can find. In Part Two of this book, where specific bug-out locations for each region will be described, I will provide information on the types of animals and edible wild plant foods that can be found in each location. Fortunately, in most of these areas in the lower 48 states, there is an abundance of both if you know what to look for.

THE OMNIVORE'S ADVANTAGE

Meat-eating in general is going out of fashion at a surprising rate as vegetarian and vegan diets continue to gain converts. These finicky eating habits are easy to sustain in a comfortable environment where foods from anywhere in the world can be purchased in the store or ordered from the menus of an endless variety of cafés and restaurants. But in a wilderness situation, where the search for sustenance is a daily struggle, the omnivore is at a tremendous advantage.

The "hunter" in the "hunter-gatherer" way of life is there for a reason. No primitive culture past or present has found a way to subsist off what the land provides without including some form of meat in their diet, whether red meat, fish, or fowl. Completely vegetarian diets are possible only when a culture becomes stable enough to engage in dependable agriculture. Small bands of people on the move have always had to depend on a mixed diet that includes anything nutritious they can find. If you have to bug out to the wilderness today and stay there after you exhaust whatever food supplies you bring with you, you had better be prepared to hunt a variety of animals and birds, catch fish, and eat reptiles, amphibians, bird's eggs, insects, mollusks, grubs, or whatever else you can find that contains protein. Animal protein in one form or another is available in any environment you might realistically bug out to.

If you utilize all the edible parts of the animal, including fat and internal organs, you can remain healthy on animal foods alone. Finding an adequate variety of plant foods for a balanced diet can be much more difficult, depending on the location and the season. If you are squeamish about eating creatures not usually thought of as food, or killing cute, furry animals, don't worry—several days or more of real hunger will convert you right back to an enthusiastic hunter and carnivore.

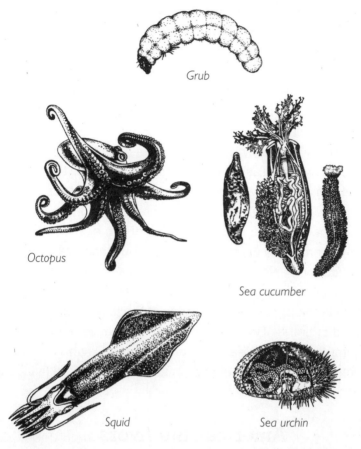

Grub

Octopus

Sea cucumber

Squid

Sea urchin

Here are some examples of protein-rich omnivorous foods found in the wild.

In discussing the hunting of animals for food, it should also be pointed out that much of what is recommended in this book is illegal in normal times and that I'm not advocating the breaking of game laws or laws against taking protected species of animals, or in some cases, plants. In addition, in some of the federally protected lands recommended as bug-out locations, such as National Park Service lands, any form of hunting or gathering of plants is forbidden. You have to be careful about breaking these laws if you are out scouting bug-out locations or honing your skills before a disaster occurs. There are plenty of species you can take legally, in season and with the proper license, as well as some that are not regulated or protected by regular hunting laws.

Some tracts of public land, such as National Forest Service lands, allow hunting and fishing, and on private lands you can often get permission from the owner. If things ever get bad enough that you have to bug out for real, however, wildlife laws will be the least of your concerns. The only laws that will matter are the laws of nature and survival. If you are hungry, you have the right to eat, just like a hungry coyote or any other predator in the wild.

In Chapter Two, I will discuss tools for hunting and food-gathering in more detail as I describe bug-out bags and the equipment you should think about including in them. For the rest of this chapter, to put more perspective on the fantasies and realities of living off the land, I think it will be helpful to look at the lives of some who have actually done it. In recent years there have been a few accounts of "modern-day mountain men" who have turned their backs on civilization and sought out lives in the wild. Even as you are reading this, it is likely that somewhere in the big wilderness areas of North America someone is attempting this. Some of these people are so disillusioned with modern life they simply decide to leave it—just as Henry David Thoreau in his time rejected the life of his peers by building a cabin and living alone in the woods.

American Survivors

Chris McCandless
One of the most publicized accounts of a young man who no longer wanted anything to do with money, material possessions, and other trappings of modern life is the story of Chris McCandless. After he perished in the Alaskan bush during his final experiment in living off the land, his story was brought to a wide audience in Jon Krakauer's best-selling book *Into the Wild*, which in 2007 was made into a successful movie.

McCandless came from a well-to-do family and was attending college when he started taking longer and longer trips into the wilderness. Soon after, he gave away most of his possessions, abandoned his car in the desert, and burned his remaining cash at the beginning of a multiyear odyssey of drifting about in the American West, hitchhiking, working odd jobs, and exploring the wild. His longing to leave everything else behind him eventually took him to Alaska, where he hiked to a remote, abandoned hunting camp and took up residence for the summer.

In the journal entries he recorded up until his death, he describes how he successfully lived as a hunter-gatherer, foraging for edible plants and hunting with a .22 caliber rifle. Although he mainly shot birds and other small game with the rifle, he also took down a moose with it at one point. McCandless was by no means an expert at wilderness survival, as is pointed out in Krakauer's book. That he fared as well as he did indicates what someone with more skills and the right equipment could accomplish. That he was able to kill big game, as well as small animals, with the .22 illustrates the versatility of his choice in firearms. But McCandless didn't know how to preserve the meat he'd secured, and so most of it was wasted. At one point he was satisfied with his experience and tried to leave, but the small stream he had crossed months earlier on the way in was now a raging torrent, barring his exit, so he had no choice but to return to his camp. He later made a fatal mistake when he misidentified what he thought was an edible root, inadvertently eating quantities of a toxic look-alike that soon rendered him too weak to hunt or even leave his camp. He died of starvation, alone in the wilderness, because of this mistake. But as Krakauer points out, other than this one mistake, McCandless was succeeding in his wilderness living experiment, and up until that point he was well-fed and healthy.

Martin Price

In the 1980s, another man who felt as if he was born 150 years too late attempted to recreate a mountain-man lifestyle in New Mexico's Gila Wilderness, one of the wildest areas in the lower 48, and a first-rate bug-out location that will be described in Chapter Eleven. Price learned some of his survival skills in the military while serving as a paratrooper with the 82nd Airborne. He liked the training, but hated the discipline. Before taking up residence in the Gila, Price put what he'd learned to use by living for months at a time in the Chiricahua

Mountains and Mazatzal Wilderness in Arizona, and in the Sawtooth Mountains of Idaho. In the Gila he survived by spearing fish, building fish traps in the streams, and hunting with a .22 rifle, a .270 rifle, and a .41 Magnum revolver.

Martin Price became a legend in the Gila Wilderness for a number of years, occasionally spotted by hikers and pursued by law enforcement for his survival poaching. He might have succeeded in living the lifestyle he chose there had he been a little more low-profile. The main reason for his undoing was not the poaching of deer and other wild game, but his occasional killing of the free-range cattle from ranches neighboring the Gila. He was arrested and jailed more than once, but none of this deterred him from heading back into the wild to live his chosen lifestyle each time he was released. Years after his prolonged stay in the Gila, he once again took up a wilderness lifestyle near Prescott, Arizona, resuming his deer poaching and cattle killing. When local sheriff's deputies went to arrest him, he refused to surrender and go back to jail, and died in the ensuing shootout.

Kayak Bill

Like the rugged and game-rich Gila Wilderness, the coastal islands of the Pacific Northwest from Puget Sound to Southeast Alaska are an ideal place for living off the land. The diversity of edible plants, game, fish, and other sea life makes hunting and gathering relatively easy. For about 30 years, this rich environment along coastal British Colombia was home to a solitary wilderness dweller known as Kayak Bill.

Kayak Bill had a family and sometimes returned to civilization, but spent most of his time alone, with everything he needed fitting into a sea kayak—the ideal vehicle for traveling and living in this island wilderness. Kayak Bill lived off the land from his kayak, moving between a series of hidden camps that he established on the most remote and inhospitable shores of these forested islands. From sometime around 1975 until his death in 2004, he drifted like a ghost on these waters, occasionally letting himself be seen and talking with recreational kayakers transiting the area. Prior to discovering the kayak as his ultimate escape vehicle, he is said to have lived for a year and a half in the

Canadian Rockies, hunting with a bow and arrows. Kayak Bill's story came to light not long after his death in a feature article in *Sea Kayaker* magazine.

Tom Brown Jr. and Jim Corbett

Some wilderness wayfarers have been more interested in spiritual quests than escaping from a society they did not fit into. Many of these have written their own first-person accounts of their journeys into the wild, though it is often hard to distinguish the facts from embellishments that make for more interesting reading. One such writer is Tom Brown Jr. (also known as "The Tracker"), who has written several field guides to survival skills as well as narratives of his personal vision quests and his apprenticeship under an elderly Apache medicine man. If half of what he claims is true, Tom Brown Jr. is certainly one of those few modern masters of wilderness survival who can go into the woods with nothing but a knife and come out well-fed. He claims to have done just that when he turned eighteen, walking naked into the New Jersey Pine Barrens and living off the land for more than a year with Stone Age tools he made himself. His books are quite popular among those studying survival skills, and he also operates a survival and tracking school he established to pass on his knowledge.

A lesser-known spiritual seeker and desert wanderer is Jim Corbett, who wrote the fascinating book *Goatwalking: A Guide to Wildland Living*. Corbett writes of spending long periods of time wandering in the deserts of the southwestern U.S. and northern Mexico. What is unique about his approach is that he wanders alone or sometimes with a few companions, accompanied by a small herd of milk goats, like the ancient desert nomads of the Old Testament he so frequently references in the book. He claims that the milk and occasional meat provided by the goats, along with few wild plants, were all he needed to survive this harshest of environments. The goats are completely self-sufficient and can find forage in places no other large mammal can survive. According to Corbett, "goatwalking" is the surest way for an individual or small group of people to disappear into terrain so inhospitable that no one would think to look for them there.

Eric Robert Rudolph

The other men described in this chapter chose to live in the wilderness in search of solitude or spiritual solace. A much different case is that of accused domestic terrorist and abortion-clinic bomber Eric Robert Rudolph, who was the subject of a highly publicized, five-year-long manhunt.

After being named as a suspect in the 1996 Olympic bombings in Atlanta, Rudolph was listed on the FBI's Ten Most Wanted list in 1998. Evading capture, Rudolph disappeared into the Appalachian mountain wilderness of North Carolina and was hunted by federal police, the U.S. military, local law enforcement, and amateur search teams without success. He may at times have had the assistance of anti-government sympathizers during his lengthy years of evasion, but in his writings he tells of eating acorns and salamanders, raiding vegetable gardens and even dumpsters on the outskirts of small towns, and retreating to hidden camps on the thickly wooded ridges. Rudolph was, by all accounts, no expert wilderness survivalist, but his success at such long-term evasion under the stress of an intense manhunt illustrates how a willingness to suffer the discomfort of hiding out in the wild can allow even those with marginal skills to survive and avoid capture for long periods of time. He was eventually apprehended by a local policeman while on a dumpster raid in the wee hours of the morning behind a small-town grocery.

Rudolph's arrest is typical of what happens to most wilderness fugitives, who are caught because they can't stand the isolation and either turn themselves in or let their longing to be near other people put them in situations where they are more likely to be discovered. A determined individual or small group with the right skills can avoid detection in a big wilderness area almost indefinitely if the temptation to return to civilization can be resisted.

Since the premise of this book is that you will bug out to the wilderness because you have a very good reason to do so, it will likely be easier for you to adopt the proper mind-set to stay away from places that could mean trouble. And unlike the lone fugitive, you may be able to ally yourself with other individuals or small groups who are in the same predicament. In all likelihood, if the situation is bad enough for you to leave town to begin with, either you will not want to go back or there will be nothing to go back to. And since going back is not an option, you will be wise to bring what you need with you when you first bug out. The specifics of this will be the subject of the next chapter.

2

THE BUG-OUT BAG & STUFF YOU'LL NEED TO SURVIVE

The subject of what to include in a survival kit or bug-out bag comes up frequently in books, articles, Internet discussion forums, and campfire conversations about wilderness survival. People have a tendency to become fixated on the gear that they imagine they will need much more than the skills that will enable them to succeed with or without help from their equipment. Skills require a lot of work and large investments of time to learn; gear can be bought off the shelf or ordered through the mail. Gear is impressive to show off and talk about with your friends, while skills are intangible and may not be apparent until they are needed.

There is no end to the development and marketing of new survival gadgets and gear. This is a lucrative market for outdoor equipment manufacturers and they know how to take advantage of it. Some of these new developments may actually prove to be useful tools for the serious survivalist. Others are more useful for separating you from money that could be better spent on tried-and-true essentials. In this chapter, I will stick with the basics when describing items that I feel you should have ready at all times to take with you if you have to bug out to the wild.

My suggestions here are based on my extensive personal experience during long forays into many different types of wilderness environments. I realize many readers will also have extensive outdoor experience and will have other preferences regarding some of my choices of equipment. If you have a bug-out setup that works well for you, I'm not attempting to convince you to change it. But for the many that do not have such experience, I hope this will provide food for thought in gathering the essential gear. Keep in mind also that in this chapter the focus is on a basic kit of gear that can be carried on your back in a worst-case scenario where you must bug out on foot. If you are evacuating by vehicle, boat, canoe, on horseback, or by other means, you can, of course, carry more equipment and supplies. These transportation options will be discussed in Chapter Four. If you can carry more, you will have the option of carting along many extras that will be nice to have in a survival situation. But the basics as described in this chapter, if you have the skills to use them properly, will be enough to keep you alive.

Considering the Bug-Out Bag Options

In the process of acquiring your gear, I would urge you to carefully consider every single item you include in your bug-out bag, think of exactly how you will use it, and decide if it is indeed essential or not. For this reason, I also advise against buying any of the generic pre-packaged "survival kits" you will often see for sale. These kits will include things you may not need for your specific area and omit other essentials. It's much better to research and collect each item one at a time and test it in the environment where you expect to use it, if at all possible.

The concept of the "bug-out bag" means different things to different people. To some, it is a 72-hour emergency kit that will include food, water, and other essentials to see you through the first 72 hours of some disaster where you have to leave your home and head for a safe haven. For other survivalists expecting disorder and breakdown on the scale of Armageddon, it includes not only survival essentials, but combat gear such as flak jackets, assault weapons, and enough loaded magazines to equip a soldier on patrol in Afghanistan. Here, I will not assume you can find safety and comfort again within 72 hours, nor will I encourage you to prepare to engage in firefights with a heavily armed enemy. In the first case, you might be severely disappointed, and in the second, you will likely be killed before you even begin to test your survival skills.

For the purposes of this book, the bug-out bag will be a way to carry those things that will enable you to more easily escape to and live in a remote, wild area without outside help, whether for just the first 72 hours or for a much longer period of time. The focus will be on items that are durable and dependable, and not easily manufactured or duplicated from anything you will find in nature.

The bug-out bag and the things inside it should be the minimum a prepared person always has close at hand and ready to go. If you keep it at home or in a vehicle during normal times, you can keep additional clothing, food, or gear alongside it, but the bag alone should allow you to be self-sufficient in case it is impossible to take anything else. It is a good idea is to add a small belt or fanny pack that is always kept with the bug-out bag, containing a few smaller items of the most essential gear that can be worn at all times in case you are ever separated from the main bag. This pack can be worn in front at the waist while carrying the main bag on your back. The contents of the bug-out bag will be adjusted, of course, for your specific area of operation. Part Two of this book, where I describe bug-out locations, will discuss any specialized or location-specific items of gear that you may need.

Choosing a Bug-Out Bag

What you use for the bug-out bag itself can vary widely depending on your needs and preferences, but it should be rugged enough to withstand the abuse of hard backcountry travel and designed to be easily carried for long distances and over rough terrain. This narrows it down to some sort of backpack, but there are so many different kinds that making a choice can be difficult. Many of the backpacks advertised as "bug-out backpacks" do not even come close to meeting the most important requirements: number one, that everything you will need will fit in it, and number two, that it has a well-designed system of straps and a hip belt to correctly distribute the load so that it can be carried long distances. The small, mostly square-shaped daypacks you frequently see billed as bug-out bags do not have deep enough compartments for longer items, such as a sheathed machete and a take-down or folding stock–equipped survival rifle. This is important, as these will attract unwanted attention unless they are hidden inside your pack, so you need an undivided internal compartment that is at least 24 inches deep. Many of these smaller packs also omit the hip belt, so all of the weight is carried on your shoulders, which is not a good idea for any but the lightest loads.

Military Surplus Bags

Items of military gear or copies of military designs are popular with some survivalists and have a "tacti-cool" factor that sells, but contrary to popular belief, much of this gear is not of optimal quality or design compared to other options on the market. Military gear, especially camouflaged backpacks and clothing, is also commonly associated with the heavily armed paramilitary type of survivalist and will attract undue attention from law enforcement and others in the aftermath of a bug-out situation.

Backpacking Bags

The best-designed backpacks are produced by a few specialized manufacturers catering to the extreme outdoor recreation market. These are the companies that outfit mountaineering expeditions and other serious outdoor enthusiasts who depend completely on their equipment. For a good bug-out backpack, look hard at some of the medium-sized internal frame packs designed for summit attempts. More compact than a full-sized pack designed for long backpacking trips, these packs are designed to carry enough stuff to bivouac for a night or two if a climber is caught by bad weather and can't get back to the base camp. They are also increasingly popular with hikers subscribing to the ultra-light, go-fast philosophy.

These packs have the right shape and profile to keep you balanced, and will not protrude far enough from your body to snag brush or other obstructions as you move through the woods. They are typically long and narrow, to fit the profile of the back, so they usually have the necessary deep compartment to conceal your longer items. Internal stays that create the frame and padded hip belts allow you to carry heavy loads without strain. These backpacks can be found in high-end mountaineering shops, discount outdoor equipment retail stores like REI, big general sporting goods stores like Bass Pro Shops, and online. They are common and do not attract attention. Although many come in bright colors so they will photograph well on white glacial slopes, most are also offered in dull shades of green, gray, or brown that will blend into the environment. You don't have to purchase a top-of-the-line model, either; several companies offer reasonably priced alternatives based on the designs of the high-end models that are built just as well for the requirements of a bug-out bag. I recently examined a selection of such backpacks that ranged in price from under $100 up to about $250. Though you don't have to buy top-of-the-line, I would recommend sticking to name brands and spending a little more for quality.

Filling Your Bag

Once you decide on the pack that will become your bug-out bag, the next step is to think in terms of the pressing needs you will have once you're on your own away from the safety net of civilization. It helps to remember the "rule of threes" when thinking about the priorities of survival: It takes about three hours to die without shelter (assuming a cold enough climate), three days to die without water, and about three weeks to die without food. By this rule, depending on where you live, you can see that shelter—meaning some way to keep dry and keep your body temperature regulated—is the top priority when it comes to outfitting your bug-out bag.

Shelter for bug-out purposes will be a combination of the clothing you wear and purpose-designed gear, such as tarps, tents, and the tools to build shelters from natural materials. Working from the inside out, we will first take up the subject of clothing.

Clothing

Assuming that in an emergency bug-out situation you may not be wearing clothing suitable for outdoor living, a complete change of clothing should be in the bag ready to go, or strapped to the outside of it so you can quickly change at the first opportunity. This clothing should include footwear and headgear, as well as the appropriate layers of cold weather protection you will need depending on the climate of your location and the time of year.

Footwear

Footwear can range from heavy insulated and waterproof boots to lightweight hiking boots—again depending on the terrain you expect to have to traverse. The main criterion when selecting footwear is to chose boots or shoes of durable construction that you can depend on to last for an extended wilderness stay. Far too many so-called hiking boots will fall apart after a short time, especially if they are repeatedly soaked in stream crossings. In addition to your boots, I also strongly urge you to consider a pair of quality river sandals or river shoes of the type used by whitewater rafters and kayakers. They will take up little space and weigh little, but will prolong the life of your boots if you wear them for crossing streams and around camp, while keeping you from having wet boots and socks that will take hours to dry.

Socks

Under the boots or shoes, you should be wearing wool and synthetic socks, the layers depending on the temperature. There are many types of synthetic inner socks available today that wick moisture away from your feet and help prevent blistering. Wool is a time-tested material that still keeps you warm even when wet. Have at least two complete changes of whatever socks you choose so that one pair can be drying out while the other is in use.

Headgear

Head protection should include a pull-over wool watch cap or bala-clava (ski mask) for cold climates and a crushable canvas hat with a decent brim for sun protection. One piece of military gear that may prove useful is the classic "boonie" hat in plain khaki, which fills the bill well for sun protection. It's inexpensive, yet durable and comfortable.

Bandanas can be tied in various configurations to protect the head and neck in extreme sun exposure conditions, can take the place of the sun hat if you happen to lose it, and take up almost no space.

Boonie hats, such as this one, provide important protection from the sun.

Pants

Other than the boonie hat, the only other item of military surplus that I prefer over commercial alternatives is the standard ripstop BDU (Battle Dress Uniform) pants. BDUs have all the attributes of good outdoor pants: They are lightweight yet tough, loose fitting for easy movement, and offer big cargo pockets, a button fly, and drawstring cuffs to close off the leg openings. For years they have been my standard outerwear in the wilderness. They dry fast when wet, and are not too hot in the summer when I would otherwise be wearing shorts, and are surprisingly warm in cold weather. Because of their baggy fit, you can wear under-layers of synthetic long underwear or polar fleece. Like the boonie hat, BDUs are available in a wide variety of solid colors and camo patterns. Solid khaki, olive drab, or brown will allow you to blend in outdoors without attracting the kind of unwanted attention drawn by a military backpack, for instance. Ideally, you will be wearing, or will change into, a pair of these pants along with your boots when bugging out,

so you should have room for a spare pair as well as the under-layers in your bug-out bag. You should also add a final layer of lightweight outer pants with a wind- and waterproof breathable membrane like Gore-Tex if you are bugging out in winter or in high mountain country.

Belt

Don't forget a sturdy belt to go with your pants. A good belt will come in handy for carrying all sorts of things you will need close at hand later after you have reached the wilds. You can then use it to openly carry things like a sheathed knife or machete, multi-tool, and holstered handgun and spare magazines.

Upper Body Wear

For upper body protection, I don't really like the fit of BDU tops and prefer a loose, heavy cotton-canvas long-sleeve in hot, buggy environments and wool sweaters or polar fleece over long underwear for cold conditions. If conditions permit, a T-shirt in a color that blends in with your surroundings is the most comfortable option.

Waterproof Outerwear

If conditions require it, the final layer of protection over your shirt or sweater should be a good waterproof but breathable parka—the kind that comes down well over your hips and has a hood incorporated in the collar. This parka is perhaps your most important piece of clothing in cold or wet weather, and you should choose a high-quality one with a Gore-Tex or equivalent membrane.

With the wool watch cap worn under the hood of the parka, and a layer of synthetic long underwear under a wool sweater and the lightweight Gore-Tex pants over your BDU pants, as well as wool socks and good boots, you will have protection from all but the worst weather. Since you can only carry so much in a small bug-out backpack, if conditions deteriorate worse than what your clothing can protect you from, you will have to find or make a temporary shelter.

Shelter

Aside from the clothing you wear, shelter for protection from the elements falls into two categories: what you carry with you for the purpose and what you can find or make in the wilderness. Utilizing natural shelters such as caves may be an option in some locations, and in most environments you can build rudimentary shelters from natural materials found in your surroundings. Drawings and explanations for these shelter types can be found in any basic wilderness survival book, but if you are on the move and already exhausted or weak from hard travel, life will be much easier if you have with you the basics of making shelter anywhere.

Blankets and Sleeping Bags

Beyond clothing, your next line of defense against the elements will be a heavy-duty emergency space blanket, a sleeping bag, or a bivy sack. A good space blanket is the most compact and inexpensive option, but not much of a long-term solution. Sleeping bags are the bulkiest option, although some of the really good ones pack down to a surprisingly small space. In really cold regions a good sleeping bag will be essential, and this is no place to skimp when purchasing equipment. The bivy (for bivouac) sack is an outer bag designed to allow you to sleep on the ground while keeping you warm and dry. In the coldest climates, a bivy sack with sleeping bag inside and a self-inflating sleeping pad beneath could make the difference between life and death. Carrying all this, however, will force you to choose a bigger backpack or cut down on supplies and other equipment. In warmer regions or in the summer season, you can get by with just the bivy sack or a compact polar fleece blanket that zips up to form a sleeping bag.

Tents

In normal backpacking or recreational wilderness camping conditions, a small tent is standard equipment for most people. But even lightweight tents made for hikers are bulky when packed, primarily because they require poles to stand them up and hold their shape. The other down-side of backpacking tents is that, by design, they are constructed of lightweight materials and include things that don't last—like zippers. I've had firsthand experience with how poorly even the most expensive tents perform over time. On one of my longest sea kayaking trips, a top tent manufacturer provided me with their best "expedition-quality" tent. They had to replace it twice because of broken poles, failed zippers, and countless other problems. Any tent that is lightweight enough to carry simply will not last in a long-term bug-out situation.

Other Options

For a shelter that will fit in a bug-out bag that will be carried on foot, it will be wise to look at simpler options than tents. An ordinary tarp can be the ultimate shelter in many environments, and its versatility allows it to be set up in many different ways. The key to making a tarp work for a portable shelter is knowing how to rig it and having adequate line, as well as a knife or machete for cutting poles and stakes. The best tarps have many tie-down points in the form of reinforced grommets along the edges and in the corners. For packing in a bug-out bag, avoid the cheap poly tarps sold in home-improvement stores and look instead for a higher-quality tarp made of lightweight, coated ripstop nylon, of the kind used in the best tents. Tarps made of this material weigh little and fold compactly. They will also last longer in the sun's UV rays and better withstand the strain of high winds. An even more compact option in milder climates and conditions is a poncho made of the same coated nylon. A large poncho can serve as your rainwear, allowing you to forgo the parka and weatherproof outer pants described earlier, and double as a tarp shelter when you set up camp.

Hammocks

The only problem with tarps and ponchos as shelters is that they do not incorporate insect netting—leaving you with no protection from pests such as mosquitoes or more dangerous crawling things such as scorpions, spiders, and snakes. If you expect to be bugging out in one of the southern desert or swamp regions, this is an important consideration. It's worth looking at the highly refined jungle hammocks such as those manufactured by Hennessy Hammocks, a relatively new alternative on the market. These one-person shelters weigh in at around two and a half pounds and do not require poles, only trees or other structures from which to suspend them. The Hennessy Hammock design allows easy entry and exit through the bottom, and includes mosquito netting and a well-designed rainfly. This is one innovative shelter that is more than just a gimmick and could be a serious alternative for your bug-out bag shelter. Such a hammock is not ideal in cold weather, but it can be set up on the ground and rigged like a tent, and in these conditions insects and other crawling things won't be an issue.

Whether you carry a tarp, poncho, or hammock for your primary shelter, you will also need the tools to clear brush, make poles or stakes, and build a fire—the final component to a comfortable home away from home.

Axes, Machetes, and Knives

In North America, the traditional woodsman's tool is the axe. With an axe, a skilled person can literally carve a home out of the wilderness, as was often done by frontier settlers. But the shorter, lighter hatchet that is so commonly substituted in modern camping is no replacement for a good axe. The hatchet came into widespread use because it's more convenient to carry than an axe, but it is far less useful. I'm not suggesting that you carry an axe in your bug-out bag, or give up the hatchet if you are skilled and comfortable with it. What I am suggesting, though, is that you consider a far more versatile tool that is used in the tropics around the globe in one variation or another: the machete. With a quality machete, you can do anything you would do with a hatchet, and much, much more. The machete will also be lighter and will hardly take up any room in your pack if you choose one with a blade from 18 to about 26 inches long, depending on your preference. Longer is better in areas of dense undergrowth and thickets. Unlike the hatchet, the machete is an excellent tool for cutting trail, its broad swath easily taking care of vines, springy branches, and the like that would be hard to even hit with an axe-type blade.

A machete can enable you to get at many difficult to harvest edible plant foods, such as the inner bark of trees, palmetto hearts, and the edible parts of various cacti. You can cut firewood, shelter materi-

A quality machete is lighter and more compact than an axe.

als, and wooden parts for making hunting weapons and animal traps. The machete can double as a large utility knife and can be used for skinning and butchering game, peeling fruits, and many intricate tasks you would not normally associate with such a big blade. In jungle regions throughout the world, the machete is a tool of a thousand uses. In my travels in Central America and the Caribbean, I have often been amazed at the innovative ways I have seen it put to use, and I have since carried one on all my outdoor journeys.

A good machete can easily be kept razor-sharp if you include a small mill file in your kit. And since the blade is so sharp, it should always be carried in a sheath so that you can keep it inside the bug-out bag when you need to be discreet. Since a long, sharp chopping blade like a machete is also a formidable weapon in the right hands, you will want to keep it out of sight while still in urban areas and around officials on your way out of town.

The machete will also help you in making fire, enabling you to get to dry kindling and tinder in the wettest of conditions if you keep it sharp. If you have no other means of making fire, the machete will make it easier to cut and shape the parts for a bow drill as well. But since fire-making tools are so lightweight and compact, and easily carried in a belt pack or a pocket if you don't have your bug-out bag, there is no excuse for being out in the wild without some means of making a fire.

Fire-Making Tools

If you are really serious about wilderness survival skills, you should study and practice with primitive fire-making tools such as the bow drill until you are confident you can build a fire with them in any conditions. But even if you can do this, modern methods of making fire are compact to carry and much easier to use.

The simplest of all tools for making fire are disposable butane lighters, which weigh practically nothing and will last a long time if you use them conservatively. Kayak Bill, the solitary paddler mentioned in Chapter One, is said to have purchased a hundred dollars worth of these at a time—not a bad investment for someone living full time among the rain-soaked wilderness islands of the Pacific Northwest. I suggest distributing a good supply of these throughout your bugout bag in various compartments, in your belt pack if you have one, and in the pockets of your clothing. They are cheap and take up so little space you'll hardly notice they are there.

Despite the convenience of butane lighters, you need other alternatives, especially for longer

Rubbing flint against steel is a primative, yet effective, way to start a campfire.

stays, during which time you will eventually exhaust your supply of them. The combination of flint and steel has a long history as a reliable wilderness firestarter, and now you can buy improved variations of the concept in the form of "fire steel" firestarters that utilize a ferrocerium rod instead of the flint, and include a steel scraping blade for generating sparks from the rod. These tools produce a shower of hot sparks that will readily ignite dry, properly prepared tinder. They are small and lightweight, and are rated for thousands of strikes. Plan on carrying at least two of these in addition to your butane lighters and you will be set for a long time. You'll also want a few of those square, cigar-sized "firestarter" sticks that are sold in camping supply stores or some cotton balls soaked in melted petroleum jelly. These are great to aid in quickly getting an emergency fire going in cold, wet conditions when you might need it in a hurry.

Although fire can save your life in many situations and is nice to have in camp anytime, for warmth and light as well as for cooking, it can also be a dead giveaway if you are in a bug-out situation that requires evasion and keeping a low profile. If you know others are nearby or that someone is looking for you or following you, it may not be safe to build a fire at all. Otherwise, you can greatly decrease the risk of detection by keeping your fires small and burning the driest wood possible to reduce the smoke. Smoke is also diffused better if the fire is built under dense, overhanging branches. A very small fire will provide all the benefits of a large one; you just have to sit closer to it for warmth.

If the fire is only needed for cooking, you can keep it small and hot by using dry twigs about the size of a pencil instead of larger branches and logs. A twig fire like this will burn hot and fast and can be quickly extinguished when you're done.

Water

Beyond the immediate need for shelter, next on your list of priorities will be finding water. Unless you are in some of the driest desert regions of the Western U.S., water will be infinitely easier to obtain than food, and that is a good thing as you will need it much sooner to stay alive. In many parts of the country, rivers, streams, lakes, and swamps will be found in abundance and you will never be far from a source of water. The best places to look for sources of drinking water, including in arid regions where it is scarce, will be discussed in more detail in each regional chapter where specific bug-out locations are described. For the purpose of this bug-out bag discussion, what is important is that you have a way to carry some water with you and a way to purify that which you do find, which in all likelihood will be unsafe to drink as is.

No matter how clear a creek, brook, or remote lake may appear, chances are it is contaminated with either man-made pollutants or naturally occurring biological pathogens such as Giardia. Only springs at their source are safe to drink from as is, and you will not likely find many of those while on the move, so you will have to treat or filter any ground water you find. One of the most effective ways of purifying water is simply bringing it to a boil. But this is time-consuming and requires building a fire when it may not be safe to do so because of the risk of detection. Today, there are better options that fit into two categories: chemical treatment to destroy any waterborne pathogens, and micro-filtration systems that remove these as well as some inorganic pollutants.

Chemical Purifiers

In my bug-out bag, I have one simple solution that has always worked for me, from every part of the United States to the jungle rivers of Central America where there are many more exotic parasites than are found in

North America. That solution is in the chemical purifier category—an iodine water treatment called Polar Pure. Polar Pure is a small glass bottle of iodine crystals, specially designed with a particle trap so that they cannot come out when it is filled with water to make a treatment solution. You simply fill the bottle with any water, pure or contaminated, shake it up well, and let it sit for an hour. This concentrated solution is then measured into your quart drinking bottle by the capful; the number of capfuls required is dependant upon the temperature of the water in the Polar Pure bottle, which has a built-in thermometer. Polar Pure is simple to use, the bottle is tiny and weighs little, and the supply of iodine in it is enough to last for many years of water treatments. For approximately 15 dollars, it's really hard to beat. If you want to carry an alternative, backup means of chemical purification, several varieties of tablets are available, such as Potable Aqua and Micropur. The disadvantages of these is that the tablets dissolve and so the amount of water that can be treated is much more limited.

Filtration Systems

Some people prefer the excellent water filtration systems that are available, such as those made by Katadyn. These are especially useful on the shorter trips they were designed for, but the filters will eventually need replacing, and the pump and filters are much bulkier and heavier than a bottle of Polar Pure. The one situation where filters are better than chemical treatment is where you have to drink from larger streams and rivers that are muddy and turbid with lots of particles in suspension. Iodine will do nothing to clear up water like that, but in most areas you can avoid taking your drinking supply from major waterways and instead find small tributaries or standing rainwater. For extra insurance in areas where pollution is more prevalent, you can carry a compromise of sorts in the form of a compact drinking straw filter such as the Aquamira Frontier. Then you can treat questionable water with Polar Pure and use the straw to filter it through for an extra measure of safety. An even more specialized type of water filter is the reverse-osmosis desalinator, which can render seawater drinkable. These are expensive and require expensive filters, but could be invaluable if you plan to bug out to places like remote barrier islands where there is no fresh water supply.

Water Bottles

Regardless of how you purify your water, you will need a way to carry some with you. I highly recommend the 1-quart-sized Nalgene water bottles that are found everywhere camping supplies are sold. These are leak-proof, sturdy, and will last for years. Get the wide-mouth models for easier filling, and carry at least two in your bug-out bag—four or more if you are in one of the arid regions of the country. Needless to say, they should be filled with pure water from the beginning when you are packing your bag, so you will have a ready supply of water when you first move out.

Food

Finding food while on the move is going to be more problematic than finding water. Remember, if you have to bug out in the first place, you will probably be doing so because you have a good reason to get out of town in a hurry. You will be under stress and will need energy to keep you going. This is why it is essential to have a supply of high-energy food items in your bug-out bag to sustain you during the early stages of your evacuation. Think in terms of calorie-to-weight ratio and choose the highest-calorie foods that you can pack into a small space. You can choose from a vast array of high-energy sports bars, meal replacement bars, lifeboat rations, or military MREs. Some of the lifeboat rations such as Mainstay or Datrex come in daily supplies of 1200, 2400, or 3600 calories, allowing you to budget calories for a given number of days. Like MREs, lifeboat rations are designed to have a long shelf life, and taste is of secondary importance.

There are also options for high-energy foods that are available in any grocery store. I always carry a trail mix I make up myself from ingredients such as almonds, sunflower seeds, raisins and other dried fruit, and semisweet dark chocolate chips. (These mixes are not suitable for long-term storage, but I use them regularly for day trips and such, so I always have a fresh supply available for the bug-out bag.)

Granola bars and many types of "breakfast bars" can also be found at the grocery store, along with specialized energy bars such as Power Bars and Clif Bars. You can add a few small packages of beef jerky to your bug-out bag as well, and just about anything else that has a high calorie-to-weight ratio. For bugging out, you will want to have foods that can be eaten right out of the package. But since hot food can be extremely comforting when you are under stress and are tired, it can't hurt to have a few items that can be quickly prepared with hot water—such as some oatmeal (which can also be eaten uncooked), packages of flavored instant rice, and a small supply of hot chocolate or coffee. Once you reach a sufficiently remote area, there will be plenty of time for foraging and hunting for more substantial meals that require cooking.

Cooking Pot

On the subject of cooking, one veteran desert traveler said that if he could take only one item from civilization on an extended stay in the wilderness, he would choose a metal pot above all else—even over a steel knife. His reasoning is that you can make a variety of cutting blades from flint and other stones that can be broken into sharp flakes, but making a cooking pot from what nature provides is much more difficult. A metal pot allows you to utilize many plant foods such as roots, leaves, and stalks that would be inedible raw. It also allows you to boil water, not only for drinking, but also for making soups from scraps of meat and bones you may have left over from a kill. In addition, it provides a way to render other animal parts into usable materials such as hide glue.

All you need is one simple pot, made of good stainless steel so that you can cook in it using fire. The ultra-light backpacking cookware sold for use with stoves will not last long used this way. I prefer a stainless steel pot of 4-quart capacity, which is sold in any department store's cookware section. I remove the handle and throw it away to make the pot more packable, and likewise remove the plastic knob from the lid. You can handle the pot with a spare T-shirt or bandana, or the pliers in a multi-tool (more on these later).

While I was sea kayak camping on a remote stretch of tropical coast in the Dominican Republic, some local coconut growers taught

me a super-simple trick for cooking with a metal pot over a tiny
fire. They simply cut three green
stakes of equal size from a small
sapling with their machetes, and
used a rock to pound them into the
ground at converging angles, creating a sturdy tripod that supported
the pot about four inches off the
ground. A twig fire using sticks
about the size of a pencil had the
water boiling as fast as I could
have done it with my Coleman gas
stove. I've since used this trick everywhere I've traveled in the wil-

How to set up your cooking pot over the campfire.

derness, though in some rocky areas where the ground is too hard to
drive stakes, large stones can be substituted for the wooden tripod.
Whatever you do, don't leave out a suitable metal pot and lid when
packing your bug-out bag. It doesn't take up space because the interior of the pot can be packed with small items, such as your energy
bars, trail mix, ammunition, or whatever.

Firearms for Hunting and Defense

Now it's time to look at everyone's favorite subject of discussion, debate,
and argument when it comes to survival gear: firearms. Unfortunately,
when it comes to firearms you can choose from for a bug-out situation, compromise is the operative word. For survival hunting and self-
defense, there is no perfect solution and no one gun—whether pistol,
revolver, rifle, or shotgun—that can do everything best in all situations.

Like many outdoors enthusiasts and wilderness travelers, I feel a
deep affinity for my guns and own many more than I could ever use
in a given situation. Growing up in a small town in Mississippi with
woods just a short walk from my door, I started hunting at an early age
and learned to shoot and handle guns of many different calibers and

configurations. I learned the advantages and disadvantages of different weapons by carrying them in the field, and over the years I have owned a wide variety of rifles, shotguns, and handguns designed for small- and big-game hunting, as well those suited for self-defense and combat.

To optimize your selection of firearms to take with you in a bug-out situation, you must first balance the priorities of food gathering versus defense against threats of the two-legged and four-legged variety you may encounter in your bug-out location. Then, you must realistically assess how much weight you must carry in other essential items besides firearms and the weight of the requisite ammunition to keep them useful for the longest period of time. This can be a complex equation to work out. I'll go right ahead and state my personal choices, then explain my reasoning for them and provide some alternatives that may suit some readers better. Keep in mind that we are talking about bugging out, not remaining in a fortified bunker armed with AK-47s and stacks of loaded magazines in preparation to fend off waves of attacking zombie hordes. I love my semi-automatic, military-style rifles dearly, but none of them will be my first choice if I ever have to bug out to the wilderness.

The .22 Caliber Rifle

If I could only take one firearm and nothing else, it would be a compact .22 caliber rifle. The rimfire .22 rifle is one of the most versatile weapons you can own when it comes to survival hunting, and the cartridges for it are tiny and lightweight, allowing you to carry 500 or more rounds in the same space and weight as just a couple of boxes of larger-caliber ammunition. A good .22 in the hands of a skilled shooter can be used to bring down a wide variety of small game such as birds, rabbits, and squirrels, and can also be used for larger game at close range with

Bolt-action .22 caliber rifle

carefully placed head or neck shots. Because it is more effective for this purpose than many people realize, the .22 rifle is a favorite choice of professional deer poachers, as the report is much quieter than any center-fire rifle more commonly used for deer hunting. I'm not suggesting the .22 as a deer rifle in normal hunting circumstances, but in a survival situation you can make it work if it's all you have. On numerous trips in the jungles of Central America, Indian guides I have traveled with routinely hunted everything from small to turkey-sized birds, monkeys, iguanas, and deer, even shooting submerged fish near the riverbanks with the battered old *veinte-dos* rifles they always carried in the bush.

On my own voluntary experiments in wilderness survival, I've had much success finding meat with my .22 rifles. At various times I've carried the Marlin Model 60, the Ruger 10/22 with folding stock, the Marlin Papoose take-down survival rifle, the AR-7 Explorer survival rifle (now made by Henry Repeating Arms), and the Winchester 94/22 lever action carbine. All of these met my needs when I depended on them. My current favorite is a compact Ruger 10/22 with the short, 16-inch barrel and a shortened wooden stock. By removing one screw I can take it apart into two pieces less than 24 inches long and conceal it in my bug-out bag. I feel that the purpose-made survival rifles like the Marlin Papoose and the AR-7 compromise too much for the sake of portability. Many standard rifles like the Ruger 10/22 can be fitted with folding stocks or simply taken down by removing the stocks. The Henry Youth lever action .22 is another lightweight, handy carbine that is 33 inches long and can be shortened for packing to 24 inches by removing one screw that secures the buttstock.

Quality .22 caliber pistols or revolvers can serve as an alternative to a rifle for skilled handgun hunters, but in my experience the ease of shooting accurately with a rifle makes it a clear winner. Small game can be elusive and difficult enough to hit even with a rifle, but compared to hunting with a pistol, most people will see a higher success rate with a long gun. In a bug-out survival situation, even more so than sport hunting, you have to make every shot count if possible, and get something to show for each precious round expended. When it comes to rifle sighting, open sights are simpler and more compact than scopes, but may compromise accuracy somewhat.

Weapons for Defense

When it comes to defense against human or animal attackers, .22 caliber rimfire weapons are woefully inadequate, but are still better than nothing. One advantage of the semi-automatic Ruger 10/22 is that it will accept high-capacity magazines of 25 or more rounds, allowing you to get off a lot of rapid-fire shots if need be. Some people make the mistake of totally disregarding the killing power of the .22, but it has in fact been used at one time or another to kill just about every species of animal on the continent, including bears (with lucky, well-placed, shots of course). It is certainly capable of killing humans and because of its low report that so appeals to poachers, it has seen use by assassins, snipers, and criminal hit men around the world.

Despite this, to be totally prepared for self-defense as well as hunting, it is best to have a larger caliber weapon as well as the .22 rifle you will use for most of your survival hunting. To keep the weight and bulk down as much as possible, as well as making it easier to conceal the fact that you are armed, I recommend a center-fire handgun in addition to the .22 rifle if you are bugging out with only two weapons. A handgun can be concealed in a ready-to-go location, unlike the rifle, which will be disassembled and stored in your pack, making it too slow to bring into action.

Although I would always prefer to be armed with a semi-automatic AK-47 or other rifle with high-capacity magazines if I knew I was going to be in a shootout with armed aggressors, for a bug-out situation where avoidance of trouble is top priority, I would not feel unarmed with a reliable handgun. Caliber choice again must be based on the weight of the ammunition and how much of it you can reasonably carry. Good choices for bugging out to the wild include the venerable .45 ACP, the .357 magnum, the .44 magnum, and the 10 mm Auto. I've had several scary encounters with bears, so if I were bugging out in any area where they were present, I would choose my handgun cartridge accordingly. At the least I would carry a .357 magnum revolver or a

Glock Model 20 in 10mm Auto. These are adequate for black bear and for mountain lions, another predator that has been responsible for quite a few recent attacks on humans. The Glock 20 with its 15-round magazines also provides plenty of firepower if you run into bad guys. In big bear country, such as the Northern Rockies where you might encounter a grizzly, the .44 magnum is much better insurance and serious big-game chamberings like the .454 Casull are even better.

The .357 Magnum

Although I switch back and forth from time to time between my Glocks and my revolvers, I'm currently in favor of the .357 magnum revolver for the purposes of bugging out as described in this book. This round carries plenty of punch, yet the cartridges are relatively compact and lightweight. Most weapons chambered in .357 magnum can also fire the cheaper and lower-powered .38 special as well. These are popular calibers and can be found everywhere. A good revolver in this caliber with at least a 4-inch barrel can do double duty as a hunting weapon, and many handgun hunters routinely use them for taking deer. Firing .38

The .357 magnum is a versatile weapon for hunting and defense.

specials, it can take smaller game such as rabbits without destroying the meat. Revolvers are rugged and simple, rarely failing under harsh conditions, and have the advantage of not requiring magazines. The disadvantage, of course, is limited capacity and slower reloading, but having a few speed-loaders ready to go negates this somewhat.

The Pistol-Caliber Carbine

Another reason I'll be carrying a .357 magnum is that it can share ammunition with my favorite rifle other than the Ruger 10/22—a Winchester .357 magnum lever action carbine of the "Trapper" variety, with the 16-inch barrel. This handy rifle is only 34 inches long overall, weighs just 6 pounds, and easily can fit in the bug-out bag with the buttstock removed. I'm not suggesting that carrying three different firearms is the right way to go for everyone in every situation, but the fact that the carbine and revolver share ammunition simplifies matters somewhat. The lever-action carbine is fast-handling and much more accurate than the revolver, excellent for hunting and for self-defense. It's also less conspicuous and less threatening in appearance than the AK-47 or AR-15, making it less likely to be confiscated by the authorities in a disaster scenario. Once you're in the wilderness, the little carbine can be slung on the outside of the bug-out bag or easily carried in hand, ready to be put into immediate use. With this combination you are ready for just about anything when it comes to close-range survival hunting. And again, if you are in big game and big bear country like the Northern Rockies, the revolver and carbine can still be had in a matched pair in .44 magnum or .454 Casull.

Ammunition

How much ammunition should you pack in the bug-out bag? I would suggest a minimum of 500 rounds of .22 long-rifle cartridges for the survival rifle, and 150 rounds for your handgun. More would be much better; it just depends on how much total weight you'll be packing, the terrain, and your fitness level. These numbers can be greatly increased if you bug out by vehicle, boat, canoe, or kayak, or if you utilize caching techniques in your advanced planning, as will be discussed in the next chapter.

Knives and Multi-Tools

Other than the machete, already described, you should carry another good knife of high-quality steel that can be kept razor-sharp for skinning and dressing the game you take while survival hunting. Avoid the oversized "Rambo" survival knives that are often marketed for the purpose, as most are poor quality and too big to be useful. Remember, the machete will meet all your needs in a larger blade. I prefer a folding or fixed-blade Bowie or drop-point style blade of about five inches in length for my main wilderness knife. This size is handy for detail work, yet still big enough to be deadly in hand-to-hand combat if you are ever were forced to that extreme. My favorite that goes with me everywhere is my Cold Steel Voyager, a five-inch folding Bowie with a strong pocket clip and easy, one-handed opening. It's more concealable than a fixed-blade knife of the same length, but if you don't mind wearing a belt and sheath, fixed-blade knives can certainly be a good option and are less likely to break in extreme use. Just as you should carry a small file for sharpening your machete, you should also carry a sharpening stone or diamond sharpener for keeping an edge on your knife.

One other tool in the knife category that you should not be without is a good quality multi-tool, such as the Leatherman Wave. This tool includes two knife blades, one plain and one serrated, a saw blade, and a file and rasp combination. It also features needle-nose pliers with wire cutters, screwdrivers in plain and Phillips, a can opener, and mini-scissors. Although at first I dis-

A good quality multi-tool can be extremely useful.

missed these multi-tools as gadgets or toys, after receiving this one as a gift and using it for a while, I realized that it was a quality tool and extremely useful. It comes in its own sheath that can be worn on a belt alongside your main knife.

Survival Fishing and Trapping Gear

There are many ways of obtaining animal protein other than hunting with firearms. If you expect to be bugging out in any but the most arid of desert regions, it goes without saying that your kit should include hooks and line for fishing. These take up little space but can provide rich returns if you know how to use them. You can carry a selection of sizes from the smallest bream hooks with monofilament line to heavy catfish hooks with nylon trotline to set out "drop hooks." Artificial lures are not required, as you can bait hooks with everything from berries to insects, worms, and grubs, or in the case of scavenging catfish, chunks of meat or organs from other fish or game you take. In a bug-out camp situation, drop hooks can be set up to work for you round the clock while you are busy doing other things. If your bug-out location will be along a river, large lakeshore, or seashore, you should also consider carrying a cast net. A small one of the type used by fishermen to catch bait will easily keep you well-fed on small fish if you know how to use it.

Just as you can set hooks for fish, you can also catch a variety of animals from squirrels and rabbits all the way up to deer if you have some snares available, or wire or strong cordage to make some with. It's much simpler if you carry two or three pre-made wire snares with

Hooks can be made from cord and found materials like wood and bone (left) or a nail (right).

you, preferably sized for small animals, as these will be the easiest to catch.

While simple snares, bare fishhooks, and line are easy to carry, there are also many great designs for fish and animal traps that you can build in nature once you are in a secure location. Most of these were derived or copied directly from proven Native American or other aboriginal designs, so it is worth the time to study their construction and use. A small field guide to survival skills that illustrates traps of this nature is a worthy addition to your bug-out bag if you don't already have a working knowledge of building them.

Navigation

Navigation will be discussed in more detail in the next chapter, which focuses on choosing suitable bug-out locations. The minimum navigation gear that you should always have on you is a high-quality, reliable compass, ideally of the orienteering type so that you can easily take bearings and navigate a course. In addition to a compass of this type, I have recently come to rely on a multifunction Casio Pathfinder watch that has an accurate electronic bearing compass as one of its primary functions. This watch also features an altimeter, which is another useful navigation tool in mountainous terrain. The watch is solar-powered, so batteries are not a concern. Having a compass on your wrist at all times is a great advantage and a good backup.

The only electronic device that I would suggest including in a bug-out bag is a small hand-held GPS receiver, preloaded with topographic maps of the region you will likely bug out to. Although you can't carry enough batteries to use such a device indefinitely, and there is the possibility of the entire GPS system crashing in times of a real crisis, it will be invaluable in the early stages of bugging out. With the GPS you can confidently move at night through unfamiliar terrain

A watch with a compass function can be an invaluable tool.

and be assured of finding your preplanned bug-out location, and any prearranged caches of supplies you may have hidden in advance.

Whether or not you carry a GPS with electronic maps, you should also carry paper topographical maps of your most likely bug-out location. Although you may end up having to go somewhere else, having a map of where you intend to go will give you a lot more confidence as you are fleeing into the wilderness.

Other Important Gear

There are many other assorted and miscellaneous items that you will probably want to include in your bug-out bag. I won't go into detailed discussions of all of these, but a sample checklist that you can work from can be found in the appendix of this book. These items include sunglasses, first aid supplies, any special needs medications or prescriptions that you will need to keep you alive (such as the Epipen syringe I carry because of my allergy to wasp stings), an Extractor snakebite kit, documents such as your passport and driver's license, and a supply of cash or even a few gold coins that may allow you to barter your way out of trouble or trade with other survivors. A basic survival manual has already been mentioned; make sure it also includes information on edible plants in your region, as well as basic first-aid techniques. A simple sewing kit consisting of a few needles and some strong Dacron thread such as that used in canvas work will go a long way toward keeping your backpack, shelter, and clothing repaired and in usable condition. A supply of 550 paracord (preferably 100 feet or more, as it is lightweight and compact) is invaluable. It can be used as is or unraveled to provide smaller cordage and thread. A mini-flashlight or headlamp is a useful luxury. You can't carry enough batteries to use it indefinitely, but if you choose one with LED lamps it will last a long time if used with discretion.

When choosing an item to pack in your bug-out bag, remember to always favor the proven wilderness basics over the latest innovative gadgets. The old ways, in both methods and tools, are often better than the new when it comes to the unchanging realities of life in the wild. In closing this chapter, I strongly suggest that you go out and test your equipment to see for yourself what works, what doesn't, and why. Have someone drop you off on the edge of a wild place for a weekend or a week. Give the bug-out bag a real shakedown and then come home and throw out the things that either didn't work or weren't needed, and add anything you discovered that you really wished you had.

3

ADVANCE PLANNING & LOCATION SELECTION

Now that you've selected your gear and carefully packed your bug-out bag, ready to leave at a moment's notice, it's time to get serious about planning where you're going to go if you actually have to use it. In this chapter, I will examine the criteria for a good bug-out location and discuss the factors that determine the suitability of an area for survival living. The focus here will be to help you analyze your particular surroundings, wherever you live and work, and explain how to use maps and other tools to find uninhabited or unused areas where you could feasibly bug out and survive if the need arises. I'll also discuss advance scouting and the option of caching supplies and equipment.

Regional Considerations

Your starting location in any bug-out situation is going to be determined by where you live and work, unless you happen to be traveling at the time an emergency occurs. This starting location can severely handicap you or aid you in bugging out, depending on factors such as the size of the city or town, population density of the surrounding counties and nearby countryside, and the amount of development and suburban sprawl found there.

Population Densities and Development

In many parts of the country, the suburban sprawl is so vast that the transition from city to countryside to the next city has become blurred

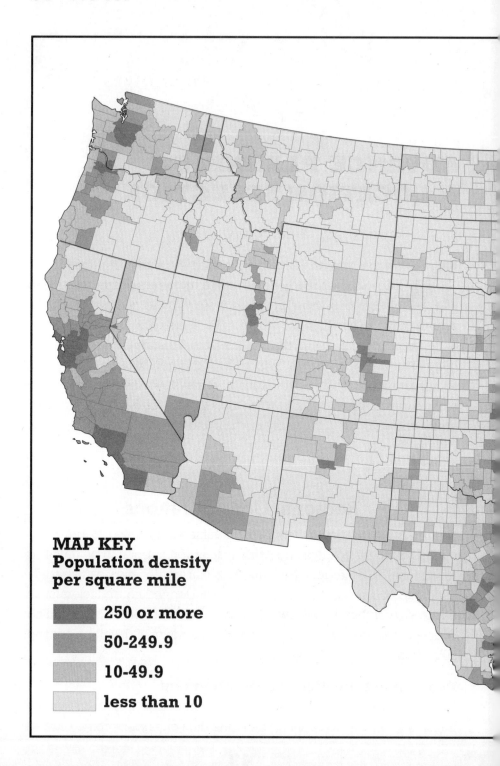

MAP KEY
Population density
per square mile

250 or more

50-249.9

10-49.9

less than 10

U.S. Population Density
(by County)

in an unending array of parking lots, strip malls, and tract housing. Naturally, someone attempting to bug out from such an area will be at a disadvantage to begin with, but ironically, it is this very population density that will increase the probability of a situation arising that will require a fast exit. The advantage you will have over other residents, however, is the information in this book and a plan to act on it accordingly. The majority of any given population will be utterly unprepared and uninformed, and will therefore not be competing with you to get to your bug-out location. What they will be doing is getting in your way and impeding your progress with mass confusion, panic, and traffic jams. It goes without saying that if you are in such a populated urban or suburban area when something bad happens, you need to act as fast as possible to try and get out ahead of the stampeding herd.

The other factor related to living or working in such an area is that because of the expanding sprawl surrounding any population center, you will have to travel farther in most cases to find uninhabited or unused land where you can evade, hide out, and survive. But as we shall see in Part Two of this book, there are such areas within reach of even some of the largest urban areas of the country, thanks in part to the large number of national parks, national forests, wildlife refuges, wetlands, and other protected areas—many right at the doorsteps of major cities. If you live in a heavily populated area, it is critical that you identify such lands and weigh their suitability against the option of traveling farther to more remote areas. In some areas it may be advisable to plan on going the extra distance, if there is a bug-out location within reach that will offer better options for evasion and survival living. Remember, although most of the residents of urban areas will not be prepared to bug out to wildlands, there will certainly be some that will try if they are desperate enough, and you may encounter fleeing refugees of widely varied skill levels in your favorite bug-out location. The farther you travel from populated areas, the fewer you will likely run across.

Climate and Terrain

The climate and terrain found in the diverse regions of the lower 48 states is incredibly varied, ranging from subtropical, jungle-like swamps to baking deserts and frigid glacial peaks. The type of terrain and the weather patterns in your home region will greatly impact your decisions when it comes to how you will travel and the gear you will need to survive in the uninhabited areas nearby. To be truly prepared to survive a bug-out emergency in your area, it is essential to become familiar with what it will be like to live outdoors in the region. Nothing can prepare you for this better than taking exploratory trips to hike, paddle, hunt, fish, or camp in your local natural environment. Only by getting outside will you understand what is needed to stay alive and comfortable in extreme heat or cold, and to cope with heavy rain, snow, or biting insect populations.

If you live in a rugged, mountainous area, it is essential to become familiar with methods for safely traversing steep terrain, and to maintain a level of physical fitness that will allow you to do so while carrying your bug-out bag. Those living where rivers or swamps predominate should know how to navigate a small boat or how to paddle a canoe, pirogue, or kayak—which ever fits their local waters best. Confidence in finding your way through a dense forest comes with understanding basic navigation skills and with time spent in the woods, getting used to the feeling of being closed in by trees that can be so unnerving to those not familiar with it.

Natural Hazards

Natural hazards in one form or another are present in every region. Some of these hazards are related to climate, such as blizzards, lightning strikes, tornadoes, hurricanes, and other storms. Other natural hazards are terrain considerations that can make travel difficult and dangerous. This can include steep, rocky slopes and deep canyons that are difficult to negotiate, avalanches and rock falls, and powerful, fast-moving rivers that may have to be crossed. In most wooded areas of the United States there are one or more varieties of poisonous plants that can cause severe skin reactions to those who are allergic to them.

Aside from these hazards, wildlife encounters are the first thing that comes to mind among those who are not accustomed to spending time in the wilderness. Most wildlife threats are imagined or greatly exaggerated, but some are certainly real. Attacks on humans by bears and mountain lions are becoming more frequent as these predators are increasing their range and numbers and more people come in contact with them. In the South, alligators are on the increase in most waterways and occasionally attack humans as well. Even more likely than an attack by a big predator, though, is the possibility of being bitten by a venomous snake or spider or stung by wasps or bees (which can be fatal to those who are allergic). Smaller animal hazards include disease-carrying ticks and mosquitoes.

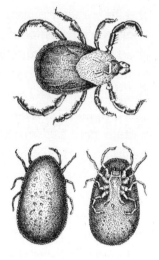

Ticks get embedded in the skin and can transfer diseases.

Although you can't do anything to change the fact that natural hazards are present in a given area, it is essential in your planning that you make yourself aware of which ones are there and take steps to avoid or protect yourself from them. In Part Two, I will discuss any particular threats encountered in each bug-out location and suggest ways to deal with them.

Natural Resources

Every region has its share of natural resources, but in some areas they can be more dispersed and harder to find than in others. The factors that can affect your efforts to survive in a bug-out situation include the species and numbers of edible plants, game animals, and useful trees and other plants; the amount of available water; and the availability of natural objects such as stones that can be fashioned into primitive tools. Not all ecosystems offer large varieties of useful animal and plant life. Some forests that are devoid of edible plants are teeming with wild game, while other places lush in plant variety may be home to fewer species of animals.

How Much Space Will You Need?

In an ideal bug-out survival scenario, you would have access to a large tract of roadless land composed of many thousands of acres of uninhabited wilderness. As we shall see in Part Two, there are many such places in the United States—some, in fact, contain millions of acres without a single road of any kind. But one evading survivalist or even a small group can subsist on much smaller parcels of wild land, especially in heavily wooded regions where staying out of sight is easy, if the necessary natural resources are present. If you are there long enough to hunt it out, you will have to do the same thing our hunter-gather ancestors frequently did—move on to new hunting grounds.

In most parts of the country, the largest wildlife populations and most diverse plant life are found along drainages, ranging from mostly dry arroyos and canyons to streams, creeks, and major river systems. If you bug out to such a drainage area, you can easily move up- or downstream as need arises in search of more resources.

Swamps are another area where you don't need a lot of space. With aquatic life as well as the plants and animals found on higher ground in the swamp, you have lots of food sources to draw from. Since swamps are by nature inaccessible and unpleasant to most people, if you can adapt to the conditions and have the right watercraft to reach the best spots, you can easily stay hidden there.

In mountain country, ridges and steep slopes are often the wildest places in a given area, due to the difficulty of traversing them and the lack of a water supply. But if you can locate a spring or other water source high above a main drainage, chances are you can avoid any human contact, as most people will tend to follow the creeks or, if traveling ridges, stay on established trails. As mentioned in Chapter One, the fugitive Eric Robert Rudolph disappeared into the wilderness of the Nantahala National Forest and had hundreds of thousands of acres available to him. But after his capture, authorities learned that he stayed hidden for most of that five years camped on a single ridge just outside of a small town. This is a good example of how mountainous country, especially in regions of heavy forest cover, can provide infinite hideout locations almost anywhere off the beaten path.

Potential Bug-Out Locations

To get more specific about areas that we can consider for possible bug-out locations, it will be helpful to look at the different kinds of uninhabited land available today in the United States. The pros and cons of each category will be discussed in the following sections.

Federal Lands

Residents of the United States are blessed with an abundance of federal lands that are available to all citizens for recreational uses such as hiking, camping, hunting, and fishing. Few countries in today's overcrowded world can boast such a high acreage per capita of open lands that are free to all to use and enjoy. In the U.S., the federal government owns nearly 650 million acres of land, accounting for almost 30 percent of the entire nation's land area.

Naturally, those living in cities and suburbs who do not own private lands in the country will probably look first to public federal lands when formulating a bug-out plan. Chances are that wherever you live, there is federal land within reach in the form of national parks, national forests, national wildlife refuges, Bureau of Land Management (BLM) land, U.S. Army Corps of Engineers land, or others. These different federal holdings are managed according to their intended purposes.

National Park Service Lands

The parks managed by the National Park Service are perhaps the most high-profile and well-known of all federal holdings, as they tend to be established in areas of spectacular natural beauty or historical significance, and are often set up as tourist destinations as well as protective sanctuaries for the plant and animal life found within their boundaries. The National Park Service manages its lands with a strict set of rules governing what visitors are allowed to do within the parks, forbidding many activities such as hunting or even the collecting or taking of plant life and inanimate objects such as rocks. Entry fees and user fees of one kind or another are charged at most national parks. Those using the remote wilderness areas of national parks are required to obtain "backcountry permits" for camping, which means that adherence to a preplanned itinerary is required. Until a bill allowing concealed carry in parks was signed into law in 2009, firearms of any kind were forbidden on National Park Service lands, including those weapons that would be carried for the purpose of self-defense against dangerous animals. This right to carry in parks is still regulated by individual states, however, so if you are a non-resident you may not be able to legally carry a firearm on park lands even with a concealed-carry permit.

Because of the strict rules governing national parks in the U.S., I have seldom made them my destination when seeking out places to practice wilderness living or survival skills. But these very rules that make them so unsuitable in normal times can be advantageous to the bug-out survivalist. Some national parks contain millions of acres of nearly pristine wilderness, and are teeming with game that has not been hunted in decades. In a bug-out situation, you won't likely have to worry about patrolling rangers enforcing park service rules, as they will have their own problems to worry about. Not to mention that, in most national parks, even the heavily visited ones like Yellowstone and the Great Smokey Mountains, the areas frequented by tourists and accessible by roads and trails are only a small percentage of the backcountry acreage within park boundaries. Even in ordinary times, park service rangers cannot possibly cover all this ground, and professional poachers occasionally slip into these big wildlife-rich sanctuaries and bag their prey undetected.

From a bug-out standpoint, national parks can be a good option, primarily because of their size and mostly untouched natural state. You must keep in mind, however, that most residents in every region will know about the major national parks near their homes. It's possible that a number of less-prepared survivors of a catastrophic event will head to these known public parks, simply because they don't know anywhere else to go. But most will not be prepared to bug out into the remote, off-trail backcountry.

U.S. Forest Service Lands

The U.S. Forest Service manages eight percent of all the land in the United States, with national forests totaling about 193 million acres. The mandate of the U.S. National Forest Service is somewhat different from that of the National Park Service, in that national forest lands are designated for "multi-use." This multi-use management includes recreational uses, as in the national parks, but also allows for limited use of natural resources, including hunting and fishing, timber cutting, mining and prospecting, and livestock grazing. National Forest Service lands can vary widely from clear-cuts to tree plantations, and include areas crisscrossed with dirt roads as well as designated wilderness areas where no motor vehicles are allowed.

U.S. Forest service lands have long been my preferred destinations when seeking out wild places to explore in the lower 48 states. A lot of freedom is allowed on these lands, especially in regard to camping, which in most national forests is allowed anywhere, as long you don't stay in one site longer than fourteen days. The freedom to carry firearms and to hunt on Forest Service lands (in accordance with state wildlife laws) is also a big plus. Outside of designated wilderness areas, a network of forest service and logging roads often makes access by vehicle, ATV, or off-road motorcycle easy and convenient. In many of the biggest national forests, you can drive for miles on remote, seldom-used roads and find surprisingly wild areas to camp in right out of the vehicle without the need to hike farther in.

The best of the National Forest Service lands, however, are the designated wilderness areas, especially the big ones in the Appalachian Mountains and throughout the huge national forests of the West. Designated wilderness areas can be visited only on foot or horseback, or by use of non-motorized watercraft such as canoes or kayaks. No mechanized vehicles of any kind, not even bicycles, are permitted. The purpose of the wilderness designation is to preserve tracts of land in a pristine state, and allow lands that were once logged or otherwise changed by man to revert back to a natural state. As a result, the Forest Service does not do any road-building or timber harvesting in these wilderness tracts. They are, however, open to recreational pursuits such as backpacking and camping, as well as hunting. In most cases, national forest wilderness areas are the best examples of wild land available today for those who would seek to re-create a wilderness lifestyle and experience a bit of what early explorers found when settling what is now the United States. As we shall see in Part Two, some of the biggest Forest Service wilderness areas comprise as much as three million acres of completely roadless land where little if any sign of human impact can be seen.

Naturally, resources as large and widely dispersed throughout the United States as national forest lands are well-known to hunters, adventurers, and would-be survivalists. Undoubtedly, in a bug-out situation, other like-minded individuals and groups will have their sights set on a national forest near you, and competition for resources may be the result. But once again, a willingness to forsake roads, trails, and obvious drainages will make it easy to leave the crowds behind and evade pursuit or confrontation.

Bureau of Land Management Lands

The Bureau of Land Management (BLM) is a government agency that manages 264 million acres of federal lands, including forests, grasslands, and desert, in 12 western states including Alaska. As will be seen in the chapters in Part Two that deal with the western regions, many large tracts of BLM land are desolate wilderness areas that are suitable for potential bug-out locations. Most of these lands are managed under a "multiple-use" policy similar to U.S. Forest Service lands. Some of these BLM tracts are little-known except to locals and are extremely remote. If you live in the western states, they are well worth looking into.

U.S. Army Corps of Engineers Lands

The U.S. Army Corps of Engineers oversees thousands of miles of navigable inland waterways and recreation areas along rivers and man-made lakes built for flood control, water supply reservoirs, and hydroelectric power. Lesser known to the general public, much of the uninhabited land along these major rivers and lakes is Corps of Engineers land that is available for hunting, camping, and other recreational use. Having traveled thousands of miles on the river systems of the nation by kayak, including a descent of the length of the Mississippi River, I have made good use of these mostly forgotten lands and found them ideal for long-term camping and living off the land.

National Wildlife Refuges

In some areas of the U.S., national wildlife refuges take in even more wilderness acreage than national forests and parks. Some of the larger ones are places like the Okefenokee Swamp of Georgia and the

Cabeza Prieta wilderness in Arizona. Some of these national wild-life refuges are well-known, while others receive little, if any, human traffic. Set up for the preservation of wildlife habitat rather than rec-reation, most national wildlife refuges do not permit activities such as camping. Many large tracts managed by the federal government under this system were purchased by private organizations such as the Nature Conservancy.

State Lands

On a smaller scale than national parks and national forests, many states also maintain state parks and state forests, both for recreational use and as resource preserves. Some states also offer wildlife refuges or game management areas overseen by their own state wildlife depart-ments. Many of these state-owned preserves are extensive in size and can rival federal tracts as viable bug-out locations. Since the size and types of management of state lands vary widely, I won't include all of them in this book, but in the regional sections of Part Two, I will high-light exceptional ones that qualify as obvious bug-out locations.

Private Lands (Individual and Corporate Holdings)

Despite the huge tracts of lands owned by state and federal govern-ments, privately owned lands still account for most of the uninhabited acreage in the United States. Not all of this uninhabited land is in a natu-ral state, of course. Much of it is cultivated farmland, ranch land, mining or petroleum drilling land, or timber plantations. Areas less suited for commercial use are often utilized for private hunting clubs and other recreation. A smaller percentage of private lands are truly abandoned or seldom visited by absentee owners, who in most cases inherited family lands but live and work far away in other states or cities. Other large tracts are owned by various corporations, often as investments or holdings for future development. Because there is so much private land in every region of the country, it would be unwise to discount the potential of such tracts as bug-out locations, and in many areas they may be better choices than the public options.

Trespassing on private property can have serious consequences even in normal times if the owners are serious about keeping intruders out. In a SHTF scenario, most landowners who see trespassers on their property will probably shoot first and ask questions later. But with this warning, I will go on to say that there are many situations where private land is so inaccessible and hard to patrol that the owners cannot possibly know about every person passing through or even temporarily living there in a bug-out situation. I've had a lifetime of experience with this as one of many part-owners of a family farm that was passed down from generation to generation on my father's side. Located on a small river in Mississippi, this property is mostly heavily forested hardwood bottomland—perfect habitat for deer, wild turkey, squirrels, and other game animals. The property is bounded on two sides by highways, and consists of about 200 acres. As long as I can remember, despite "Posted" signs along the boundaries and repeated attempts to keep them out, trespassing hunters have slipped onto the property each year and bagged deer and other game on a regular basis. To effectively patrol even a small private holding of thickly wooded terrain, you would need a small squad of armed men on duty 24 hours a day. It's simply not feasible.

Finding a Bug-Out Location

The time to find your bug-out location is now. If you wait until something happens and just head off into the unknown, even with a well-prepared bug-out bag, you are just going to be another refugee instead of a knowledgeable survivalist. Taking into account the regional considerations discussed at the beginning of this chapter, and the types of potential bug-out locations discussed above, you can now get specific in your planning and locate the best place within reach that will meet all or most of your needs. With today's technology, you can begin the first phase of this from the comfort of your own home. You can do quite a bit of research into potential bug-out locations using old-fashioned paper maps, electronic maps, Google Earth, and GPS.

Paper Maps

Paper maps are, of course, the traditional tool for advance study of an area of interest, and will give you most of the necessary information, including how to get there from your present location. There are many different kinds of maps available, from road maps to topographical maps, and specialized maps detailing specific destinations such as trails, parks, waterways, etc. To get the up-close details you will need for specific bug-out location selection, as well as routes to get there, you will need a lot of maps if you are using traditional printed maps. A state road map or, better yet, a regional road atlas, will get you started. The road map will provide an overview of the larger area, showing your home location in relation to potential bug-out locations and the routes to them. Most public lands of any significance are shown on state road maps, so by using them you can at least get a sense of what's out there. Rivers and important smaller streams, coastlines, and areas of marsh or swamp are also shown. The state road map will show all Interstates, state and federal highways, and many county roads. By looking for roadless areas, you can somewhat deduce where the uninhabited locations are, but what maps at this scale will not show are the locations of private roads, residences, and farms that may be present in many of the blank spots.

A state road atlas with separate maps for individual counties is the next level of detail you will need, as these will often show houses and other buildings, as well as private drives and lanes, allowing you to get a much better sense of what areas are truly uninhabited. Even better than this is the Delorme Atlas and Gazetteer series of state atlases that are now available for each of the 50 states. These full-color atlases include detailed topographical maps for every area of a given state, and show recreation sites, federal and state lands, rivers, lakes and seashores, and trails and back roads. They are useful for advance planning and for navigation in the field. If your bug-out location is in your home state and you won't need to carry an atlas for more than one state, a Delorme atlas will fit in your bug-out bag.

The next level of detail in paper maps is the large-scale topographical maps available from the U.S. Geological Survey (USGS). The most popular of these are the 1:24,000 scale maps known as quadrangle or "quad" maps. These quad maps are so detailed that it takes about 57,000 maps to cover all of the United States and its territories. They can be ordered directly from the USGS website. Detailed topographical and trail maps are also printed by most federal and state land management agencies for the areas in their district, and are available directly from the U.S. Forest Service, the National Park Service, the U.S. Army Corps of Engineers, and others.

Electronic Maps

Most the above-mentioned maps that are available in printed form are also available electronically in the form of scanned raster maps (these look just like the paper version) and vector navigation charts and maps for use with GPS mapping systems. Except for those that can be viewed on a hand-held GPS receiver, which will be discussed shortly, electronic maps are best suited for planning purposes at home on your computer. You do have the option of printing paper copies, however, so they could meet all your needs, especially if you waterproof or laminate the copies.

Electronic maps are available online for free from sites like Google Maps and government agencies like the USGS, or you can purchase a CD-ROM version of a mapping software program like Delorme's Topo U.S.A., which includes electronic versions of the maps in the above-mentioned Atlas and Gazetteer series. Electronic mapping programs usually feature a lot of extras as well, and can give you information you can't easily get with a paper map, including 3D views, search capabilities, and detailed info about specific points of interest on the maps.

Google Earth

Google Earth, a free program you can download to your computer, can be even more useful than any map for your bug-out location planning. This program allows you to access satellite imagery of any location on Earth and then zoom in close enough to see details like buildings and parked cars. The downside to Google Earth is that some specific areas may not be available in high-resolution images, so you may be limited in how close you can look. In addition, if there was cloud cover obscuring some of the detail on the ground on the day the image was taken, you will be out of luck. And one other point worth mentioning—the photos are usually recent, but may not be updated for a few months

CACHING TECHNIQUE

It is essential that food and other items in your cache that must stay dry be sealed in waterproof containers of some sort. In the survivalist market, there are now companies that offer specialized containers for this use, including waterproof burial tubes for firearms. Many types of waterproof boxes and "dry bags" are available for kayakers, canoeists, and whitewater rafters. Some of these will be good for long-term use, while others are more suitable for temporary storage.

You can make your own firearms containers from sealed sections of large-diameter PVC pipe. The key is to make sure the seals are truly watertight. If you use screw-in end caps for access, seal the threads with marine silicon caulk when closing the container for long-term burial or above-ground storage.

Items that do not require the lengthy tubes needed to contain rifles or shotguns can be stored in commonly available five-gallon buckets with gasket-sealed lids. For food storage, first line the buckets with heavy-duty trash bags and tie these off before sealing the bucket lid. I've successfully used buckets of this type for caching food supplies to be picked up en route on longer hiking or paddling trips and found them to work well as long as you can keep them out of reach of bears. In heavily wooded areas where they are not likely to be discovered, this can be accomplished by hoisting the buckets into the trees after first stringing a long line between two trees so the cache will be out of reach of climbing bears. You can get the line between the trees by weighting one end and throwing it over branches. It takes some effort, but is well worth it in bear country.

The best way to hide a cache from discovery by other humans is to bury it. This takes considerable effort, and must be done well in advance, preferably at

and in some cases, a couple of years. Things can change in this length of time, including the construction of new buildings and roads.

Fortunately, most areas you'll be interested in, especially in the United States, are well-covered by the program, allowing you to virtually "fly over" the area with a bird's-eye view and see the big picture as well as the up-close details. The ability to do this makes Google Earth an amazing tool for bug-out location planning. With this aerial overview, you can determine exactly which areas are heavily wooded, clear-cut, bisected by roads, or covered in swamp. You can use the measuring tool to assess how far a given location is from the nearest night when you are less likely to be seen or heard digging the hole. A buried cache is not convenient for casual retrieval, so this method is best used for long-term storage of items you won't likely need before a true emergency situation. Buried items have to be especially well protected from water intrusion.

Aboveground caches may be more practical in some areas, particularly in rocky, mountainous regions where digging will be difficult. In this kind of terrain, you can often find small caverns or rock overhangs that will make good hiding places, especially if you conceal the entrance with stones and other natural debris. Non-food items like firearms that will not attract bears can be hidden in camouflaged PVC tubes like those described above by lashing them to tree trunks high up amongst the branches where no one is likely to look. The more remote your bug-out location and the farther off any road or foot path you get, the better your chances that the cache will remain undiscovered until you need it.

Other than keeping it hidden from others, being able to find your cache again when you need it is the most important consideration. Recording the coordinates from an accurate GPS fix is a good first step. To assure you can find it without electronic aids, though, you should also record the cache location in relation to natural landmarks, preferably permanent ones that are unlikely to change over time. When doing this, consider the effects of strong winds, floods, forest fires, and rockslides. With care, you can pick a location that will remain identifiable despite localized natural disasters. If circumstances in a bug-out situation permit you to return to your cache, you will be grateful for the effort you put into securing it when you uncover your treasure trove of survival goodies.

road, dwelling, or other man-made structure, and you can mark spots of interest and get the exact GPS coordinates to them so you can be sure of reaching them on the ground. Google Earth images will give you a clear picture of the terrain of a given area, allowing you to find the most inaccessible hideouts. Along rivers and streams, you can easily see which stretches of a particular waterway are remote from farms and fields, and pick the densely forested stretches that offer good hiding and hunting. Just as with the electronic maps previously discussed, you can print imagery of an area from Google Earth and take the hard copy with you as part of your navigation equipment.

Global Positioning System (GPS)

The GPS satellites put into orbit for commercial and military use have had an enormous impact on recreational boaters, hikers, hunters, and others who can now benefit from knowing exactly where they are at all times. A handheld GPS receiver that weighs only ounces and costs about the same as your bug-out backpack can give you an accurate location fix and show your position on its built-in mapping software, allowing virtually anyone to navigate unerringly through any terrain, even in the dark. There's little not to like about GPS receivers, except for the fact that they are electronic devices, so they require batteries to operate and are subject to failure. This rules them out for a long-term bug-out situation, unless you have cached a large supply of batteries in advance. But for your initial exit from a disaster area, with a goal of reaching your pre-planned bug-out location, a GPS receiver is indispensable, and should definitely be part of your kit.

For advance planning purposes, the real value of the GPS is the ability to input the coordinates of locations or "waypoints" that can be given a filename and stored, allowing you to navigate to them with the receiver. These waypoint coordinates can be entered manually or with a click of the mouse if the GPS receiver is connected to your computer. You can input waypoints from paper maps, electronic maps, or Google Earth. Storing these waypoints in your GPS is the last essential step in the process of researching likely bug-out locations. The next step is to actually find them and scout them in person.

Advance Scouting

There is no substitute for on-the-ground advance scouting if you want to truly do everything you can to be prepared for a bug-out situation. Now that you've located a potential bug-out location, whether you've zeroed in on a particular spot or just have an idea of a general area that might be good, you need to make every effort to get out to it and spend some time on the ground there. By conducting some advance scouting, you will become familiar with the terrain, the resources, the weather, and the natural hazards of the area. Taking your bug-out bag with you is a good way to see if you packed what you need, and after a few scouting trips you should have it fine-tuned and ready.

While scouting a bug-out location, the primary thing to be on the lookout for is signs of human activity. You should be able to get a feel for how much use an area gets by whether or not you find primitive roads and trails, and the condition you find them in. Remains of campfires and trash left behind are also good indicators that people use the area, as are, of course, tire tracks in places that can be accessed by motor vehicles. If your bug-out location is in a public recreation area, such as a national park or national forest, you can expect to see signs of visitor use, especially on and near designated trails. To find out if the off-trail areas in the location are sufficiently remote, you'll need to bushwhack some and see for yourself if others have done the same. In most areas, this is not likely. Make every effort to find the places that are the most difficult to access. Features that discourage most people should be the very things you seek out. These include thickets and areas of dense undergrowth; muddy or swampy ground with lots of sloughs and other nasty bodies of water to cross; steep, rugged routes over difficult obstructions like rock fields and talus; and steep canyons and ravines with no easy or obvious access.

Scouting trips to your bug-out location are also great opportunities to see what the area offers in terms of edible wild plants, water sources, and game. Take a field guide if necessary to help you identify plant and tree species. By being observant and moving quietly, you will likely see some of the resident animal population, and even if not, the presence of tracks, runs and trails, droppings, hair, feathers, and other indicators will give you a good idea of the kind of hunting you can expect. If the area is national forest land or other land where you can get away with it, actual hunting and gathering activities can be included in your scouting trips, giving you an even better idea of what it will take to live in the area.

Caching Supplies and Equipment

If you've found the ideal bug-out location and are quite certain of your ability to reach it in times of crisis, it might be worth your while to consider supply and equipment caching. Caching is one way of making sure you will have things that you can't carry with you in a bug-out bag, but it is important to remember that it cannot be a substitute for what you have on your back. No matter how careful you are in your planning, things can happen that prevent you from reaching a cache, or it could be found by someone else or damaged by the elements or the local wildlife.

If your cache is successful, however, it can greatly aid in your survival, as you can stock it with staple foods like rice, beans, and other non-perishables that will reduce your dependence on living off the land, at least for a while. Extra gear to aid you in survival living can be included as well, such as additional firearms and ammunition, hunting weapons such as a bow and arrows, animal traps, snares, fishing equipment, and nets. You may also consider caching shelter-building materials and tools such as axes, and other heavy items you would not want to carry in your bug-out bag.

Exit Routes and Exit Planning

The biggest obstacle to reaching a bug-out location could well be your fellow citizens, who in all likelihood will be much less prepared than you are. In any situation that warrants executing your bug-out plan, you can expect to see mass confusion and even panic, as well as runs on the local supermarkets and gas stations as people who have waited too long desperately try to get food, other supplies, and the gasoline to get out of Dodge.

In hurricane-prone areas of the country, such as the Gulf Coast and parts of the East Coast, you can see examples of this every time a tropical storm threatens to make landfall. Grocery store shelves are stripped bare, batteries and propane cylinders are sold out, and long lines form at every gas pump in the region. People never seem to learn, even when dealing with known and predictable threats such as hurricanes. You can expect it to be much worse in a true SHTF scenario.

Be Prepared and Leave Early

The only way to avoid all this chaos and have a hope of escaping a major city at all in such a situation is to leave almost immediately, well ahead of the masses. Fortunately, with your pre-packed bug-out bag and a well-formulated plan, you will be ready to do just that. Your preparations should include having everything you will need in your bug-out bag, as discussed in the previous chapter, and having the fuel or whatever else you need for your bug-out vehicle, which will be the subject of the next chapter. If you are truly prepared, there will be nothing to stop for, shop for, or look for. While everyone else is wasting their time standing in line to get the things you already have, you can be well on your way out.

Even so, leaving early is not a guarantee of beating the traffic, because if the situation is bad enough, many people will take off without supplies or sufficient gas. This also happens in every major hurricane evacuation, and soon disabled vehicles out of fuel compound the problem and choke already backed-up roadways.

Study Your Escape Route

Part of your advance planning should be devoted to studying roads and back roads out of your city or town to find routes that the masses are less likely to use. This is an effective strategy I've often used in hurricane evacuations, as the authorities try to route everyone onto major Interstates and other highways, frequently leaving small county roads and more indirect routes free and clear. Many of these secondary routes parallel the larger highways that have replaced them, and you can often travel just as fast on them.

Study your maps to make sure they offer a completely separate route and do not eventually merge with Interstates or dead end. If you live in a city bounded by a large river or located on a coastal barrier island, there may be only one or two routes with bridges that cross the waterways separating you from your bug-out location. If this is the case, you will have to be doubly vigilant to know when to leave in order to cross these obstacles before they become impassable.

Don't make the mistake of doing all your planning with maps alone. Go out now and drive, ride, or walk your exit routes, just as you plan to do in a real bug-out situation. Observe the traffic patterns under normal conditions, and make note of the populations that live and work along the way, assessing the potential threats they may pose to your exit plan. Explore not only alternatives to the main routes, but alternatives to your chosen alternative routes. Familiarity with the area is the most important part of your strategy and will do more to ensure your success than any amount of gear or any specialized bug-out vehicle. But how you will travel is an important consideration—both for bugging out to your pre-planned location and for getting around in the area once you are there. In the next chapter, I'll discuss my thoughts on this and present some alternatives you may not have considered.

4

TRANSPORTATION TO & WITHIN THE BUG-OUT LOCATION

How will you travel if there is no alternative but to bug out? Do you plan to drive or ride a motorcycle, bicycle, or other wheeled vehicle? Would some sort of boat be best for quickly leaving your living or working area? In the worst-case scenario, are you prepared to walk if you have to? If you've researched potential bug-out locations and studied routes to them, as well as your best exit routes, I'm sure you've given some thought to transportation.

Since the majority of people in this country rely on private automobiles for everyday commuting and basic transportation, I'll look at the pros and cons of motor vehicles first. Like the independence which led settlers ever westward to explore a wilderness continent, private car ownership is an integral part of American culture and as a result, public transportation is woefully inadequate in most areas except a few of the largest cities. Even if you live in one of those cities where it is available, you can forget about public transportation being an option in a bug-out situation. There will simply be far too many people with no other means of leaving for such systems to function for long. Again, hurricane evacuations are prime, smaller-scale examples of what you can expect. Big storms like Katrina completely bog down the public system, as was seen in New Orleans, where thousands of people were bused out of the city only after waiting many days while crowded into the Superdome. You don't want to be stuck among those crowds, so it is essential that you plan to get out on your own power, even if it means walking.

Motor Vehicles: Cars, Trucks, and SUVs

Driving your own private vehicle will likely be the fastest method of bugging out and traveling to your pre-planned bug-out location, especially if it is far away. A vehicle will give you some measure of protection and allow you to carry extra supplies and gear beyond what will fit in a bug-out bag. If you have family members who are too young, too old, or simply not fit enough for more physical means of travel, a motor vehicle could be your best chance of getting them to safety. The downside to private motor vehicles is that there are so many of them, as anyone who commutes in traffic even in normal everyday life can attest.

In a bug-out, SHTF scenario, there will be many obstacles and hazards to getting anywhere in a vehicle that must travel on roadways. There will be traffic jams caused by the sheer numbers of vehicles on the road, in addition to those caused by accidents, breakdowns, and possible roadblocks. However, one advantage to bugging out by vehicle is that you can carry in or on the vehicle some of the alternate means of transportation discussed later in this chapter, including dual-purpose motorcycles, bicycles, canoes, or kayaks, and of course, your bug-out backpack for when it's time to walk. This gives you the means to strike out for your bug-out location with everything in the vehicle, but the option to abandon it and travel lighter if you reach an impasse or suffer a serious breakdown.

Vehicle Maintenance

If you plan to use a motor vehicle for bugging out, whether it is an ordinary sedan, economy car, SUV, or pickup truck, you should ensure that it is mechanically sound and regularly maintained. Even if there is an orderly evacuation and you are able to drive out of the city where you live, traffic will likely be moving at a crawl. A long period of slow driving in such a stop-and-go situation is hard on engines and cooling systems, and overheating is frequently the result. To prevent this, make sure your radiator hoses are in good shape, and replace them if they show any signs of becoming dry or brittle.

Broken drive belts are another common cause of breakdown, but can be prevented by regular inspection and replacement when

VEHICLE CHECKLIST

SPARE PARTS:

- ❏ spark plugs
- ❏ spark plug wires
- ❏ alternator
- ❏ spare alternator or main drive belt
- ❏ spare battery (fully charged replacement for main battery)
- ❏ thermostat
- ❏ starter
- ❏ fuel pump
- ❏ fuel filter
- ❏ headlamps
- ❏ taillights and other bulbs
- ❏ spare wiper blades

OTHER SUPPLIES:

- ❏ engine oil
- ❏ transmission fluid
- ❏ power steering fluid
- ❏ brake fluid
- ❏ coolant/antifreeze
- ❏ WD-40 lubricant
- ❏ electrical tape
- ❏ duct tape
- ❏ nylon zip ties
- ❏ JB Weld metal glue
- ❏ misc. fasteners (sheet-metal screws, nuts, bolts, etc.)
- ❏ baling wire

TOOLS:

- ❏ jack (supplied with vehicle)
- ❏ jack (hi-lift jack with long handle, can also serve as a winch)
- ❏ lug wrench
- ❏ socket set (standard and metric)
- ❏ open-end and adjustable wrenches
- ❏ channel lock pliers
- ❏ Vise-Grips
- ❏ screwdrivers in several sizes (both flathead and Phillips)
- ❏ pry bar
- ❏ spark plug wrench
- ❏ Allen-wrench set
- ❏ jumper cables
- ❏ voltmeter or circuit tester
- ❏ heavy-duty wire cutters/ stripper
- ❏ 36-inch bolt cutters

they show signs of age. Since many newer vehicles have a single belt that drives the alternator, air conditioning compressor, fan, and water pump, losing this belt will render your vehicle inoperable. If you really want to be prepared, you should carry a spare parts kit in the vehicle, as well as the tools to install them. For a complete list of parts and tools you should consider carrying, see the "Vehicle Checklist" above.

In addition to tools for repairing the vehicle, it's a good idea to carry what you need to get through locked gates and barbed wire or chain-link fences. Most such obstacles can be defeated with a pair of heavy-duty wire cutters for fences and a pair of 36-inch or larger bolt cutters for padlocked gates. Even in public national forests, you will occasionally come upon service roads that have been closed to the public with a locked iron gate. Having the means to open these will greatly increase your options. A powerful winch mounted on the front bumper (and better yet, one on the rear as well) will get you out of a lot of trouble if you get stuck, and can be an aid to clearing broken-down vehicles and other obstacles out of the roadway.

Fuel

Other than mechanical breakdown, running out of fuel will be your biggest worry when bugging out by motor vehicle. As already mentioned in the previous chapter, you cannot count on being able to obtain any additional fuel after the onset of a bug-out situation. This is seen time and time again when hurricanes threaten to make landfall. People rush to the gas station to fill up their vehicles and extra jerry cans. On September 11, 2001, the same thing happened across much of America.

In addition to making it a habit to top off your vehicle's tank as often as is reasonable, you should keep on hand enough jerry cans for a complete refill once you burn that first tank. This will give you quite a long range in most vehicles, and enough reserve to allow for long delays and for possibly helping a less-prepared neighbor or family member. Gasoline should only be stored in approved containers, of course, and it is essential to keep the containers vented and stored in a safe place. Another thing to keep in mind is that stored gasoline will not stay fresh and burn reliably unless you use a conditioning additive like STA-BIL to prolong its storage life. The other alternative to doing this is to rotate the fuel in your jerry cans every few weeks by pouring it into your tank to be burned and buying new fuel for the containers.

Carrying jerry cans when you bug out can also be problematic, depending on the vehicle. In a sedan or other passenger car, you will have no option but to carry it them in the trunk or inside the vehicle. You must vent the cans, especially in hot weather, but in an enclosed car the fumes could be a problem if you have to store them this way for long. Pick-up trucks are the easiest, as you can simply carry the jerry cans in the open bed, provided you secure them with lashings or straps so they don't slide around or fall over and spill. Many SUVs feature racks for carrying a jerry can or two, and you can add such a rack if you don't have one.

In a bug-out emergency when there is a shortage of gasoline, you don't want to advertise the fact that you have plenty by riding around with your jerry cans in plain sight. In the aftermath of Katrina, some drivers were targeted by looters and carjackers for this very reason, so you should make every effort to conceal the jerry cans under a tarp or some other cover so that they are out of sight, yet still vented.

Choosing a Vehicle for Bugging Out

If you're bugging out by motor vehicle, obviously some form of rugged four-wheel-drive SUV or pickup is more versatile than a Honda Civic or Mini Cooper. That's not to say that you can't bug out in an economy car or sports car if that's all you have, but vehicles with some off-road capability will give you more options for dodging or going through obstructions or traveling damaged roadways.

In the decade or so before the unprecedented gasoline prices of 2008, large trucks and SUVs enjoyed a tremendous popularity in the

WHAT TO LOOK FOR IN A BUG-OUT VEHICLE

Some survivalists who are prepping for a bug-out situation advocate older, pre-1980 trucks or SUVs, based on the fact that these vehicles do not use electronic computer modules that would be vulnerable to an EMP (electromagnetic pulse) attack. In reality, such an attack is probably the least likely bug-out scenario, but older vehicles do have the advantage of simplicity of systems, making them easier to work on in the field with a minimum of tools. Newer vehicles are less likely to break down to begin with, of course, and may get better gas mileage.

If you are looking for a dedicated bug-out vehicle rather than simply making do with what you drive every day, then you might as well try to find one with the following features:

- four-wheel-drive
- full front axles rather than independent front suspension
- trailer hitch and heavy-duty tow package
- at least one winch, preferably two (front and rear)
- skid plates to protect the drive train and fuel tank
- brush guards and heavy-duty front and rear bumpers
- cargo racks on the roof
- room for jerry cans and two spare tires on the roof or mounted on the rear bumper or gate

U.S., even among residents of urban areas and suburbia, who used them for nothing more adventurous than trips to the mall or hauling the kids to soccer games. This popularity and the resulting competition among manufacturers led to the introduction of a wide variety of such vehicles in many sizes and configurations. While these vehicles had long been used by those working in construction, surveying, or other outdoor pursuits, when the general public took an interest, they demanded not only the exterior looks that portrayed the owner as an outdoorsy individual, but the creature comforts of the finest luxury cars. The result was a steady escalation in size, amenities, and price, until most SUVs and some pickups reached the same status category as expensive sports cars and luxury sedans.

Because of the popularity of these vehicles, you may already own one as your everyday ride. If not, the used market is flooded with examples that owners are getting rid of in favor of smaller vehicles with better gas-mileage ratings. If you are looking for one to purchase, avoid the larger, fully loaded models, as these will cost the most and be least suitable for setting up as a versatile bug-out vehicle. Fuel consumption can be outrageous in some of the largest examples.

Some examples of suitable older model SUVs and trucks:

- Jeep Cherokee XJ
- Jeep CJ series
- Jeep Wrangler
- Suzuki Samurai
- Toyota 4WD pickup or 4Runner with 22R engine
- Toyota Landcruiser
- Nissan Pathfinder
- Ford Bronco
- Chevrolet Blazer
- Land Rover Discovery

Unless you have a big family and need the room to haul all the people and necessary gear, keep in mind that bigger is not always better when choosing an SUV or pickup for bugging out. A lightweight, narrow Suzuki Samurai or Toyota four-wheel-drive pick-up can go more places on narrow fire roads or in dense woods than an extra-wide Hummer or Ford F-350.

Alternative Motor Vehicles: Motorcycles and ATVs

Motorcycles and ATVs (all-terrain vehicles) can in many cases make excellent bug-out vehicles. They are smaller and lighter than standard vehicles, get better gas mileage, and many can go places automobiles cannot. Large street bikes and road touring machines such as Harley Davidsons, Honda Goldwings, and others are not in this category and have less of an advantage over cars. While these larger motorcycles can work as bug-out vehicles, they will still be confined to roads that are in generally good condition, and may not be more fuel efficient than many cars.

Dual-Sport Motorcycles

A better choice for a bug-out vehicle is the dual-sport or on-road/ off-road type of motorcycle. Dual-sport motorcycles are designed to be street-legal, with lights, turn signals, and other required features, while offering the additional capability to handle dirt roads, trails, and even some cross-country riding. Motorcycles in this class are generally smaller and lighter than the big street cruisers. They are also much simpler, with basic single- or two-cylinder engines, chain drive, basic instrumentation, and rugged frames. Many of these motorcycles have evolved to meet the requirements of demanding races that combine both paved and unpaved surfaces, such as the famous Paris to Dakar Rally.

Dual-sport motorcycles are available in a range of sizes with engines anywhere from 100cc up to about 900cc. The bikes with 500cc or larger engines are more suited to use on the road and can comfortably travel at highway speeds when appropriate. These bikes are popular with long-distance motorcycle tourists, who ride them to remote locations in Alaska and undeveloped countries. Rack and pannier systems allow you to carry everything you would carry in a bug-out bag securely on the motorcycle. A good dual-sport motorcycle like this can get you quickly out of the city, allowing you to take off-road shortcuts around stalled traffic and across open ground, and then take you deep into the wilderness of your bug-out location on service roads, fire roads, and trails. In the more open country of the West in particular, such a motorcycle can literally become a "steel horse," taking you far out into the desert or mountains to places no other motor vehicle can go. The fuel supply is limited, of course, but some of these bikes have large enough tanks for a 300-mile range and you may have room for a small jerry can on the rack to extend this even further.

Some examples of suitable dual-purpose motorcycles:
- Kawasaki KLR 650
- Suzuki DR 650
- Honda XLR 650
- BMW R1150GS
- KTM 640 Adventure
- KTM 950 Adventure

Four-Wheeler ATVs

ATVs appeal to many who do not want the challenges of riding rough terrain on two wheels, or to those who need to carry heavier loads or negotiate mud and other obstacles that would stop a two-wheeler. Most of these ATVs have fat mud-grip tires that can easily negotiate deep sand and cross shallow creeks or water-filled mudholes. The best of them feature four-wheel drive and reverse gears, making them able to navigate very treacherous terrain. The disadvantage of such vehicles compared to dual-sport motorcycles is that they are generally slower and not as suitable for use on roads, and are heavier, larger, and more difficult to hide in the woods.

Four-wheeler ATVs have become ubiquitous in rural America and are popular with the deer-hunting crowd because they can be fitted with

large racks to carry climbing tree stands and hunting weapons, as well as pack out the deer after a successful hunt. They are also used by farmers and ranchers to carry tools and fence-building supplies and serve other utilitarian purposes that motorcycles would not be good at.

Like SUVs, four-wheeler ATVs started out as simple machines and evolved into something much more complex. For the most versatility as a bug-out vehicle, I would suggest a simple, open machine with front and rear racks rather than the larger vehicle-like giants such as the

Kawasaki Mule. Like a dual-sport motorcycle, a smaller, open ATV can easily be transported in the bed of any pickup, or pulled behind other vehicles on a small trailer, allowing you to abandon the tow vehicle and take to the desert or woods on the ATV if necessary. This type of ATV has a simple straddle-style seat like a motorcycle and can carry one passenger behind the operator. The larger, side-by-side ATVs like the above-mentioned Mule have bench-type seating for two or even four passengers. This type of ATV could be useful if you need to move that many people on one vehicle or carry heavy loads, but it will not be able to go as many places off-road as the more compact open four-wheeler. Another drawback to these larger side-by-side ATVs is that most of them cost as much as many small cars or more than what you would pay for a good used SUV.

Some examples of suitable ATVs:

- Kawasaki Brute Force 650
- Polaris Sportsman 850 XP
- Arctic Cat 550 H1
- Polaris Ranger 800 HD (side-by-side ATV)
- Kawasaki Mule 4010 Trans 4x4 Diesel (4-passenger side-by-side ATV)

Alternative Transportation

As we have seen, motor vehicles can offer many advantages and will likely be the first choice of most people bugging out from suburban areas and U.S. cities where private car ownership is high. But even in urban areas there are those who do not own vehicles or even know how to drive. At the other extreme, in some rural areas there is so much open land that travel by road is too limiting and better options are available. And finally, if you happen to live along the coast, a bay shore, a large navigable river, or an inland lake, bugging out on the water in some type of boat may be a far better option than jostling with millions of others on overcrowded roads.

Bicycles

As those who use them for commuting, long-distance touring, or serious competition already know, modern bicycles are a serious and viable means of transportation. Bicycles have evolved into dependable, lightweight, and efficient machines that can take a fit rider unlimited distances at a surprisingly fast pace. Even without training, an average person can cover much more ground on a bicycle than by walking or running. The right type of bicycle also has the added advantage of being able to carry a fairly heavy load of gear with a system of racks and panniers or a trailer. After the failed evacuation from New Orleans during Katrina, one avid cyclist pointed out that if this kind of scenario occurred in a city like Seattle, where so many people commute to work on their bicycles, most of them could have simply pedaled out of town past the impossible traffic jams on the freeway.

Bicycle Advantages and Disadvantages

Like dual-purpose motorcycles, many bicycles can easily negotiate road shoulders and sidewalks, jump curbs, and cross medians and other unpaved areas. Like the motorcycle, a bicycle is narrow and can slip between lines of traffic and squeeze past jammed cars. The bicycle is even more versatile in that it is lightweight enough to pick up and carry over bigger obstacles or can be walked through deep mud, sand, and other terrain that cannot be ridden. Bicycles can also be easily carried in most any type of motor vehicle, even small cars, by removing the wheels. This makes them a good secondary choice even if you initially bug out in a car.

Another obvious advantage a bicycle has over all motorized vehicles is that they are much quieter, and in fact virtually silent from even a short distance away. Especially when traveling at night, bicycle riders can pass by camps and occupied residences unheard and unseen. In the backcountry, mountain bikes operating on trails or cross-country can also go undetected unless they pass close enough to hear the hum of wheels or sounds of shifters or brakes.

ROUTE PLANNING FOR BICYCLES

In many U.S. cities and communities today, there are networks of recreational bike paths and trails that are inaccessible to motor vehicles. Some of these bike-only routes are dozens of miles long and many will take you all the way out of the city to the surrounding countryside. Some are paved, the most extensive network of these being the converted railroad beds that are part of the National Rails-to-Trails Conservancy. Other bike trails intended for mountain bikes may be rugged dirt single-tracks, but if you have a suitable bike, they can be great escape routes. If there are such bike trails in your area, maps will be available from the agencies that manage them, and you should obtain these in advance and get out and ride the trails you might need to use in an emergency.

Since they require no fuel to operate other than the rider's own energy, there are no limits on the ultimate distance you can travel on a bicycle, given enough time. A bike is a relatively simple machine; one made with quality components can travel almost indefinitely, as long as you have a few basic tools and spare parts. The most common issues are flat tires, and those are easy to deal with if you carry a pump, spare tubes, and a patch kit. Other spares to carry include an extra tire of the folding variety, extra spokes, derailleur cable, brake cable, and brake pads. As with motor vehicles of course, you must carry the tools needed to replace these parts, but they are relatively few and are small and lightweight.

On the downside, compared to drivers of motor vehicles or motorcycles, bicycle riders are significantly more vulnerable to attack because of their slower top speeds and lack of protection. This is especially true on the open road, where automobile drivers could hit a cyclist with thrown objects or even the vehicle itself. But in a mass evacuation the cyclist would be able to move while drivers enclosed in their vehicles would be trapped in traffic and possibly more at risk from gangs of attackers on foot. As the everyday commuting cyclist who rides in city traffic knows, the key to survival on a bike in the street is constant vigilance and the ability to react quickly and take evasive action.

Because of the many specialized interests in the field of cycling, a variety of bicycle types have been developed, from racing and touring to commuting and off-road trail riding. Some of these are more suitable than others for bug-out purposes. Ultra-lightweight and somewhat fragile racing bikes are not ideal. For potential bug-out vehicles, there are three main choices: touring bikes, mountain bikes, and commuting or hybrid bikes. Whichever you choose, it is important to find one of quality construction. This does not mean you have to buy the most expensive model out there, as new bikes can be outrageously pricey, but you should look for a name brand and if buying new, shop at a bike shop rather than a department store. Bike shop bikes will have better-quality frames, all-aluminum wheels and components, and will be properly assembled. It's far better to buy even an older, used bike of this type than a cheap imitation built with inferior materials and incorrectly assembled and adjusted.

Touring Bicycles

Touring bicycles usually resemble road racing bikes in outward design, but are much more substantially built and are fitted with threaded mounting eyelets for attaching racks and panniers. The frame geometry is more relaxed to better absorb road shock and allow all-day riding comfort. Purpose-built touring bicycles are the best choice if your goal is to travel a long distance as quickly as possible. These bikes have lightweight but sturdy wheels fitted with road tires. They are not

BIKE TRAILERS

Another option that will allow you to carry your fully loaded bug-out bag without repacking is a tow-behind bicycle touring trailer. These trailers are available with a single wheel or in a two-wheel configuration, and connect to the bike at the rear axle or the rear seatpost. A lightweight aluminum frame with a built-in fabric bottom allows you to strap in your fully-loaded backpack and protect it with a rain-proof cover. This is much more convenient than loading and unloading panniers, and it's easier to keep everything protected from the elements. Around camp the trailer can also be used as a utility trailer to haul firewood or water. A touring trailer keeps your bicycle free of bulky luggage and can be quickly disconnected if you need to ride somewhere fast without the burden. The disadvantage of trailers compared to panniers is the extra wheel or two to deal with and maintain, as well as the extra length of the whole rig that may limit quick maneuvering in some situations. Single-wheel trailers are better in this respect and are more versatile for trails and rough terrain.

the best for rough conditions, but on pavement they allow much higher average speeds than mountain bikes. With some training, most bicycle tourists can cover 50 to 80 miles in a day's time with a fully loaded touring bike. Serious touring cyclists can do well over a hundred miles a day, even in the mountains. This is enough to get you a long way in the span of a few days—much farther than walking.

The pannier system that has been developed by those who enjoy traveling on bicycles is a superb way to carry all the gear necessary for living on the road or bugging out. The weight is distributed evenly and low around the front and rear tires so that the bike's handling is not affected. This is much better than trying to ride with a pack on your back, which raises the center of gravity too high. If you are using a bicycle as a bug-out vehicle, you will have to redistribute your gear into the smaller panniers, but you should be able to easily carry everything outlined in Chapter Two. The bug-out backpack itself can still be carried, even if mostly empty, by strapping it across the rack over the rear panniers. This is essential, because if you are bugging out to a roadless wilderness on a road touring bike, you will eventually have to ditch the bike when you reach your destination.

Mountain Bikes

Mountain bikes are designed for off-road riding and are the bicycle equivalent of four-wheel-drive vehicles, ATVs, or off-road motorcycles. Like other bicycles, the advantage mountain bikes have over motorized vehicles of any sort is that they do not require fuel and they are light enough for you to pick up and carry over large rocks, streams, and other obstacles. A good mountain bike can get you to a bug-out location and in some areas serve as transportation within the area, if the terrain is suitable for riding off-trail. It can be easily hidden when not needed and retrieved if there is a need to cover long distances faster than is possible by walking.

From relatively simple beginnings, mountain bikes have evolved into expensive, high-tech machines optimized for different recreational and competitive pursuits, from cross-country racing to fast downhill and stunt performance. Many of these have features you do not want in a bug-out bike, as they add weight and complexity and are more likely to break down. Mountain bikes are heavier than most road bikes, and with their fat tires, they will be slower and more tiring to ride long distances on pavement.

The best compromise is to look for an older style of mountain bike: a simple, strong frame with no front or rear suspension and rugged off-road rims with knobby tires designed to negotiate rough terrain. You may have to search the used market to find a rigid-frame bike, as simplicity has fallen out of favor with the mountain bike crowd. Failing that you could choose what is called a "hardtail" mountain bike, which is set up with a rigid rear frame and front suspension only. Racks and panniers can be attached to most of these basic rigid-frame mountain bikes, or you can do as many off-road bike tourists prefer and tow a touring trailer.

Commuting Bikes

Another class of bicycle that falls between the fast road touring machine and the rugged mountain bike is the commuting or hybrid bicycle. Bicycles in this class were designed to have some of the toughness of mountain bikes, for dealing with potholes and other dangers of city streets, while retaining most of the speed of road bikes. They are generally set up with handlebars for an upright riding position, which allows good visibility in traffic but less comfort on really long distance rides. The other advantage of this upright position in traffic is improved handling and the ability to perform evasive maneuvers that would be harder with the drop bars of a road bike. Most bicycles designed for commuting come with racks or can easily be fitted with them.

Some examples of suitable bicycles:
- Surly Long-Haul Trucker
- Trek 520 (road touring)
- Cannondale Bad Boy
- Trek 7500 FX (commuting)
- Trek 4500
- Specialized Rockhopper (hardtail mountain)
- Older non-suspension models such as the Trek 970 or 830 (rigid frame mountain)

Bugging Out by Boat: Canoes, Kayaks, Motorboats, and Sailboats

In many ways you will have an advantage if you live along the shores of navigable water. Even in coastal areas where boating is popular, the vast majority of the population will not have access to a boat of any kind and will remain shorebound, with no choice but to deal with the problems of traffic and crowds. Those who have their own boats will have the option of bugging out by water, and all waterways lead to places that are inaccessible to those who do not have a boat.

Your bug-out boat can be as simple as a canoe or elaborate as a cruising yacht, and the following sections will examine the advantages and disadvantages of several types of boats. Much will depend on the type of waterway you live near, but there will likely be a boat that will serve your purpose just right. In many cases, the boat can not only be your bug-out escape vehicle for when the SHTF, but also your primary means of transportation within your bug-out location of choice, serving as a platform for hunting, fishing, and gathering. Obviously, for this purpose, the best type of boat is one that requires no mechanical parts such as an engine, is quiet while underway, and is small enough to keep a low profile and to be hidden when not needed. The simplest boats of this type are human-powered with paddles or oars.

Canoes

Canoes in one form or another have been used by indigenous people around the world for thousands of years and are still in use today in many places. Since they can be made with simple methods and tools from materials found in nature, they were ideal for groups living a hunter-gather lifestyle. In a long-term bug-out situation, you could still make your own dugout canoe from a suitable log if you had a need for one, but if you plan in advance, you can take advantage of modern materials and design to have a lightweight, long-lasting canoe that will be more versatile.

A good canoe is an easily propelled vessel that can carry a sizeable load over a variety of water conditions, from placid rivers and lakes to whitewater rapids and windblown bays. Canoes are the epitome of simplicity in boat design—just an open, double-ended hull reinforced with only the necessary thwarts and seat racks. There are no moving parts and if you choose a model made of aluminum, fiberglass composite, or one of the new plastics such as Royalex, there is no maintenance required. The canoe paddle is also a simple design that can be replaced without much trouble from the materials found in nature.

The open canoe with no decks is easy to load and easy to get in and out off for dragging over logs and other river obstructions, and is lightweight enough to be portaged between lakes and other waterways. Being open, it is also easier to fish and hunt out of, and most designs can be paddled from a standing position if desired, especially if you are carrying a good load of gear that increases stability. In swamps and other still waters, the canoe can be paddled slowly and silently, allowing you to approach game that would be difficult to stalk on foot. All but the smallest canoes can accommodate two paddlers, but can still be handled by one if necessary.

Choosing a Canoe

Like bicycles, canoes have evolved from their more utilitarian origins and are now offered in many specialized configurations for recreational and competitive pursuits. Reading through manufacturer's literature on the array of choices, one would conclude that a different canoe is needed for every type of waterway encountered. This marketing hype can be ignored, however, if you stick to proven parameters in canoe design and select one that may be a compromise in some areas, but will do the job most anywhere.

In boat design, waterline length equals speed, so the longer the hull the faster it will be. In the case of a narrow hull like a canoe, extra length also increases stability, reducing the likelihood of capsizing. Too much length, however, decreases maneuverability, making it more difficult to negotiate the obstacles and sharp bends of creeks and smaller rivers. The best all-around canoes seem to fall in the range of 15–17 feet in length, with a maximum beam (width) of around 33–36 inches. Although a wider canoe may appear more stable to the uninitiated, it will be slower to paddle and will actually have less secondary stability in really rough water. Other design considerations are the amount of rocker (curve) along the keel and the shape and height of the ends. A straighter keel with slight or no rocker will track better and be faster than a banana-shaped hull designed to do tricks in whitewater rapids. The bow and stern ends should be high enough to rise over waves and deflect spray, but if too high they will catch too much wind and make the canoe difficult to paddle straight in open water.

One reason a canoe makes such a great bug-out vessel is that is can be launched at a moment's notice practically anywhere and with little hassle. You can store it in your garage or upside-down in the backyard, transport it on the roof of a vehicle, or carry it on your shoulders to the launch site. Your bug-out backpack can be thrown in and tied down as is, or put inside a larger waterproof dry bag made for the purpose. Canoes can travel on mere inches of water, so if there is a small stream or creek near you, chances are you can negotiate it in a canoe with the option of heading downstream to a larger river or body of water. A good used canoe can be picked up for a couple hundred dollars in most places, and even new ones are not expensive. They certainly represent the most boat for the money of any vessel you can choose from.

Some examples of suitable canoes:

- Old Town Tripper 172
- Mad River Expedition 186
- Wenonah Boundary Waters 17
- Buffalo 16
- Grumman Aluminum 17 (frequently available on the used market)

Sea Kayaks

Despite the utility of a good canoe, I have a strong bias in favor of sea kayaks when it comes to human-powered watercraft. I've traveled literally thousands of miles in sea kayaks, along coastlines, down rivers, and island-hopping in the open ocean. My trusty 17-foot sea kayak has taken me from the Canadian north woods to the Gulf Coast and through the West Indies from Florida to the Virgin Islands, an adventure I wrote about in my book *On Island*  *Time: Kayaking the Caribbean.* Like the canoe, the modern sea kayak is a lightweight, simple vessel derived from the aboriginal version, used in this case by the natives of the arctic and sub-arctic regions of North America and Greenland. When modern adventurers rediscovered the oceangoing kayak and started exploring its potential, they soon realized that here was a boat that could do things no other vessel could. Light and small enough to be carried to the beach by the paddler, it is still seaworthy enough to negotiate breaking surf and make long journeys on the open ocean.

The key to the kayak's extraordinary seaworthiness is the watertight deck. A decked boat with no place for the water to enter can survive almost any wave, bobbing back to the surface like a cork even after being completely submerged. Using modern technology to make the hulls stronger and more durable, today's sea kayak designers have created watercraft that can go just about anywhere there is water. Sea kayaking adventurers have completed expeditions far more difficult than my own island jaunts, including rounding Cape Horn, paddling from California to Hawaii, and circumnavigating Australia.

Because of this ability to go anywhere on the water, from rough seas to inland rivers, you should give sea kayaks serious consideration if you are planning to bug out from anywhere along a coastline, barrier island, or other open waterway. With some experience and training, you can plan on averaging 20 miles or more per day even when paddling against wind and current, and much more if conditions are more favorable. A touring-sized sea kayak can carry everything that would go in your bug-out bag and more. Wielding the double-bladed sea kayak paddle becomes as easy as walking after a while, and you can travel at a steady pace while observing the scenery and marine life.

Like the canoe, the sea kayak is a good platform for hunting and fishing. Although you can't stand in it, you can cast a fishing rod, use a drop line, or shoot a hunting rifle from the seated position. Everywhere I've traveled by kayak I've frequently come in close contact with game animals that were not frightened by my silent approach. This stealth aspect would be a great advantage when bugging out, especially when traveling at night or in bad weather, as you would be almost invisible to those ashore or on other vessels and too small to show up on most ships' radar. I have often paddled silently past unsuspecting people ashore, close enough to hear their conversations. Living out of the kayak, I would frequently find an inaccessible location along a remote river, seashore, or island and set up camp out of sight from the water, hiding the kayak in camp as well. This is something you can only do with small boats like kayaks or canoes.

Kayak Advantages and Disadvantages

Decked touring kayaks are a little more inconvenient to get into and out of than canoes, and packing your gear through the small watertight hatches means it will take more time than simply throwing a bug-out bag in and going. But what you gain by putting up with this inconvenience is secure dry storage for your gear and supplies, and a boat that is far more versatile than a canoe. A good sea kayak can handle conditions no canoe could survive, and even on waters a canoe could handle the kayak will be faster and easier to paddle. This speed will permit you to travel upstream on most rivers, something that is much more difficult in a canoe.

Sea kayaks are more expensive than canoes and require more basic equipment to function—such as the more complex, double-ended paddle, a watertight spray skirt, and safety accessories such as bilge pumps and a paddle rescue float for re-entry after a capsize. But as with canoes, there are good deals in the used market, as most owners never subject their boats to the rigors of an expedition and many secondhand ones will be as good as new. My preference in a sea kayak is one of high internal volume that allows me to carry lots of gear. This generally means a length of 17 or 18 feet and a beam of 23 to 25 inches. Avoid the more performance-oriented narrower boats, as they will not have sufficient volume for your bug-out gear. Larger tandem sea kayaks are available if you are bugging out as a couple, but most seasoned touring kayakers would prefer the versatility and greater carrying capacity of two single kayaks in this situation.

Some examples of suitable sea kayaks:
- Current Designs Solstice GT
- Eddyline Journey
- Necky Tesla (only available used)
- Pygmy Arctic Tern 17 High Volume (available as a build-it-yourself kit)

Other Boat Options

Canoes or sea kayaks are the most useful small boats for wilderness use, particularly for extended stays in your bug-out location, for the reasons already mentioned—silent operation, low profile, and the ease of carrying and concealing them when not in use. Nevertheless, there are many other types of small boats that can be used as bug-out vessels, ranging from a wide assortment of human-powered rowboats, outboard-powered skiffs, runabouts and fishing boats, and small sailboats. The variations of such boats are far too many to describe here, but those who prefer something different than a canoe and kayak can choose from many capable small boats that can carry a good load and negotiate a variety of water conditions. Some of these have the added benefit of being large enough to sleep aboard under a tarp

BOATING SKILLS AND EQUIPMENT

Regardless of the type of boat you choose, from a simple canoe to a cruising boat, if you plan to bug out by water you need to acquaint yourself with marine navigation and include in your kit the relevant nautical charts that cover your home waters and the route to your bug-out location. Navigation skills are more critical on open water than on land, and beyond getting lost, marine navigation also involves understanding shoreline and bottom structures and how they interact with wind and currents that can create dangerous waves. Running aground can also have serious consequences, especially in larger boats. Because of these factors, you have to know where you are at all times when navigating on the water, and a good GPS and reliable compass are two essential tools. Like the electronic topo maps available for land navigation, electronic nautical charts can be plugged into your GPS receiver and will show your vessel's position on the screen.

The spare parts, repair materials and tools needed on your bug-out boat will depend on its size, construction material, and complexity of systems or rigging. At the very least, even in a canoe or kayak, you should carry the materials needed to patch a hole or other damage to the hull. Duct tape can do wonders in an emergency, and with some fiberglass cloth and epoxy resin, you can make permanent repairs to many types of hulls. You should carry spare paddles or oars, as well as parts to maintain engines and sails if you are relying on those.

Since cruising boats are larger, heavier, and generally deeper in draft than the other classes of boat mentioned, they require more equipment such as anchors, dinghies, mooring lines, etc., and consequently require more skill to operate. Cruising boat seamanship is not something you can learn overnight, so if you plan on bugging out in this type of vessel, you should begin getting in as much time on the water as possible in the boat of your choice. Offshore waters of the coast and open ocean are unforgiving of beginner's mistakes and are no place to venture without proper skills and preparation.

or purpose-made deck tent, allowing you to shelter in places such as marshes or swamps where there is no dry land for camping.

Except for the smallest and lightest rowing dinghies, most boats of this type will be too heavy to carry far from the water and more difficult to conceal. But the tradeoff is greater load-carrying capacity and the ability to carry more than one or two people. Larger boats in this category are good bug-out choices for families, as they can accommodate several people and their bug-out bags.

Motorboats

Like motor vehicles, boats with outboard engines will require spare parts, tools, and plenty of reserve fuel to make them reliable for a SHTF situation. The advantage of outboard power, of course, is the speed with which you can make your getaway, as well as the distance you can cover with little effort. If you choose a late-model four-stroke engine, an outboard-powered boat can be extremely dependable and relatively fuel-efficient. Avoid the popular tendency to mount the biggest outboard you can fit on the transom. You will see this done all the time by fishermen who put enough power on small boats to pull water skiers, but for a bug-situation this is a bad choice because such a boat will guzzle fuel and you won't be able to go far before it becomes useless and will have to be abandoned. If you outfit your boat instead with an engine designed to push it along all day at a comfortable cruising speed, you will have a long-range bug-out vessel that will get you where you're going with fuel in reserve.

Flat-Bottom Skiffs

On inland rivers, swamps, and smaller lakes, a flat-bottom skiff with square ends is an excellent choice. Known among those who use them as "Johnboats," boats with this hull design have the benefits of shallow draft and great stability and load carrying capability—which is why the same shape is used for huge river barges that carry cargo. They are also among the cheapest outboard-powered boats you can buy, ranging from 10- to 14-foot lightweight aluminum hulls to much heavier boats of 20 or more feet in length. For exposed open water however, especially on windswept bays and along the coast, the Johnboat is a poor choice and should be ruled out in favor of a more seaworthy V-hull or power catamaran design that can slice through breaking waves.

Sailboats

In locations where there is open water there is usually more wind, so sailboats also become a viable option for bug-out vessels. If you live along an open coast, or on a barrier island, a small sailboat can take you as far as you need to go without requiring any fuel, although it is wise to have a small auxiliary outboard for times when the wind is too light. Since they are designed to be operated in windy conditions, most small sailboats are more seaworthy than small powerboats. Some of them are partially or fully decked, allowing them to withstand severe conditions, and a few small day sailers can double as "micro-cruisers," complete with a minimal cabin that allows sleeping aboard and the possibility of long, open-water voyages.

Some examples of suitable small boats:
- Whitehall Tyee 14
- Little River Marine Heritage 15 (rowing)
- Sea Pearl 21
- Drascombe Lugger 18 (sailing camp cruisers)
- West Wight Potter 15 (cuddy cabin sailboat)
- Tracker Topper 1432 (Johnboat)
- Panga Marine 18
- Boston Whaler Montauk 170 (outboard skiff)
- C-Dory 16 (cuddy cabin motor cruiser)

Liveaboard Cruisers

Longer voyages become even more of a possibility with the final category of potential bug-out vessels—the liveaboard cruiser. Cruising boats are quite popular in coastal regions everywhere and are also widely used in places like the Great Lakes and along navigable inland rivers. The price of entry into the world of cruising can be a lot less than what most non-boaters imagine. A fixer-upper used liveaboard sailboat can be had for the price of a good used truck or SUV. Of course the sky is the limit on how much you can spend on boats of this type, and if you choose a luxury motor cruiser it could cost the equivalent of several houses. But an interesting point to consider is that a cruising boat can be your bug-out vehicle and bug-out location all in one, as you can live aboard it anywhere you go. This type of bugging out is a bit beyond the scope of this book, but is something to think about if you have knowledge of navigation and especially if you already own a suitable cruiser.

Cruising boats are designed as both motor vessels and sailing vessels. Most motor yachts of any size consume far too much fuel to make them viable for a long-term bug-out vessel. A sailing cruiser, however, can go indefinitely with no fuel or perhaps a small amount for occasional maneuvering with an auxiliary engine. Cruising sailboats of many designs from about 20 feet on up offer open-ocean capability, giving you an option others in a SHTF situation will not have: the ability to simply sail away to an unaffected part of the world. Although this may be the best bug-out strategy of all, a cruising boat can also be used as a liveaboard platform in many remote parts of the United States, such as among barrier islands and coastal marsh areas, many of which are uninhabited. Such a boat can also carry stores for six months or more of independent living. The key to choosing a cruising boat that is suitable for a bug-out vessel is simplicity. The fewer complex systems the better, and a smaller size boat that can be easily maintained in remote locations will be easier to keep going for a longer period of time.

One cruising boat disadvantage to keep in mind is that such a boat cannot be easily hidden, and if you choose one as a bug-out boat you will tied down to it, as you cannot leave such a tempting target filled with gear and supplies unattended. Even if you are on board, a high-profile cruising boat could attract the attention of gangs of looters. It's always a good idea to anchor among islands or other locations not easily reached by shorebound people, and to do so far enough from land to discourage swimmers. You'll still have to contend with potential attacks from those in smaller boats, so someone should be on deck to keep watch anytime there is a potential threat.

Some examples of suitable cruising boats:
- Catalina 27 or 270 (sail)
- Maine Cat 30 (sailing catamaran)

- Pearson Triton 28 (offshore sail—available used)
- Nordic Tug 26
- Mainship Pilot 31 (motor yacht)

Horses and Pack Animals

Horses and pack animals, including mules, donkeys, and llamas, have a long history of aiding man's travel in the wilderness. The use of such animals to either ride or carry your gear will not likely be an option to most readers who live in cities or suburbs, unless the animals are kept boarded at a secure location in the country that you can be sure of reaching. For those who already live in rural areas or on farms or ranches, horses and other livestock may be a part of daily life and could be a viable option. Even if you don't ride, walking along with a packhorse or other beast of burden will make it much easier to carry your basic bug-out gear, as well as extra supplies and equipment.

In the old days, when fences were nonexistent, it was much easier to strike out on horseback or lead a pack train of mules through the mountains. In most parts of the lower 48 today, a cross-country rider will come across fence after fence in one form or another. The only exception will be in large tracts of federal land, such as national forests or BLM holdings. Everywhere else, it is essential to carry wire cutters if you expect to get far in a bug-out situation.

Horses

Horses are the obvious choice if you intend to ride. A single rider and horse can cover a lot of ground in the wilderness in a hurry. At a trot or a gallop on a horse, you can really eat up the miles. But if you are bugging out on horseback, you're probably going to want an additional packhorse as well to carry your gear and supplies. Even at a walking pace of three miles per hour, riding with a packhorse in tow sure beats humping a backpack through the mountains on foot. Horses can carry up to twenty percent of their weight, so a load of 200 or more pounds is not unreasonable for a good-sized packhorse.

Mules

Mules can be more valuable than horses in really rugged terrain, which is why they are commonly used for tours with inexperienced riders in places like the Grand Canyon. They don't spook as easily as horses and are not fearful of narrow trails that lead beside precipitous cliffs. A mule can climb a slope up to forty-five degrees with little effort, and can carry as much or more weight than the average packhorse. Like a horse, a mule can be ridden as well if you prefer not to walk.

Donkeys

Donkeys are less expensive than horses or mules, but are also generally smaller and somewhat slower. The larger ones can be ridden at a walking pace, but they are more useful for simply carrying the load, led by a walking handler. They are easier for a beginner to train for packing than a horse, and are generally intelligent and congenial, bonding with their human companions in much the same was a dog would. They are good browsers and can forage off the landscape quite well, eating thistles another rough plants that horses and mules would turn their noses up at.

Llamas

Llamas from South America have in recent years found favor with many backcountry travelers as pack animals. Pack llamas can carry loads of between 60 and 100 pounds, depending on the individual animal and the speed and daily distance traveled. Llamas are sure-footed in rough terrain and reliable enough to be a good alternative to larger pack animals, though, like donkeys, they are a little slower than horses. Since they are browsers like deer, they can generally find their own forage, eliminating the need to carry any extra food for them.

CONSIDERATIONS FOR BUGGING OUT WITH ANIMALS

Just as motor vehicles, bicycles, boats, and other man-made machines have their various maintenance issues, beasts of burden are no exception. Like their owners, they have to eat, can get sick or injured, and have personality quirks that can be difficult to deal with. They can be easily frightened and will occasionally panic, breaking free and running from their handlers if not kept in control at all times. The advantage of living animals as a method of transportation or carrying your gear, however, is that they can offer a form of companionship in the lonely backcountry, and their keener ears and sense of smell can warn you of approaching dangers.

No matter which type of pack animal you chose, you will have to obtain the right gear for rigging the pack load on the animal's back. To do so incorrectly, with uncomfortable or painful pack saddles, is unfair to your load-bearing companions and could possibly cause injuries that will render them useless for the purpose. The best way to learn the intricacies of caring for pack animals, securing the loads, and leading them into the wilderness is to take some preliminary trips with a guide or knowledgeable friend before you need to rely on them in a bug-out situation. Utilizing and caring for pack animals as transportation in the wilderness can involve quite a steep learning curve if you are a greenhorn with no livestock experience.

Goats

Goats are not often thought of as pack animals, but in the mountains they excel at the task because of their ability to climb over rocks and up slopes no other pack animal could negotiate. Their use in this manner is becoming more common in the West as selective breeders pick the best animals for the purpose. A single goat cannot carry nearly as much as a mule or horse, or even a llama, maxing out at about 50 pounds per animal. But because they eat anything and can forage on their own, goat packers simply take more of them, as a string of six can carry the load of a mule. Goats are a good choice if you need a pack animal to travel off-trail in really steep and difficult country. As discussed in Chapter One, they also can be a source of milk and, in a pinch, make better eating than any other kind of pack animal.

On Foot, Carrying Your Own Pack

The final transportation option for bugging out is simply walking. While walking may be slow, it is certainly sure and you won't have to worry about fuel (other than food), mechanical breakdowns, or traffic jams. If you plan to walk, your packed bug-out bag, along with suitable boots and clothing as described in Chapter Two, will be all the gear you need. Walking gives you more route options than any other bug-out method on land, as you can use bike paths and walking trails, cut through alleys in the city, and travel cross-country over parking lots and neighborhoods in the suburbs.

In most cities and towns there are many hidden routes you may not have thought of. Drainage culverts and ditches are among these. A good example is the small creek that runs right behind my fiancée's house in the city of Jackson, Mississippi. Most residents of the area pay it little mind except when the creek  gets out of its banks in heavy rain. When I first saw it, however, I immediately zeroed in on it as a great exit route. The creek bed has been paved and walled in by the city in an attempt to control flooding. As a result, it is mostly out of sight behind thick vegetation and the privacy fences of adjoining yards. Except in times of high water, the stream is only ankle-deep. The paved streambed leads out of the neighborhood, passes under busy streets in great culverts, and just a few miles down leaves the city to merge into the swamps of the nearby Pearl River. It would be a simple matter to walk out of town unobserved along this route.

Such drainages can be found in most cities, either open and mostly above ground, or in underground storm drains that can be accessed by opening manhole covers in the streets. Like Jackson, many cities are built along the banks of rivers that periodically flood, and the buffer zone between the river and inhabited neighborhoods is often a no-man's land of levees, sewage lagoons, swamps, and woods. In mountain country, many cites are likewise built in valleys along streams or rivers. The population situation may be reversed in these areas, with more habitable areas along the drainage and the wild areas on the steep slopes above. In this case, it may be faster to escape by simply hiking up the nearest slope and crossing the first ridge beyond the valley.

If you're going to have to walk out of town anyway, you might as well consider all these alternate routes that can get you to safety quicker than if you simply try to follow the roads that will be packed with cars and other vehicles. By doing so, you will be living in the bug-out mode immediately, with only the things in your backpack, as you slowly make your way to your pre-planned bug-out location.

PART II
BUG-OUT
LOCATIONS

The balance of this book will consist of a region-by-region run-down of some of the best bug-out locations in each part of the United States. For the purposes of this discussion, I've broken the lower 48 into eight distinct regions, each of which will be covered in a separate chapter. Each individual state within a region will have its own separate section if there are noteworthy bug-out locations within that state.

Many states have more options than I can possibly cover in detail in a volume of this length. My purpose instead is to highlight a few prime examples so that you can deduce on your own whether you want to choose one of these specific locations or find an area with similar attributes that meets the requirements for evasion and survival. Most of the areas described here are the obvious tracts of public lands that are available to anyone. Keep in mind that the surrounding areas beyond the boundaries of national forests, parks, and wildlife refuges will be much the same in many cases, and may prove even more remote, as discussed in Chapter Three.

Each regional discussion begins with an overview and sketch map, as well as region-specific information on weather and climate, land and resources, edible plants that are found there, hunting and fishing prospects, wildlife hazards, and recommended equipment. The bulk of each chapter will then be organized by state or groups of states and each bug-out location will be defined in regards to its rough boundaries, size, and potential for providing refuge and resources. At the end of each location description, the nearest cites and towns to the area are listed to help you find them on more detailed maps.

5

RIVERS, SWAMPS, & ISLANDS OF THE GULF COAST

EAST TEXAS, LOUISIANA, MISSISSIPPI, ALABAMA, AND FLORIDA

The Gulf Coast Southeast is not a region of spectacular mountain ranges or breathtaking views around every curve of the highway. Instead, the wild nature of this part of the United States might easily be overlooked by those who only see it from the windows of a moving vehicle. But away from the roads, along the big, slow-moving rivers, is a land of mysterious swamps and thickly forested hills and hollows. And along the coastlines of these states that border the Gulf of Mexico, there are still many uninhabited barrier islands and vast areas of salt marsh and bayous.

Heat, humidity, swamps, and mosquitoes kept much of the Gulf Coast Southeast wild and undeveloped, and many acres of wilderness remain today in the more difficult areas. Though most are not large tracts such as can be found in the mountains or deserts of the West, in the Gulf Coast Southeast, they don't have to be as large to qualify as excellent bug-out locations. Dense, jungle-like woods make for easy hiding, and the essentials of survival—shelter, water, and food—are all easy to obtain here. Winters are mild, water is practically everywhere, and a great variety of plant and animal life flourishes in this subtropical environment.

Gulf Coast Southeast Bug-Out Essentials

Weather and Climate

This region stays hot and humid for more than six months of the year; the short winters are mild, with few nights below freezing along the coast and slightly colder temperatures farther inland. Rainfall across most of the region is significant, averaging from around 50 to 70 or more inches per year, except for the southern half of the Texas coast, which gets less than 30 inches per year. The hurricane season from June through November brings a significant threat each year to one or more parts of this region. Tornadoes and thunderstorms can also pose a hazard in the spring and summer.

Land and Resources

A variety of federal and state-managed public lands are scattered across this region, and include large swamps, marshlands, and uninhabited barrier islands. National forests and national wildlife refuges account for most of the largest tracts, although one of America's most outstanding wilderness national parks, the Everglades, is also located in this region. Although a large percentage of the land here is privately owned, population densities are low in many areas and large areas of private land are, in effect, wildlands. Forest, swamp, and saltwater marsh are the primary ecosystems, each supporting a diversity of plant and animal life. Water is abundant in the form of rivers, streams, and plentiful rainfall. No ground water here should be considered safe to drink without treatment (see Chapter Two).

Edible Plants

The warm climate and long growing season make this region especially diverse in plant life. Abundant species include cattail, wild rice, wapatu (arrowhead or duck potato), pokeweed, dandelion, burdock, amaranth, chicory, wild onions, ferns, saw palmetto, acorns, hickory nuts, blackberries, huckleberries, elderberries, wild grapes, prickly pear, persimmons, paw paw, and wild plum. Farther south, many tropical species can be found in the wilds of Florida, including cabbage palm, papaya, sea grapes, seaside purslane, and coconut palms.

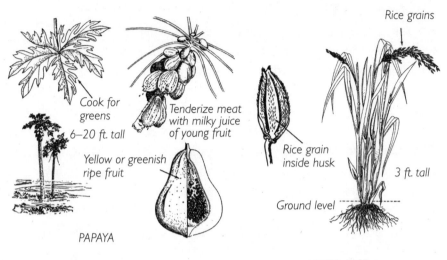

Cook for greens

6–20 ft. tall

Tenderize meat with milky juice of young fruit

Yellow or greenish ripe fruit

PAPAYA

Rice grains

Rice grain inside husk

Ground level

3 ft. tall

WILD RICE

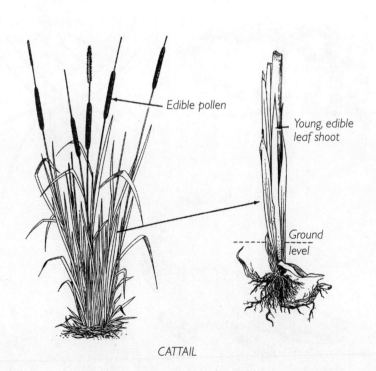

Edible pollen

Young, edible leaf shoot

Ground level

CATTAIL

Hunting and Fishing

Abundant wildlife in the region includes whitetail deer, wild hogs, wild turkey, doves, bobwhite quail, American alligator, gray squirrel, fox squirrel, opossum, armadillo, rabbit, muskrat, beaver, a variety of snakes and lizards, and amphibians such as land and aquatic turtles and frogs. The inland rivers and lakes offer bass, bream, catfish, gar, eels, and many other fish, as well as freshwater mussels and crawfish. The coastal marshes, bayous, and lagoons contain oysters, shrimp, clams, blue crabs, flounder, speckled trout, redfish, and many other saltwater species. In addition to more palatable animals, the warm climate breeds a thriving insect population with easily obtained grubs and other edible small creatures to be found practically everywhere.

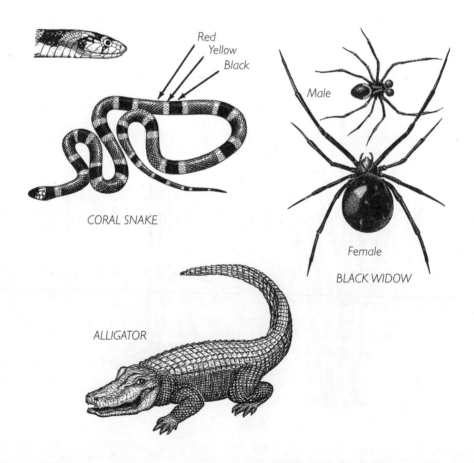

Red
Yellow
Black

Male

CORAL SNAKE

Female

BLACK WIDOW

ALLIGATOR

Wildlife Hazards

Reptiles are the most prevalent dangerous animals in the region, with large alligators in any body of water—fresh, brackish, or salt—as well as American crocodiles in the extreme southern parts of Florida. Four varieties of poisonous snakes can be found here: The coral snake, the cottonmouth, the copperhead, and the rattlesnake (including the Eastern diamondback and pygmy rattler). Smaller venomous creatures include the black widow, the brown recluse, and a variety of wasps and bees. Although black bears are making a comeback in the region, and a few Florida panthers remain in the wild, neither of these are present in enough numbers to pose a threat.

Recommended Equipment

Cold weather is rarely a threat in the Southeast. Instead, you must be prepared to deal with heat, humidity, periods of torrential rainfall, and voracious populations of biting insects. The insect problem calls for mosquito netting, whether in the form of a tent, jungle hammock, or separate mosquito bar. Sleeping on the ground under an open tarp is fine in the cooler months, but for most of the year it's probably not a good idea due to the nocturnal nature of rattlesnakes and other crawling creatures. In this environment of dense undergrowth, a machete is as essential as it is in the jungle. Waterproof boots, good rain gear, and bug spray are also priceless here. Most hunting can be done with nothing more than a .22 rifle, as it is easy to get close to game in these thick woods. For self-defense all you need is a weapon capable of stopping an aggressive human, as the few bears in the region are generally much too shy to attack humans. The best bug-out locations can only be reached with a boat of some type, but there are areas that can be driven to or accessed on foot.

◆ ◆ ◆

The following sections, organized by state, will discuss the various regions of the Gulf Coast Southeast in terms of their suitability as bug-out locations.

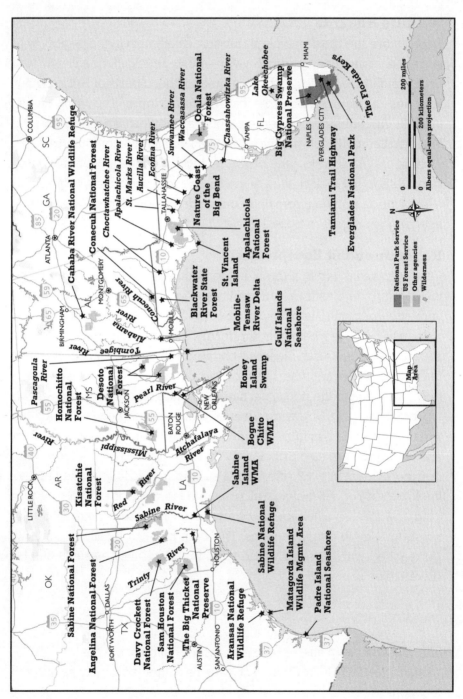

Bug-Out Locations of the Gulf Coast

Texas

Most people think of ranches and plains when they think of Texas, but the southeastern part of the state is ecologically part of the Gulf Coast Southeast. Pine woodlands in the hills and drier lands and bottom-land hardwood forests along the rivers, along with the same heat and humidity found elsewhere in the South, make much of eastern Texas almost indistinguishable from neighboring Louisiana. The rivers and streams are the key to accessing the most remote and often forgotten lands, and you will find plenty of places here—both private and public—unfrequented by landowners or anyone else. In this eastern part of the Lone Star State you'll find cypress sloughs and alligators, magnolia and beech forests, and wild hogs, black bear, and whitetail deer.

In addition to woods and inland swamps, Texas has hundreds of miles of uninhabited seashore along the Gulf on its barrier islands, sounds and lagoons, and marshland estuaries. Most of these undeveloped coastal areas are protected in national seashore and wildlife refuge lands.

The Big Thicket

The Big Thicket is a heavily wooded area of the Texas coastal plain north of Beaumont that would at first appear unremarkable, but is actually one of the most biodiverse areas in the world, with 85 different trees and 1000 other varieties of flowering plants, as well as 186 kinds of birds and 50 different reptile and amphibian species. The Big Thicket is roughly 40 miles long by 20 miles wide, interspersed with private lands but still containing lots of wild areas. Little known outside the region, The Big Thicket National Preserve, managed by the National Park Service, was established in 1974 to protect 97,500 acres of this wilderness along the Neches River and Pine Island Bayou. The Big Thicket also gained international biosphere reserve status in 1981.

Although parts of the Big Thicket can be reached on foot, and there are established hiking trails and primitive roads in some areas, much of the area is swamp, bogs, and river and bayou country. A canoe or kayak will allow you to access the best parts of the preserve, as well as travel farther upstream along the Neches River.

During the Civil War, many locals of eastern Texas fled into the dense woods of the Big Thicket to avoid conscription. Other outlaws through history have used it as a hideout, and a legend of a Big Thicket "Bigfoot" or hairy relative of the Sasquatch of the Pacific Northwest has persisted among some people in this part of Texas for decades. That the locals view the Big Thicket as wild enough for this possibility is a good testament to the suitability of the area as a bug-out location.

Nearest Cities: *Beaumont, Houston*

Sabine National Forest

The Sabine National Forest includes more than 180,000 acres of public lands on the Texas side of Toledo Bend Reservoir, a huge man-made lake that is bordered on the east side by Louisiana. Toledo Bend Reservoir is roughly 65 miles long by 5 miles wide and situated in a land of rolling, piney hills, featuring many convoluted bays and finger coves reaching far into hollows and up streambeds, offering a total of more than 1200 miles of shoreline, including the parts on the Louisiana side. On a lake so vast, also bordered by national forest lands, it's easy to pick an isolated cove that can be reached by canoe or kayak and set up a hidden camp that no one is likely to find, despite the popularity of the lake with fishermen.

The entire area is heavily wooded with mixed pines and hardwoods, much of it mature second growth that resembles the original forest. Smaller areas of designated wilderness lands are located within the Sabine National Forest, including the Indian Mounds Wilderness Area, which shelters stands of virgin beech and southern magnolia forest.

Nearest Cities: *Jasper, Lufkin*

Other National Forests of East Texas

In addition to Sabine National Forest, there are three more separate national forests in eastern Texas. The Angelina National Forest, totaling 154,000 acres, lies in the Neches River Basin upstream of the Big Thicket, and also surrounds much of Sam Rayburn Reservoir, a 114,000-acre lake on the Angelina River. Unlike the Big Thicket, the terrain in Angelina National Forest is rolling hills and open woodlands of longleaf pine.

Sam Houston National Forest is located just fifty miles north of Houston, and contains 163,000 acres of public land intermixed with tracts of private land. A 128-mile-long hiking trail, the Lone Star Trail, winds through the national forest land and offers a backpacking bug-out option to those who may not have a boat or care for swamps like the Big Thicket.

Davy Crockett National Forest is another 160,000 acre area of public lands in the Neches and Trinity River basins. Within the forest management area along the Neches River, the Big Slough Wilderness Area protects a 3000-acre stand of old growth forest. In times of heavy rain the entire area can be explored by canoe.

Nearest Cities: Lufkin, Nacogdoches, Huntsville, Livingstone

The Texas Gulf Coast

Southwest of Houston and Galveston, the Gulf Coast of Texas becomes a series of barrier islands and big, protected lagoons and bays that separate them from the mainland. Many areas of this coast are still uninhabited and offer possibilities for living in isolation on a small boat or out of a seaworthy canoe or kayak. The Intracoastal Waterway provides an inside route all the way to Mexico, protected from storms of the Gulf behind the low-lying barrier islands. The key to using these coastal locations as a bug-out location is to travel in a small enough boat to keep a low profile and to avoid staying in any one area for too long. This is not difficult to do along a coastline that is over 300 miles long and includes more than 3000 miles of tidal shoreline, counting the islands and estuaries.

One example of the wild Texas coast is Matagorda Island, a 38-mile long barrier island that varies in width from a half mile to four and a half miles. It has an area of 56,000 acres, protected within the Matagorda Island Wildlife Management Area. Aransas National Wildlife Refuge is another tract of 115,000 acres along nearby San Antonio Bay and Black Jack Peninsula, just across the Intracoastal Waterway from Matagorda Island.

Farther south, Padre Island National Seashore encompasses 130,000 acres and includes 70 miles of uninhabited seashore—one of the longest such stretches found anywhere in the United States. The island is sun-drenched world of dunes, grassland, and salt marsh, and is inhabited by deer, coyotes, rabbits, and over 300 species of birds.

Nearest Cites: *Port Lavaca, Corpus Christi*

Louisiana

Louisiana is probably the first state that comes to mind when residents of other regions of the U.S. think of swamps. With more than 40,000 miles of rivers, bayous, and creeks, plus a half a million acres of back-waters and natural lakes, not to mention 3.6 million acres of saltwater marsh, it's easy to see how the state got that image. Although much of the land in Louisiana is high and dry and resembles neighboring east Texas and Mississippi, it is the swampy southern bayous that the state is known for.

Disappearing into the swamp and living off the bounty it provides is a tradition with a long history in this state. In remote places like the Atchafalaya Swamp and other areas of south Louisiana, there are still holdouts practicing the old ways and living the lives of subsistence hunters, trappers, and fishermen back in the maze of hidden bayous. Wildlife enforcement officials have always had a tough time keeping up with poachers and other outlaws who make these swamps their home; there are simply too many waterways and too many square miles of remote swamp to patrol.

Sabine River Bottomlands

The Sabine River forms the border between Texas and Louisiana, flowing through Toledo Bend Reservoir (which was described in the Texas section) and south to the Gulf of Mexico. The Louisiana side of the giant reservoir is much the same as the Texas side, offering mile after mile of remote woodlands along the many finger coves of the convoluted lake. Downstream of the lake dam, the Sabine River flows through remote bottomlands and swamps, offering plenty of seclusion and options for backwoods hideouts.

The Sabine River has a long history as a haunt for outlaws since the frontier days and today the Sabine River bottomlands are still a prime bug-out location, with many areas accessible only by canoe or small boat, such as the Sabine Island Wildlife Management Area just north of Interstate 10. Cut off from roads by the Sabine River to the west and the Old Sabine river on the east, this nearly 9000-acre "island" is laced with bayous and hidden lakes. This is one of many options on both the Louisiana and the Texas sides of the Sabine River. South of the interstate, the 124,000-acre Sabine National Wildlife Refuge is another federal sanctuary that is made up of mixed marsh and bottomland forest.

Nearest Cities: DeRidder, Lake Charles

Atchafalaya Swamp

The Atchafalaya River Basin is the largest river basin swamp in North America and, at over 800,000 acres, one of the largest tracts of wilderness and semi-wilderness in the Southeast. The area contained within the basin is roughly 15 miles wide by 100 miles long, and is crossed by only one road, the four-lane Interstate 10 that bisects it east to west. Within the basin there are numerous man-made pipelines, navigation canals, and other oil-field related structures, but despite this, most of the area is quintessential Louisiana swamp. It is a maze of bayous, sloughs, and dead lakes and home to alligators, black bears, and bald eagles.

It's easy enough to disappear into the Atachafalaya Basin in a canoe, a kayak, or the more indigenous Cajun pirogue. The trick is to leave the main river, the larger bayous, and the man-made canals and travel the smallest sloughs and dead lakes. Get far enough off the beaten path in the Atchafalaya and you'll have it all to yourself.

Nearest Cities: Baton Rogue, Lafayette

Honey Island Swamp

People get lost in Honey Island Swamp all the time, though not usually on purpose. The 160,000-acre labyrinth of bayous is so confusing it's hard not to get lost there. Honey Island Swamp is located along the lower Pearl River, at the eastern boundary of the state with neighboring Mississippi. This part of the Pearl splits into three rivers as it nears the Gulf, creating a five-mile-wide elongated wilderness of flooded forest and intricate bayous between the separate branches. Most of the swamp is on the Louisiana side, but it is equally wild across the state line as well. A lot of it is protected by the Bogue Chitto and Pearl River wildlife management areas.

Honey Island Swamp is not a place you can get around in without a boat of some sort, but the swamp and all the surrounding bottomlands of the lower Pearl River Basin offer first-rate bug-out locations if you have a canoe, kayak, or pirogue. The swamp is a rich foraging, fishing, and hunting ground, and a prepared survivor can thrive there.

Nearest Cities: *Slidell, Picayune*

Kisatchie National Forest

Not all of Louisiana is swamp and bayou country. Those who are looking for a bug-out location that does not require a canoe, kayak, or pirogue can find plenty of dry land in Louisiana's only national forest: the 604,000 acre Kisatchie, which is broken up into five units.

The Kisatchie Hills Wilderness area contains some unusual topography for Louisiana, including steep and rugged hills, and sandstone bluffs and outcrops. Old growth longleaf pines cover the hills, and sandy, rock-strewn stream beds course through the hollows. The wilderness designation keeps all manner of mechanized traffic out, and leaves hiking or horseback riding as the only means of entry. This is one part of Louisiana where alligators are not a worry. Trails into the Kisatchie Hills bring recreational hikers, of course, especially since this area offers scenery unlike any other part of the state. As always on public lands that are popular with weekend adventurers, the wildest areas are along drainages and ridges that are far enough removed to be out of sight and earshot of established routes.

Nearest Cities: *Alexandria, Natchitoches*

Mississippi

Mississippi is the heart of the Deep South and known more for its history of cotton plantations, antebellum mansions, and Delta blues music than for its wild lands. What many outsiders may not know is that other than Maine, Mississippi has the lowest population density of all the states east of the Mississippi River. As a result, this southern state contains lots of uninhabited wild and semi-wild lands. Like Louisiana, it is a land of rivers and streams, but not nearly so wet and low in most places as the Bayou State. Mississippi certainly has its share of big swamps, bottomland hardwood forests, and coastal marshes, but in addition there are large tracts of public forest lands in the drier rolling hills of the Pine Belt.

But what Mississippi really has in abundance is a network of creeks and small rivers of the size that is just right for a small Johnboat, canoe, or kayak, but too small for larger vessels or commercial traffic. These waterways wind through seemingly unending forests, as even in agricultural areas the stream banks are left wooded. And more and more, the main cash crop in the state is pine timber, so forests cover most of the uninhabited land.

Pascagoula River Basin

A treasure little-known outside of the region, the Pascagoula River is the last unaltered large river system in the entire lower 48 states. Although the Pascagoula itself is only 81 miles long, it gathers more than 750 miles of tributaries navigable by canoe or kayak. The longest of these are the Leaf River, the Chickasawhay River, and Black Creek. Black Creek is remote and beautiful enough to have earned a designation as a National Wild and Scenic River in the stretches where it flows through the half-million-acre Desoto National Forest.

Few towns and no major cities are built along any of the tributaries of the Pascagoula, until you reach the last couple miles at the coast. What makes the river system especially unique is that the river itself and none of its major tributaries have been dammed, channelized, or altered in any significant way. Although much of the land along the river and its tributaries is private, there are also vast holdings containing old-growth forests, some purchased by the Nature Conservancy and some parts of national and state wildlife preserves.

As a bug-out location, the Pascagoula River system is unrivaled in the state of Mississippi. With a canoe or kayak you can travel both upstream and down in the relatively slow current. There are almost limitless opportunities for camping along its side sloughs and backwaters, where you will rarely see a fellow human.

Nearest Cities: *Pascagoula, Lucedale*

Pearl River Basin

The Pearl River is the second major river basin in the state that empties into the Gulf. The Pearl has been used as a river highway in the region since the days when the Choctaw lived along its banks. In early frontier days it was used by steamboats carrying goods between the capital city of Jackson and the coast. Today, the Pearl lies forgotten by commerce and winds in lonely isolation through miles of big woods and impressive swamps.

Wildlife is abundant along the Pearl, and includes deer, wild turkey, wild hogs, plenty of big alligators, and the occasional black bear. The river is used by fishermen in Johnboats and small bass boats, but there are plenty of fantastic bug-out locations in the long stretches between the few bridges that cross it. With more than 400 miles of the Pearl flowing through the state, plus two tributaries navigable by canoe (the Strong River and the Bogue Chitto), this basin offers plenty of wild river land in central and southern Mississippi.

The lower reaches of the Pearl form the border between Mississippi and Louisiana and the river eventually splits into an east Pearl, a middle Pearl, and a west Pearl, with the wilds of Louisiana's Honey Island Swamp in between.

Nearest Cities: *Jackson, Monticello, Columbia, Bogalusa*

Homochitto National Forest

After the Desoto, the Homochitto National Forest is Mississippi's second largest national forest, totaling 189,000 acres in the hilly southwestern part of the state. This national forest is named for the Homochitto River, which also drains into the Mississippi River instead of directly into the Gulf. The Homochitto River resembles a river of the Southwest, with a broad sandy bed up to a mile wide in many places, the river threading through in a shallow maze of channels, diverging and converging along the way. Many parts of the river are inaccessible except by long canoe trips from distant bridge crossings. The sandy bottomlands are home to big herds of deer and bear tracks are common along the river.

Away from the river, Homochitto National Forest is a land of rolling, sandy hills covered in longleaf pines on the ridges, with clear brooks and hardwoods in the deep hollows. Many parts of the forest are seldom visited, as the hikers and hunters tend to stick to trails and forest service roads. Far from the roads among the lonesome wooded hills, all you can hear is the whisper of wind in the pines.

Nearest Cities: *Brookhaven, Natchez*

Gulf Islands National Seashore

If you have a sea kayak or some other kind of seaworthy boat to reach them, Mississippi's barrier islands could be an attractive bug-out location. Located between 7 and 12 miles offshore, these are among the most remote islands on the Gulf of Mexico. On these islands one could spend weeks living a beachcomber's lifestyle, camping among wooded sand dunes with the kayak hidden from the eyes of rangers and other boats cruising by. The five islands of the Gulf Islands National Seashore offer more than 200 miles of empty, wave-washed shoreline, maritime forests, and salt marsh lagoons.

Although they are not well-known to many residents of inland Mississippi and elsewhere, those who own boats and live in the cities on the state's coast frequent them on good-weather weekends. In the late summer and fall, hurricanes are a threat, but can easily be avoided by keeping track of the weather and having a boat in which to head for the mainland. The islands are no place to be in one of these storms. The worst ones, like Katrina in 2005 and Camille in 1969, can completely bury them under a raging storm surge.

Nearest Cities: *Gulfport, Biloxi, Pascagoula*

Alabama

Like Mississippi, Alabama is rich in long rivers with many tributary streams and includes navigable waterways that traverse the state from top to bottom. The big rivers in Alabama have been altered by the hand of man more than those in Mississippi, especially with the construction of locks and dams to open them up to commercial barge traffic. Despite this, even on these rivers one can find plenty of seclusion, and long undeveloped and uninhabited stretches of waterway where passing vessels are few and far between. Even better than the big rivers, many smaller creeks and unaltered rivers offer a near-wilderness experience equal to those in other states in the region.

Canoeing and kayaking enthusiasts have created the 631-mile Alabama River Trail across the state that is the longest of its kind in any single state in the country. The route begins at the Georgia state line in the northeast part of the state. Much of central and northern Alabama is rocky and hilly, belonging more to the Appalachian Mountain corridor discussed in Chapter Seven than to the swamps and rivers we are considering here. But this long water route continues south to the Gulf, changing to sluggish, muddy rivers and passing through big bottomland hardwood forests en route to the wild Mobile-Tensaw Delta.

Mobile-Tensaw River Delta

The Mobile-Tensaw River Delta is the second only to the Mississippi as the largest river delta in the country. It is formed by the confluence of the Alabama and Tombigbee Rivers, which combine their flow to form the Mobile River. At nearly 50 miles long and 10 miles wide, this 300,000-acre tract of wetlands and forest is one of the best bug-out locations to be found in Alabama. The waterways in the delta are used by fishermen in motorboats, but as with the Atchafalaya and other semi-wild river basin swamps in the Southeast, there are many opportunities for solitude to be found in such a vast labyrinth. The 150-mile Bartrum Canoe Trail has been established to take paddlers to some of the most scenic and out-of-the-way parts of the Mobile-Tensaw Delta, and offers a clearly marked route for those new to navigating in delta swamp country.

Unlike many river deltas, the Mobile-Tensaw has relatively high banks, as it was formed by a sinking of the land between two geological faults. This makes finding good campsites in the area easier, and one can simply disappear by dragging a canoe or kayak a few yards back from the bank of any of the waterways and setting up residence in the jungle of head-high saw palmettos.

If you decide to keep moving, the Mobile-Tensaw River Delta offers good escape options by water. Downstream takes you to Mobile Bay and Gulf. Upstream you have a number of route choices beyond the confluence of the Tombigbee and the Alabama. Heading up the Alabama, you can make your way to North Georgia on the Alabama River Trail mentioned previously. Alternatively, the Tombigbee River can take you north to Tennessee by way of the Tenn-Tom Waterway; beyond to the Land Between the Lakes of Tennessee and Kentucky; then to the Ohio River and, ultimately, the mighty Mississippi. Many good tributaries off of these major rivers can also be found in Alabama, including the Cahaba.

Nearest Cities: Mobile

Cahaba River

A major tributary to the Alabama River and part of the Mobile-Tensaw drainage, the 200-mile long Cahaba River is Alabama's longest free-flowing river. Originating far to the north in the central part of the state, the Cahaba River is navigable by canoe for most of its length. With the exception of the upper reaches of the Cahaba River basin near Birmingham, most of the area of its drainage is relatively undeveloped and many wild stretches with long distances between bridges can be found. Efforts to protect lands along the river have led to the establishment of the Cahaba River National Wildlife Refuge and to purchases of several tracts by the Nature Conservancy. Like most southern rivers in sparsely populated areas, the private lands along the Cahaba are often as wild as the federally owned stretches.

Nearest Cities: Selma, Centreville, Birmingham

Choctawhatchee River

The Choctawhatchee is biggest of several southeast Alabama rivers that originate in the state before running into the Florida panhandle to reach the Gulf of Mexico. The Choctawhatchee is quite remote in many parts of its 170-mile length, with limited access and much potential as a bug-out location. Not only is it remote, it is also scenic, with its upper reaches defined by steep limestone banks, swift water, and even some rapids. Farther downstream the river broadens and slows, the surrounding bottomland forests becoming swampy and more characteristic of a big Gulf Coast river.

A sizeable tributary of the Choctawhatchee is the Pea River. It joins the Choctawhatchee just north of the Florida state line, but upstream offers 85 miles of river suitable to canoes and some kayaks. The Pea River alternates from swampy bottomlands to rocky shoals and sandbars.

Nearest Cities: Dothan, Enterprise

Conecuh National Forest

South Alabama's only national forest is also found along the Florida panhandle border. Containing 83,000 acres, this federal tract of pine and bottomland forest is bounded by two navigable rivers smaller than the Choctawhatchee, the Conecuh on the northwest corner and the Yellow along the eastern side. The Yellow River is popular with some canoeists, and the 230-mile long Conecuh is a major waterway, but this is a sparsely populated part of Alabama where even on the roads all you see is mile after mile of mostly uninhabited pinelands.

Nearest Cities: Andalusia, Brewton

Florida

Florida is the most densely populated state of the Gulf Coast Southeast. Ironically, it also has more real wilderness than any other southern state as well as a great number of sufficiently wild areas of smaller size from the Keys all the way up through the panhandle. The vast majority of Florida's urban millions live along the coasts, but surprisingly, there are still many areas of coastline in the Sunshine State that are completely uninhabited and infrequently visited.

For the survivalist seeking a near-tropical experience and an escape from winter, Florida has much to offer, especially in the southern half of the state. The extreme southern end of the peninsula and the Keys beyond are a world apart from anything else in the United States. The northern part of Florida is very similar to the other states covered in this chapter, and offers river systems, national forest lands, remote private woodlands, and some undeveloped coastal areas. I'll begin an analysis of Florida's wild places in this panhandle region, where rivers that originate in Alabama and Georgia find their way to the Gulf.

Blackwater River State Forest

North Florida's Blackwater River State Forest is contiguous with Conecuh National Forest in Alabama. The Conecuh River changes names to the Blackwater River after crossing the state line and winds some 30 miles through the state forest. This state-owned public woodland encompasses 206,000 acres of a thinly populated area north of Interstate 10. Much of the forest here is flat coastal plain pinelands with sandy soil and clear "blackwater" streams so named because of the tannic acid that leaches from vegetation and turns them the color of black tea. In addition to the Blackwater River, other canoe and kayak routes through the state forest are Coldwater Creek, Juniper Creek, and Sweetwater River.

Nearest Cities: Pensacola, Milton, Crestview

Apalachicola River

The Apalachicola River flows through some of the most scenic and least settled parts of the Florida panhandle. Fed by two major rivers in Georgia to the north, the Apalachicola runs 107 miles from the state line to the Gulf, where it empties into Apalachicola Bay. The upper reaches of the Apalachicola do not seem like Florida at all. Rugged hills, limestone bluffs along the river, and deep ravines in the surrounding forest characterize an area of the Apalachicola that is protected by Nature Conservancy holdings and state park and forest lands.

The lower reaches of the Apalachicola become a maze of deepwater bayous winding through jungle-like forests of oak and tall cabbage palms. The woods along the river here are so thick that you need a machete to enter from the river. Once you're within them, however, staying hidden is easy. Beyond the mouth of the river, the bay of the same name is ringed by several large barrier islands including uninhabited St. Vincent Island, with 12,000 acres of dunes, forests, lakes, and swamp, accessible only by boat.

Just to the east of the Apalachicola River, occupying a broad swath of mostly empty land between the river and the capital city of Tallahassee, the Apalachicola National Forest is a 575,000-acre patchwork of pine-lands and grasslands. There are many remote parts of this national for-est that can be reached on little-used dirt forest service roads, making this area a place where you can bug out with a motor vehicle, on foot, or by off-road bicycle. Spread over such a large area, the Apalachicola National Forest offers plenty of options.

Nearest Cities: Apalachicola, Tallahassee

The Nature Coast of the Big Bend

The Big Bend area of the Florida Gulf coast is so named because of the sweeping curve the shoreline makes as the peninsula extends from the panhandle region of the state and the coastline switches to a north-south orientation. This part of Florida is also often referred to as the "nature coast" or the "forgotten coast," simply because it has practi-cally none of the tourist beaches, condominiums, and other develop-ments found in other coastal areas of the state.

One reason the Big Bend of Florida was never developed is that it lacks deep-water harbors, and extremely shallow water extending for many miles out to sea from the land in this area makes navigation hazardous for any but the smallest shallow-draft boats. As if that were not deterrent enough, much of the shoreline of the Big Bend coast is low and swampy, lacking expansive sand beaches. There is not even a coastal road that follows the shoreline in this part of Florida, and there are very few settlements in the roughly 200-mile stretch from Apalachicola Bay to New Port Richey.

Just about any part of this coast is a first-class bug-out destination for those with sea kayaks or seaworthy small boats that can operate in less than two feet of water. Notable wild areas that are exceptional hideout locations are found at the mouths of the rivers that empty into the Gulf here, such as the Aucilla, the lower reaches of which is a vir-tual jungle. The Aucilla River is so remote that it was popular with drug smugglers running their cargo in from the Gulf on fast powerboats in the 1970s and '80s. Other rivers that empty here are the Suwannee, which is navigable upstream by canoe or kayak all the way to Georgia's Okefenokee Swamp (which will be covered in Chapter Six), the St. Marks, the Ecofina, the Waccasassa, and the Chassahowitzka. All of these river deltas and surrounding islands and estuaries are protected from development in wildlife refuges and management areas.

Nearest Cities: *Perry, Gainesville, Cedar Key, New Port Richey*

Ocala National Forest

The Ocala National Forest is comprised of 388,000 acres of pine and subtropical forest in the middle of the Florida peninsula north of Orlando. Although heavily visited because of its proximity to many large cities and its excellent hiking trails and lakes, the Ocala National Forest still has remote corners in difficult sections of its wet prairies, bogs, and thickets. A little off-trail bushwhacking with map and compass can get you as far from other forest users as you need to be. The area is teeming with deer, wild turkeys, and small game, and fishing and foraging is good as well.

Nearest Cities: *Ocala, Orlando, Daytona Beach*

Big Cypress Swamp

Big Cypress Swamp was once part of the Everglades but is now separated from it by the Tamiami Trail Highway. This area contains nearly 600,000 acres of terrain similar to that found in the larger Everglades proper. Named for its extensive stands of bald cypress, the area is also intermingled with sawgrass prairie and palm hammocks. Like the Big Thicket in Texas, the federal lands protecting Big Cypress Swamp are designated a "national preserve," a status which means they are under the administration of the National Park Service, but under different rules than national parks. This means you can practice survival skills such as hunting (in season and with a license) without potentially facing the consequences of getting caught by a wildlife officer or park ranger.

Less restrictive rules also mean locals with airboats and other powerboats can use the area, so some parts of the preserve might not feel like wilderness. But the fact that Big Cypress Swamp is one of the main strongholds of the endangered Florida panther, as well as home to solid populations of black bears, says a lot about its potential as a bug-out location in this part of the state.

Nearest Cities: *Naples, Miami*

The Everglades

The Everglades once reached south from the shores of Lake Okeechobee to take in practically all of the southern peninsula of Florida. Most of what remains intact is within the vast Everglades National Park, which protects approximately 1.7 million acres of sawgrass prairie, cypress swamp, mangrove swamp, and the islands and shallows of Florida Bay.

The environment of the Everglades is a difficult one to travel in, a fact the U.S. Army found out the hard way while trying to wrap up the Seminole Indian Wars that finally pushed the last holdouts of the tribe to the swamps south of Lake Okeechobee. The third and final war did not end until 1858 due to the difficulty of pursuing war parties that attacked settlers and then retreated into the most remote parts of the 'Glades. Stifling tropical heat, black clouds of mosquitoes, biting flies, and sand fleas all conspire to make the Everglades something less than a paradise for those who cannot adapt.

But as the Seminoles knew, what makes this area enticing as a survival refuge is how easy it is to disappear into it and to live off the land once inside. With a canoe or kayak, one can paddle into a maze of sloughs and creeks far from the main water trails used by most Everglades visitors and find places so remote the chances of seeing another person are slim to none. As with every other national park or national forest area described in this book, the key to not being discovered is get off the main trails and waterways.

Finding food in the Everglades should not be a problem for anyone with even the most basic hunting, fishing, and foraging skills. Most of the shallow creeks and waterways in the marsh are so thick with fish that taking them with a cast net, spear, or bow and arrow is easy. Birds, small mammals, and reptiles and amphibians such as turtles, snakes, lizards, and frogs are abundant. Plant food includes saw palmettos, cabbage palms, cattails, breadroot, sea grapes, and wild papaya.

Nearest Cities: Naples, Everglades City, Miami

The Florida Keys

The Florida Keys are known for Key West, that funky tourist town at the end of the southernmost highway in the United States, and for their diving, boating, and tourist destinations such as Islamorada and Key Largo. What the tourists miss, however, is the fact that most of the Keys are not even connected by road or bridge to the Overseas Highway, and are completely inaccessible unless you have a boat. Tiny mangrove islands dot the horizon from the tip of peninsular Florida to Key West and beyond to the Marquesas Keys. Many of these islands are not really land at all but simply clusters of mangroves growing in the shallow flats and offering no access or dry areas big enough to pitch a tent. Some of these islands do have land, though, in the form of tiny, hidden beaches and hammocks of high ground in their centers, surrounded by almost impenetrable mangroves.

Some parts of the upper Keys lie within Everglades National Park and others are protected in national wildlife refuges and state parks. Enforcement officers from these agencies and the Florida Marine Patrol are frequently seen working from small runabouts. But traveling and living out of a sea kayak or other small boat, it's easy to evade them and to move throughout the area mostly unnoticed.

The Keys are known for their clear, tropical waters and the only living coral reefs in North America. Needless to say, these waters are prime fishing grounds for all manner of tasty marine delicacies, from spiny lobster and conch to a wide variety of game fish. Seafood can be taken by underwater spearfishing, hand-grabbing, bow fishing, cast nets, improvised traps, and of course, hooks, using everything from hand lines to standard rod-and-reel tackle. Some seafood can be simply picked up in the shallows of the lagoons among the islands or, like "coon" oysters, gathered off the mangrove roots at low tide.

Nearest Cities: Key Largo, Islamorada, Marathon, Key West

6

ISLANDS & LOWLANDS OF THE ATLANTIC COAST

FLORIDA, GEORGIA, NORTH AND SOUTH CAROLINA, VIRGINIA, MARYLAND, AND NEW JERSEY

The East Coast of the United States is one of the most heavily populated regions of the nation, but despite this, the coastline between New Jersey and southern Florida still has many undeveloped areas of swamp, saltwater marsh, bayshore, and windswept barrier islands. In addition to the immediate coastal areas, numerous large rivers empty into the Atlantic in this region, many of which support expansive tracts of bottomland forests that resemble the river bottoms of the Gulf Coast Southeast.

The southern section of the eastern seaboard, especially in Florida, Georgia, and South Carolina, is similar in most respects to the Gulf Coast region in terms of climate and plant and animal species. Just as in the Gulf Coast states, an abundance of wild foods can be found in the woods, swamps, marsh, and fresh- and saltwater environments. As one moves farther north along the coast from North Carolina to Maryland and New Jersey, gradual changes in the landscape become apparent due to longer and colder winters. The population density is greater as well, especially from Virginia north to the nation's capitol and in the vicinity of New York City.

In a bug-out situation, larger populations mean more potential competition for the bug-out locations that are available. Because of this, some of these areas may only be suitable for short-term use, and a long-term plan may require alternatives farther away from population centers.

The East Coast continues farther north than New Jersey, of course, and there are good bug-out locations to be found there as well, especially in Maine. Because of the differences in climate and plant and animal species, however, that area will be considered in Chapter Eight, which covers the Lakes and Big Woods of the North.

EAST COAST BUG-OUT ESSENTIALS

Weather and Climate

The climate of the East Coast is temperate, with hot, humid summers and cool to cold winters. The southernmost stretch, in Florida, Georgia, and South Carolina, is more subtropical, with shorter winters and longer summers. Rainfall averages 40 to 70 inches per year. Flooding can and does occur in many parts of this region, especially along major river systems. Strong thunderstorms can bring dangerous straight-line winds as well as spawning tornadoes. Lightning is also a hazard during such storms. The East Coast faces the same hurricane threat as the Gulf Coast Southeast during the months of June through November. Occasionally a major hurricane will make a direct hit on this coast, causing catastrophic damage from high winds and wind-driven waves. Deeper water just offshore in the Atlantic, however, means that most of the region does not suffer from the enormous storm surges that Gulf Coast hurricanes can generate. The northern section of the East Coast is subject to frequent snow in winter and occasional severe cold, but is still generally milder than the inland areas at the same latitude.

Land and Resources

Much of the wild land remaining in the East Coast region is protected federal and state land in the form of wildlife refuges, national seashores, and other parks. Most remaining large areas of wetlands enjoy some form of government protection from future development. Because of the high population density across most of the region, the largest uninhabited areas are in the various wetlands, including swamps, river basins, coastal marshes, and along the barrier islands. Due to the abundant rainfall and the number of rivers that drain to this coast, drinking water is plentiful and easy to find in most wild areas of the region, with the exception of the tidal marshes and the barrier islands.

Edible Plants

An extended growing season and mild winters mean that at least some edible plant food can be found in the bug-out locations in this chapter year-round. Common species here include marsh mallow, sea purslane, elderberry, cattail, wild rice, saw palmetto, prickly pear, acorns, hickory nuts, pine, sassafras, blackberries, huckleberries, wild grapes, dandelion, chicory, pokeweed, bull thistle, milkweed, ferns, greenbrier, and amaranth. A variety of palms such as cabbage palms, needle palms, and exotics can be found near the coast in the southern parts of this region. At the northern end of this coastal region, cold-weather species such as bearberries, cranberries, and blueberries can be found.

Hunting and Fishing

As in most of the eastern United States, the whitetail deer is the most sought-after game animal, and is plentiful throughout most of the East Coast region. Other popular game animals found in most of the bug-out locations in this chapter include wild hog, wild turkey, dove, gray squirrel, rabbit, beaver, and a variety of ducks, geese, and other waterfowl. Non-game animals that can be important food sources include alligator, snakes, opossum, raccoon, turtles, frogs, and smaller reptiles, amphibians, and insects. The eastern seaboard is rich in marine life and coastal resources include oysters, clams, crabs, and a wide range of saltwater fish. In this region, anywhere there is water—fresh, brackish, or salt—you can find a source of animal protein if you have the gear to obtain it.

Wildlife Hazards

Just as in the Gulf Coast Southeast, the primary hazards here are in and near the water, or are of the small and hard to see variety. The southern and central reaches of the East Coast are home to many of the same species of dangerous reptiles found in the Gulf Coast Southeast, including alligators and cottonmouth snakes in the rivers, swamps, and marshes. Copperheads and rattlesnakes are present as well, ranging throughout this region all the way to New Jersey. Wasps and bees are common in this region. The coastal waters, both brackish and salt, are frequented by several species of potentially dangerous sharks, as well as other hazardous marine life such as stingrays. The best defense against these dangers is to use caution around the water and avoid swimming in murky waters, especially at night. Keep a sharp eye out for snakes and wasps nests and avoid putting hands or feet anywhere you can't see clearly. Black bears live in the larger tracts of forests and

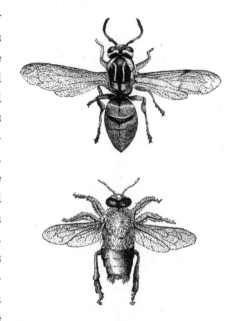

Wasp (top) and bee (bottom)

bottomlands of the region, but are rarely seen and are less likely to be a threat than in mountain regions where their numbers are greater.

Recommended Equipment

To reach the best bug-out locations in this region, a boat of some type is essential, and can range from the smallest canoe or kayak to a larger cruiser. Bugging out by wheeled vehicle is also possible, especially if you are prepared to eventually slog in on foot once you get as far as you can ride. Other recommended equipment for the region includes waterproof boots, a jungle hammock or tent with no-see-um insect netting, a machete, a snake-bite kit, and bug spray. Hunting and gathering equipment should focus on small game and aquatic/marine life, and should include a .22 caliber rifle, drop hooks and line, a cast net, and maybe a fishing spear or bowfishing rig. A rifle for taking deer could also be included, keeping in mind that most shots here will be at close range where the .22 might suffice just fine. For defensive firearms, any caliber sufficient against human aggressors will be adequate here, as the threat from large animal predators is practically nonexistent.

◆ ◆ ◆

The following sections, organized by state, will discuss the various regions of the East Coast in terms of their suitability as bug-out locations.

Florida

Unlike the western side of the peninsula and the panhandle, described in the previous chapter, the east coast of Florida has little to offer in the way of big wild areas and federal lands. If you live on the eastern side of the peninsula and there is time, you might be better off trying to make your way to one of the locations highlighted in Chapter Five.

But despite the large population, due to the nature of the state's Atlantic coastline and its string of barrier islands, sounds, and river entrances, there are pockets of hidden beach and tracts of mangrove swamp and marsh where one could disappear if needed, especially for a short time. If you live right on or near the coast, which is overcrowded in most areas, the key to successfully bugging out is to have a boat at the ready, because the best places cannot be reached any other way.

Just inland from the east coast, however, much of Florida is rural and sparsely populated, and a few parts are relatively wild, whether protected by the state or federal government or privately owned. It's a tough environment—hot, humid, buggy, and populated by snakes and other reptiles—but rich in plant and animal food for those who can endure it.

Loxahatchee National Wildlife Refuge

Loxahatchee National Wildlife Refuge is similar ecologically to the Everglades and Big Cypress Preserve, but is included in this chapter because of its proximity to the heavily populated stretch of Florida's east coast from Ft. Lauderdale to West Palm Beach. Remarkably, the refuge boundaries enclose 147,000 acres of mostly roadless wilderness within a few miles of millions of residents on that crowded coast.

The refuge is open to hunting, and is a key habitat for whitetail deer and endangered species such as the Florida panther. Beyond the refuge boundaries, much of the surrounding countryside is similar in habitat and wildlife populations. The entire portion of the state south of Lake Okeechobee to the Everglades and the west coast could become a bug-out refuge in the event of a real SHTF situation in crowded south Florida. Just remember to bring the bug spray if this is your only option.

Nearest Cities: West Palm Beach, Fort Lauderdale, Belle Glade

Cape Canaveral National Seashore

Cape Canaveral National Seashore and the surrounding area encompass the most expansive stretches of uninhabited shoreline remaining on the east coast of Florida—not that this is a large wilderness by any means, but it is better than nothing. Taking in 24 miles of shoreline, its lagoons, mangrove swamps, oak and palmetto hammocks, piney woods, and dunes total 58,000 acres.

Between the barrier island and the mainland, Mosquito Lagoon offers a maze of smaller islands, mangrove channels, and coastal hideaways that can be accessed by boat, especially sea kayaks and canoes that can go places larger craft cannot. Fishing, beachcombing, foraging, and hunting of coastal wildlife and waterfowl should be good in the event of a bug-out situation when the park's usual rules cannot be enforced.

For those bugging out with the mobility of a boat, the surrounding areas outside of the national seashore also have potential, as much

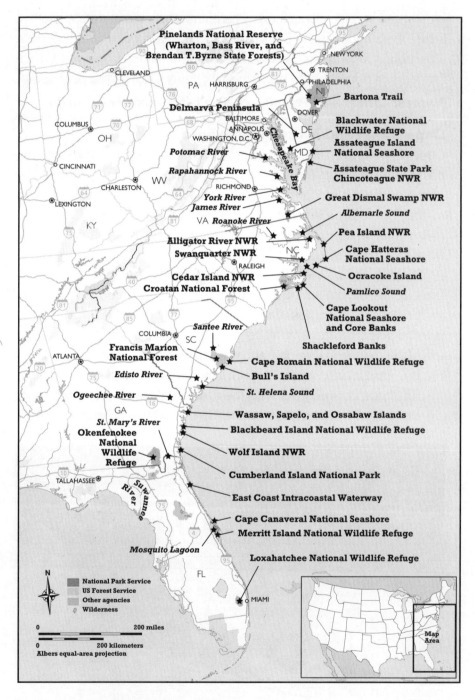

Bug-Out Locations of the Atlantic Coast

of the East Coast Intracoastal Waterway offers spoil islands, mangrove swamps, and other pockets of unused shoreline.

Just to the south of the park lies the 140,000-acre Merritt Island National Wildlife Refuge, taking in the John F. Kennedy Space Center and providing a buffer zone for it from the populated areas of Merritt Island and nearby Titusville.

Nearest Cities: *Titusville, Merritt Island, Orlando, Daytona Beach*

Georgia

Georgia is a southern state that has a bit of everything, from the biggest blackwater swamp in the U.S. to a 100-mile long labyrinth of uninhabited wilderness islands on the Atlantic Coast. Georgia even has rugged mountain wilderness areas, including one of the wildest in the Appalachians, but that part of the state will be described in the next chapter.

Georgia has tens of thousands of miles of rivers and streams. The state's biggest rivers include the Chattahoochee, which forms part of the border with Alabama and empties into the Gulf of Mexico, and the Satilla, Altamaha, Ogeechee, and Savannah, which drain into the Atlantic. The entire coastal plain of eastern Georgia is a maze of rivers, swamps, estuaries, and wet bottomland hardwood forest. Naturally, there are many excellent bug-out locations to be found in such an environment. I'll highlight just a few of the best examples in the following sections.

Okefenokee Swamp and Upper Suwannee River

The Okefenokee Swamp is a truly unique 700-square mile wetland in southern Georgia at the border with Florida that forms the headwaters of two rivers: the St. Mary's, which empties into the nearby Atlantic, and the 280-mile long Suwannee River, which flows to the Big Bend area of the Gulf Coast, as described in the previous chapter. Most of the Okefenokee Swamp is under the management of the Okefenokee National Wildlife Refuge, which totals 402,000 acres.

This vast swamp, which is approximately 38 miles long by 25 miles wide, is a peat-filled, saucer-shaped depression in the earth formed around 7000 years ago. Within this wet depression are more than 60 named lakes and 70 islands of more than 20 acres, the largest of these totaling 8000 acres. The Okefenokee Swamp also contains some 60,000 acres of naturally occurring open prairie, creating a mixed habitat that is ideal for a wide diversity of plant and animal life.

Like the Everglades of southern Florida, this prime hunting ground was a favorite of early Native Americans and was a hideout for raiding Seminole warriors as late as 1850. Such a watery labyrinth of interconnected lakes and deep southern forests is, of course, still a promising refuge for someone needing a place to hide out and live off the land. In normal times, however, access to this swamp is highly restricted within the wildlife refuge, with more rules and regulations than most any park or refuge in the country. The rangers here want to know your every move and travel even by canoe is limited to designated trails with no side trips permitted. In a real SHTF scenario, however, none of this will be enforceable, and for those living within reach of the Okefenokee, it is a prime bug-out location offering everything you need for long-term evasion and survival. An added advantage is the ability to travel by water (or with a reasonable portage, depending on water level) from the Okefenokee to either the Atlantic Ocean or Gulf of Mexico if it becomes necessary to move on.

Nearest Cities: *Waycross, St. Mary's, Valdosta, and Lake City and Jacksonville (FL)*

Georgia's Coastal Islands

If uninhabited islands, seashores, and wilderness estuaries are your idea of a great bug-out location, then the humid, subtropical Georgia coast has some of the best to offer in all the United States. This 100-mile-long coast is a maze of river deltas, winding bayous, marshland, and wooded dunes. From Cumberland Island National Park near the southern boundary with Florida, all the way north to Savannah, there is plenty of federal and state-owned coastal land along this shore. Most of Georgia's coast has been spared from the high-rise condominiums and tourist hotels of Florida's east coast farther south. While most of the individual islands are relatively small, taken as a whole network of islands and waterways, the Georgia coast offers many possibilities to those who would bug out in boats.

The coastal islands of Georgia are not separated from the mainland by wide sounds of open water like some of the barrier islands in Florida and the Carolinas. Instead, there is a four- to six-mile-wide swath of estuaries and marshlands that are safe to navigate even in small boats. The East Coast Intracoastal Waterway also winds its way inside the barrier islands, allowing for an inshore route for larger vessels.

In addition to the 16,600-acre Cumberland Island, managed by the National Park Service, several other large islands on the Georgia coast are protected as national wildlife refuges, including the 5618-acre Blackbeard Island, named for the pirate Edward Teach who used this excellent hideout as a base for attacking merchant shipping in the early 18th century. Wolf Island National Wildlife Refuge totals 5126 acres and includes Wolf Island, two smaller islands, and the surrounding marsh. Farther north, the even larger Wassaw Island, at 10,050 acres, features rolling dunes, maritime forest, and miles of trails and dirt roads. Two other large islands, Sapelo (16,500 acres) and Ossabaw (11,800 acres), while not completely uninhabited, are mostly owned by the state and are also managed for recreation and as wildlife refuges.

Nearest Cities: *St. Marys, Brunswick, Savannah*

Altamaha River

The Altamaha River drains about 14,000 square miles and is the third-largest river that empties into the Atlantic along the East Coast. This 130-mile-long river encompasses a vast floodplain of swamps and bottomland hardwood forests that have remained in a largely pristine state due to difficult access. It begins at the confluence of the Ocmulgee and Oconee Rivers, which rise at the eastern slopes of Georgia's Applachians. The river basin once flowed through 90 million acres of longleaf pine forests, most of which has been long since logged, but it is one of the few places left in the South where there are still remnants of old-growth longleaf. The Nature Conservancy has called the basin "one of America's last great places" and has established an Altamaha

Biosphere Reserve. Like many of the big river systems of the Gulf Coast Southeast, the Altamaha offers those who choose to bug out by small boat a waterborne highway into places that are otherwise inaccessible.

Nearest Cities: *Brunswick, Jesup, Hazelhurst*

Ogeechee River

The Ogeechee River is a 245-mile-long blackwater river that retains its wild quality along most of its length, offering plenty of potential for bug-out hideaways along its banks and good hunting, foraging, and fishing. The Ogeechee is popular with Georgia canoeists because of its scenic beauty and abundant wildlife. The river's namesake tree is the Ogeechee lime, a small tree in the Tupelo family, which produces an acidic bright red fruit that can be used as a lime substitute. Other exotic-looking plants of the subtropics found along its banks include pitcher plants, needle palms, and spider lilies.

The lower reaches include extensive swamps, and in high water many alternate channels become available, making it easy to get lost, whether accidentally or intentionally. This lower part of the Ogeechee turns into a broad salt marsh estuary with access to the Atlantic and the above-mentioned coastal islands just a short distance south of Savannah, at Ossabaw Island.

Nearest Cities: *Savannah, Statesboro, Louisville*

South Carolina

Like Georgia, South Carolina has a distinct coastal plain or "low country" region with a hot and humid subtropical climate, many rivers, and 187 miles of Atlantic coast. Inland the terrain changes gradually and reaches the edge of the Appalachians. The population density is relatively low for an East Coast state, and as a result there are good potential bug-out locations scattered about. The South Carolina coast is not quite the wilderness that much of Georgia's coast is, but there are still undeveloped barrier islands and estuaries, especially in the southern half below Cape Romain. All of the coast is accessible by boat from the protected route of the East Coast Intracoastal Waterway.

The wildest places in the low country of the state are along the rivers and in the swamps, both of which are plentiful. South Carolina also boasts a large tract of federal land near the coast: the Francis Marion National Forest. Farther inland, the newest addition to its protected federal lands is Congaree National Park, recently established to protect what is said to be the largest expanse of old-growth bottomland forest remaining in the United States.

Francis Marion National Forest

Located just north of Charleston, the Francis Marion National Forest protects 252,368 acres of public land. Much of the timber in this coastal national forest was devastated in 1989 by Hurricane Hugo, but nature is slowly healing the wounds and new growth is replacing the downed trees. Although the forest is crisscrossed by numerous roads and highways, there are many smaller pockets of wild lands within its boundaries, including four designated wilderness areas: the 2200-acre Hellhole Bay, 1900 acres of blackwater swamp in Wambow Creek Wilderness, and over 10,000 acres in Wambow Swamp and Little Wambow Swamp. All of these areas are difficult to access on foot except during the driest weather, and access by canoe is limited or impossible in most parts due to insufficient water. Wambow Swamp in particular is said to be perhaps the least visited area in South Carolina. This is good news for someone willing to put up with the muck and mosquitoes in a bug-out situation. Hunting and foraging will be good, with the usual wide variety of edible plant, animal, and aquatic species common in such places. As is typical of southern swamp environments, it is also replete with alligators, cottonmouths, copperheads, and rattlesnakes.

Nearest Cities: *Charleston, Moncks Corner, Georgetown, McCletonville*

Cape Romain National Wildlife Refuge

Adjacent to Francis Marion National Forest on the east side of Highway 17 and the Intracoastal Waterway, Cape Romain National Wildlife Refuge stretches for 22 miles of the Atlantic coast and takes in 34,000 acres of bayshore, marsh, and barrier island habitat. The 5000-acre

Bull's Island is an outstanding example of a wooded barrier island, covered with forests of live oak, magnolia, pine, and palmetto.

This protected seashore environment is rich in wildlife and is popular for saltwater fishing, as well as crabbing, clamming, and oyster gathering. Hunting is allowed here as well, in season, and deer are abundant. As in most national wildlife refuges, camping is not permitted. In a bug-out scenario, this would be a good choice for someone operating out of a small boat, with escape routes up or down the coast, or inland to the Francis Marion National Forest by way of the Santee River that enters the coast just to the north.

Nearest Cities: *McCleltonville, Georgetown, Charleston*

Edisto River Basin

The Edisto River is another of those long, free-flowing blackwater rivers of the South, offering much potential for bugging out along its 250-mile length. Due to its popularity among river paddlers, a 56-mile Edisto River Canoe and Kayak Trail has been established to improve river access and promote conservation.

Bottomland forests and cypress swamps border the river, and in times of high water it's possible to leave the main channel and strike out by canoe through the flooded forest. Although most of the land along its banks is private, difficult access by road means large areas of wild lands are infrequently visited by the landowners or anyone else. The surrounding countryside is by no means a wilderness, but the river provides a woodland corridor that is excellent wildlife habitat and offers good hunting, fishing, and foraging anywhere along its navigable length. In its lower reaches the Edisto becomes a broad coastal estuary and opens up into areas of marsh and maritime forest before it enters the Atlantic at St. Helena Sound, near Beaufort.

Nearest Cities: *Orangeburg, Summerville, Walterboro, Beaufort*

North Carolina

The eastern low country of North Carolina offers a vast array of huge estuaries, wide-open sounds, and isolated barrier islands. With 300 miles of coastline, and over 3000 miles of tidal shoreline, the possibilities for waterborne bugging out are tremendous. In addition to all these saltwater coastal routes and hideaways, several large rivers and freshwater swamps add to the options. More than 300 miles away, the western area of the state, of course, encompasses some of the wildest parts of Appalachia, and will be an important part of the next chapter.

The climate of eastern North Carolina is only slightly different than South Carolina and Georgia to the south, with mild winters and generally hot summers. An indicator of the similarities is the fact that American alligators are still present all the way to the northern end of this coast. Hurricanes and tropical storms are also a threat, but major hits are less frequent than on the coast to the south.

Croatan National Forest

Located midway along North Carolina's Atlantic coast, between Cape Lookout and the Neuse River, the Croatan National Forest offers 160,000 acres of public pine forests, lakes, freshwater bogs, and salt marsh. Many of the inland swamps and bogs of this national forest are difficult to access and are rarely visited, making for good bug-out locations if you are willing to bushwhack a bit to reach them. Some of the most pristine areas are the four designated wilderness areas within the forest, including the 11,700-acre Pocosin Wilderness, a raised bog area with no trails through it. Other tracts designated to remain in an untouched state are the 8530-acre Catfish Lake South Wilderness, the 9540-acre Sheep Ridge Wilderness, and the 1860-acre Pond Pine Wilderness.

For bug-out purposes, Croatan National Forest can be reached by road or by boat. Numerous small creeks flow out of the forest lands to the Neuse River estuary, which forms part of the northern boundary, and the White Oak River that runs along the southwestern edge. These rivers are also connected to the East Coast Intracoastal Waterway, allowing plenty of options for those with waterborne transportation.

Nearest Cities: *Morehead City, Jacksonville, Havelock, New Bern*

Pamlico Sound and the Outer Banks

Bounded by the windswept barrier islands of North Carolina's Outer Banks to the east, and receiving the outflow of two major rivers, the Neuse and the Pamlico, to the west, Pamlico Sound is the largest sound on all the East Coast. It stretches for 80 miles north and south, and varies in width from 15 to 30 miles. Much of the shoreline on both the island side and the mainland side is uninhabited and protected in a series of national seashores and national wildlife refuges.

Pamlico Sound is a wide-open, exposed body of water that can get nasty in windy conditions. To safely navigate it, especially to reach the Outer Banks, you will need a seaworthy boat. Sea kayaks are fine on the small end of the spectrum and can get you to remote coastal areas with shallows that prohibit other boats. Other parts of the sound are navigable in larger boats and yachts.

Cape Hatteras National Seashore, encompassing over 70 miles of the Outer Banks barrier islands, is the best-known federal tract on the sound and can be accessed by a single road that runs down the island from the north end to Cape Hatteras and Ocracoke Island. Despite the road, there are many isolated areas of beach along this seashore. Pea Island National Wildlife Refuge takes in 13 miles of dunes, brackish ponds, and salt marsh on the northern end of Hatteras Island.

Farther south across Ocracoke Inlet, the much more isolated Cape Lookout National Seashore extends an additional 56 miles south, taking in several roadless barrier islands including North Core Banks, South Core Banks, and Shackleford Banks.

Shackleford Banks is home to a large herd of wild horses. All of the barrier islands of the Outer Banks offer excellent beachcombing and foraging, and are abundant with seashore edibles, including clams, crabs, and a wide variety of fish and waterfowl.

The mainland side of Pamlico Sound is a convoluted shoreline of small bays, points, and river mouths. Most of the shore consists of tidal marshlands and thus is sparsely populated. Swanquarter National Wildlife Refuge, on the north side of the Pamlico River entrance, is a 16,411-acre preserve of coastal wetlands and forest that is a major sanctuary for ducks and other migratory waterfowl. Cedar Island National Wildlife Refuge takes in more than 14,000 acres on Cedar Island, just across Core Sound from Cape Lookout National Seashore. Overall, considering the amount of protected shoreline around much of its natural boundary, Pamlico Sound has much to offer to anyone bugging out by boat.

Nearest Cities: *Nag's Head, Morehead City, Greenville*

The Roanoke River and Albemarle Sound

The Roanoke River is a major river of the East Coast, draining a good portion of southern Virginia and northern North Carolina. This 410-mile-long river empties into the vast Albemarle Sound in coastal North Carolina before reaching the Atlantic. The lower Roanoke River floodplain contains broad stretches of relatively undisturbed bottomland hardwood forest and expansive tracts of cypress and tupelo swamp. Some of the most pristine examples of these river habitats have been purchased and preserved by the Nature Conservancy and much of it is managed as the Roanoke River National Wildlife Refuge.

Albemarle Sound is only slightly smaller than the huge Pamlico Sound to the south, and is connected to it by Croatan and Roanoke Sounds, which in effect make the whole area one vast estuary that contains many miles of undeveloped shoreline. One of the best areas is preserved in the 152,000-acre Alligator River National Wildlife Refuge, named for the reptile that reaches the northern limit of its range there. The swamp forests of the refuge are also home to plenty of black bear and to endangered southern red wolves that have been reintroduced to the wild there by the U.S. Fish and Wildlife Service. Within the refuge are numerous creeks, canals, and waterways, including the Alligator River and Milltail Creek.

Nearest Cities: *Elizabeth City, Edenton, Kitty Hawk, Nag's Head*

Virginia

Moving north to coastal Virginia from the Carolinas, the options for good bug-out locations become fewer and smaller, but there are places to go, especially if you have a seaworthy boat. The most noteworthy feature of Virginia's coast is the vast Chesapeake Bay, with its entrance to the Atlantic Ocean located between Cape Henry and the southern end of the Delmarva Peninsula. The Chesapeake is the largest estuary in the United States, with over 150 rivers and streams draining into its 64,299-square-mile area. The shorelines of this great bay and Virginia's rivers that drain into it are by no means uninhabited, but there are a surprising number of undeveloped and inaccessible pockets. Another large natural area near the coast that still retains some of its wilderness qualities is the Great Dismal Swamp in the area south of the Chesapeake along the North Carolina border.

The Great Dismal Swamp

The Great Dismal Swamp is the northernmost "southern" swamp. The swamp itself is 37 miles long and up to 12 miles wide, with approximately 40 percent of its area in Virginia. The Great Dismal Swamp National Wildlife Refuge protects 112,000 acres of forest, swamp, and a 3100-acre natural lake. This is only a fraction of the Great Dismal Swamp that once covered 3600 square miles, but it is still a significant wild area so close to the urban sprawl of the Norfolk area.

The Great Dismal Swamp can be accessed by the Dismal Swamp Canal, which connects it to the East Coast Intracoastal Waterway and the nearby sounds of North Carolina. Even a passage on this manmade canal gives a glimpse of the isolation of the swamp. The really wild areas, however, are off the main routes, in the morass of peat bogs, cypress lakes, and hardwood bottoms.

Nearest Cities: Norfolk, Portsmouth, Suffolk

Backwaters of the Chesapeake Bay

With more than 12,000 miles of shoreline in Virginia and Maryland, the Chesapeake Bay has many nooks and crannies that could offer potential bug-out locations to those with small, shallow-draft boats that can reach them. Sea kayaks are ideal for these shores, where a knowledgeable coastal forager could do quite well off the natural bounty.

These hideaways can be found on both the eastern and western shores of this vast bay, among the countless small peninsulas and shallow coves that make up the entire fringe of the bay. In Virginia, the James, York, Rapahannock, and Potomac Rivers all drain into the bay from the west, offering many more miles of waterway through both urban and unpopulated areas.

Nearest Cities: *Virginia Beach, Hampton, Newport News, Williamsburg, Richmond*

Maryland

With the teeming human populations surrounding Washington, D.C., and Baltimore, one would think that the small state of Maryland would offer little in the way of bug-out locations. But with so much of the Chesapeake Bay shoreline within its borders, as well as several rivers and a stretch of undeveloped Atlantic coastline, Maryland has some good possibilities for the short term, especially for those who are properly prepared to bug out by water and are familiar with the most remote waterways. Since none of the specific areas are particularly large, the descriptions here are brief, but taken as a whole, the shoreline of the bay, the barrier islands, and the rivers can all be considered bug-out locations for those with boats. Two of the largest areas of federally protected land are the Blackwater National Wildlife Refuge and the Assateauge Island National Seashore.

Blackwater National Wildlife Refuge

This national wildlife refuge, located just inland from the convoluted eastern shore of the Chesapeake, is one of the larger reserves of several on this side of the bay. Blackwater National Wildlife Refuge protects 25,000 acres of tidal marsh and mixed forest. Situated along the Atlantic Flyway, it is a major haven for migrating ducks and geese and provides habitat for a great variety of other wildlife. Game animals including squirrels, muskrat, nutria, whitetail deer, and an exotic Asian deer called sika deer are abundant. Small though it is, the Nature Conservancy calls the Blackwater the "Everglades of the North." It is named for the Blackwater River and the Little Blackwater River, which empty into the bay from freshwater swamps inland on the Delmarva Peninsula.

In addition to the refuge itself, many other rivers empty into the Chesapeake from the Delmarva Peninsula, including the Pocomoke,

Wicomico, Nanticoke, and Choptank Rivers, which spread out into expanses of marsh and delta at their mouths. Any of these can offer routes to and from the interior of the peninsula to the open waters of the bay, with many potential hideouts along the way.

Nearest Cities: *Cambridge, Salisbury, Crisfield, Washington, D.C.*

Assateague Island National Seashore

Assateague Island, located partially in Virginia, is a 37-mile-long stretch of undeveloped Atlantic barrier island. Although it is accessible by vehicle from bridges connecting it to the mainland at the northern end, most of the island is protected in the Assateague Island National Seashore, Assateague State Park, and Chincoteague National Wildlife Refuge. Large populations of free-roaming wild horses inhabit the island, as well as the usual shorebirds and many varieties of waterfowl.

As is true of most East Coast barrier islands, the best hideaways that are the most inaccessible are found on the western side of the island, in this case along the shores of Chincoteague Bay. Fishing and foraging from a small boat would be good here for the short term, with a protected route behind the island where you could wait for a weather window to move north or south to wilder areas if necessary.

Nearest Cities: *Pocomoke City, Berlin, Ocean City*

New Jersey

The first things that come to mind when most people think of New Jersey are industrial wasteland, the urban jungle adjacent to New York City, or the glitz of Atlantic City on the coast. Outsiders might think there is not a single place in this heavily populated state in which to bug out to the wild, but there are actually some pretty expansive forests just inland in the coastal plain area known as the "Pine Barrens" and some lonely stretches of marsh and riverbank in other areas.

Readers who are familiar with the works of survival writer and instructor Tom Brown Jr. will know that the New Jersey Pine Barrens were his childhood training ground in the skills of wilderness living and survival, and that he continues to run his survival school there. This area has so much to offer that I will focus on it as the bug-out location of choice for residents of New Jersey, though other areas to look at are Barnegat Bay, the shores of Delaware Bay, and the hills and lakes of the northwest corner of the state at the edge of the Appalachian range.

The Pine Barrens

The Pine Barrens region of New Jersey gets its name from the predominant tree species found there. The acidic, sandy soil of the area is not well suited to many other trees, and early settlers discovered the farming in the area was poor, which was the main factor that kept it relatively wild. This unique soil does support some unusual plant communities, though, including carnivorous plants and orchids. Species in the Pine Barrens have adapted to periodic fires, which are frequent and are fueled in intensity by the pine pitch.

Despite its proximity to so many large cities, enough of the Pine Barrens remained undeveloped or lightly populated rural countryside that the Pinelands National Reserve, the nation's first national reserve, was designated here in 1978. This reserve protects 1.1 million acres of the Pine Barrens, and has since been upgraded to an International Biosphere Reserve. The reserve contains three state forests: Wharton, Bass River, and Brendan T. Byrne. These state forests are connected by the Bartona Trail, a 49.5-mile trail that winds through the barrens. A network of shorter trails branch off into many of the most remote areas, opening up many options for bugging out on foot. Fire roads and logging roads offer access in to the area by bike, motorcycle or ATV, or four-wheel-drive vehicle. Game animals such as deer and squirrel are plentiful, as are wild berries such as blueberries, strawberries, and cranberries.

Nearest Cities: *Atlantic City, Vineland, Cherry Hill, Trenton*

7

THE APPALACHIAN MOUNTAIN CORRIDOR

ALABAMA, GEORGIA, TENNESSEE, SOUTH CAROLINA, NORTH CAROLINA, KENTUCKY, VIRGINIA, WEST VIRGINIA, PENNSYLVANIA, MARYLAND, AND NEW YORK

The Appalachian Mountains form the backbone of the eastern United States, dividing the drainages of the Atlantic Ocean to the east from those of the Mississippi River to the west and Hudson Bay to the north. This 1500-mile-long mountain range provides a corridor of rugged wilderness areas stretching from central Alabama and northern Georgia to Maine and the Canadian island of Newfoundland. The Appalachians as a whole are made up of many smaller mountain ranges linked together, including the Blue Ridge Mountains, Smokey Mountains, Allegheny Mountains, and many others. The mountain corridor averages 100 to 300 miles wide, with individual peaks averaging 3000 feet in elevation. The highest peak in the range and in all the eastern United States is 6684-foot Mount Mitchell in North Carolina.

The Appalachian Mountains are within easy reach of many of the biggest population centers of the nation yet contain extensive tracts of protected wild lands in a variety of national forests and parks throughout their length, including some of the largest virgin forests remaining in the East. The Appalachians create their own weather and are much wetter than much of the surrounding low country around them (as well as the more arid western mountains). This rainfall allows for a lush and diverse ecosystem and the resultant dense forests make it easy to disappear in virtually any valley or on any ridge. A wide variety of edible plants flourish in these mountains, as do healthy populations of deer and other game animals.

Unlike the Gulf Coast Southeast and the Islands and Lowlands of the East Coast discussed in the previous two chapters, the Appalachian Mountain Corridor offers many areas of wild country that can be considered true wilderness and in many cases can only be accessed by rugged foot trails. Boats are of limited use here, except on a few of the rivers and larger man-made lakes. One of America's longest hiking trails, the 2178-mile Appalachian Trail, runs almost the entire length of the corridor and makes it possible to walk from northern Georgia to Maine almost entirely in the wilderness or semi-wilderness of the mountains.

APPALACHIAN MOUNTAIN CORRIDOR BUG-OUT ESSENTIALS

Weather and Climate

The weather and climate within the Appalachian Mountain Corridor varies tremendously because of the wide range of elevations, as well as the range of latitudes the mountains span from the northern parts of the Gulf Coast states to southern Canada. These mountains create their own weather, which can be quite different from the lowlands to the east and west of the corridor. Compared to other mountains in the U.S., especially the Rockies, the Appalachians are generally wet, with annual precipitation ranging from about 55 inches to more than 85 inches on some of the peaks. Summers in the valleys and lower elevations can be hot and humid, especially in the southern parts of the range. With peaks over 6000 feet, however, the changes are significant in the high elevations and as a result, north woods ecosystems exist much farther south here than would be possible at normal elevations. Winters at elevation and in the northern part of the range can be severe, with heavy snowfall, icy winds, and occasional blizzards.

Land and Resources

Millions of acres of public lands are available in the Appalachian Mountain Corridor, including expansive national forests and national

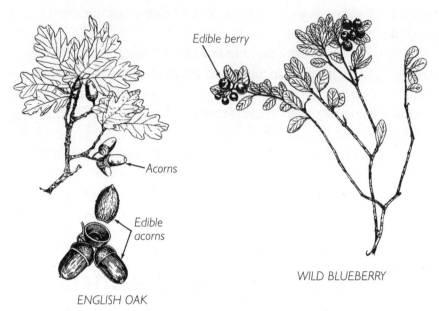

ENGLISH OAK

WILD BLUEBERRY

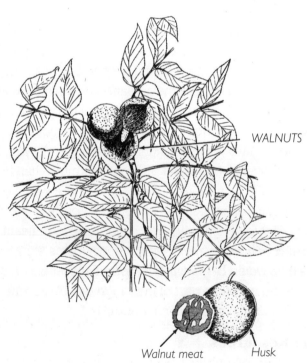

WALNUTS

Some edible plants of the Appalachian Mountains

parks. This is one of the few regions of the East with such a high ratio of public to private land, and virtually all the roadless areas of any size are part of some federal or state holding. Human populations here, as in most mountain regions, are concentrated in the valleys and larger areas of gentler terrain within the mountains, as these areas were more conducive to farming by early settlers. Many of the towns and cities are along rivers and streams, while the most rugged peaks and ridges are uninhabited. Throughout these wet mountains, an abundance of small rivers, creeks, and springs offer easy access to drinking water, though even in remote areas it should be treated before use unless you find it right where it comes out of the earth.

Edible Plants

The Appalachian Mountains contain some of the most diverse temperate forests on the planet, and as a result, many useful species of trees, bushes, plants, and herbs can be found here. Some of these are the same species found in the lowlands of these states, while others native to more northern climates grow here because of the colder weather of the higher elevations. Trees include several species of pine and spruce, which are useful for their edible inner bark and their needles that can be brewed into a vitamin-rich tea. Sassafras trees are also present in the Appalachians, as are sugar maples. A variety of deciduous trees provide nuts such as acorns, hickory nuts, and black walnuts, and fruits such as black cherries and persimmons. Fruit-bearing bushes and vines include wild blueberries, strawberries, bear berries, cranberries, mulberries, and wild grapes. In the shady understory, ferns are common, providing edible fiddleheads in the spring. Other edible plants to look for in the forest undergrowth include wild leeks, wild onions, plantain, waterleaf, toothwort, saxifrage, lady's thumb, giant chickweed, spiderwort, wood sorrel, wood nettle, burdock, groundnut, and wintercress.

Hunting and Fishing

Many species of mammals inhabit this mountain region, including whitetail deer and black bear throughout and mountain lions, coyote, wild hogs, and reintroduced elk in many areas. Smaller animals include red, gray, and fox squirrels, rabbits, beaver, chipmunks, raccoons, opossums, groundhogs, and porcupines. Game birds include wild turkeys, ruffed grouse, wood ducks, and mourning doves. Most of the streams in the Appalachians are rich in edible fish species, including minnows, brook trout, rainbow trout, brown trout, smallmouth and largemouth bass, and blue catfish. Other aquatic creatures include crawfish, turtles, and frogs. The Appalachians are home to numerous species of salamanders, many of which are found nowhere else on Earth. Look for them under logs and in the deep litter of leaves typical on the forest floor, where you will also find an abundance of grubs and other insects if you are truly desperate for animal protein.

Wildlife Hazards

The Appalachian Mountains are home to large populations of black bears, and though attacks on humans are rare, they do occur, so I would have to rate bears as the number-one wildlife hazard in this region. The bears that inhabit these mountains are frequently unafraid of humans, and problem bears in places like Smokey Mountain National Park are usually moved to remote wilderness areas where they could be dangerous to the infrequent human visitor. The threat is real enough that you should carry adequate protection when traveling in the wilds here. Another large predator native to these mountains is the mountain lion, which was long extinct from the East but is now making a comeback and is occasionally spotted in the Appalachians. Russian wild boars, imported to parts of the southern Appalachians decades ago by sport hunters, are now firmly established and can pose a threat if you surprise a herd or get too close to their young. Dangerous reptile species are not as diverse here as in the South and East Coast lowlands, but you still have the timber rattlesnake and the copperhead to worry about.

Recommended Equipment

The wildest parts of Appalachia can only be accessed on foot. You'll need good boots and a bug-out backpack as described in Chapter Two, as well as warm, waterproof clothing and sleeping gear. Cold rain that lasts for days on end is common in these mountains, and in the winter, deep snow and even blizzards can catch the unprepared off-guard. It is essential here to have good shelter and a reliable way to make fire.

Hunting equipment should include a .22 survival rifle for shooting elusive squirrels and small birds in thick cover, as well as a larger-caliber handgun or rifle that can take deer and double as bear protection. The .357 magnum is a good choice as a minimum caliber for eastern black bear. There are also other transportation alternatives besides hiking in this region, if you'd rather not walk or need to carry more supplies and equipment. Many parts of the various state and national forests in Appalachia can be accessed by four-wheel-drive vehicles, dual-purpose motorcycles, ATVs, mountain bikes, or on horseback.

◆ ◆ ◆

The number of potential bug-out locations in this region could easily fill a book this size, so I'll highlight just a few of the best. I'm also omitting the mountain sections of northern New York and the New England states, which are technically part of the Appalachians, as those areas will be covered in Chapter Eight, under Lakes and Big Woods of the North. I will also note here that because of the size of some of the wilderness areas in this chapter, it is not possible to define all of them on a state-by-state basis because of state line overlaps. Consequently, I have grouped some states together in a single section rather than keeping each separate as in previous chapters.

Alabama

Most people from other regions of the country tend to think of Alabama as a "Deep South state," which it certainly is, but they may not realize that much of its northern third is rugged foothill and mountain country at the southern terminus of the Appalachian chain. While northern Alabama does not have as much wilderness as some of the other states in this chapter, there are ample bug-out locations in these hills on both public and private lands. This part of Alabama offers many terrain options for bugging out on foot, by vehicle, or by boat. The Tennessee River, a large navigable river with a system of man-made lakes, cuts across the entire north end of the state from east to west. This is an entirely different type of waterway than the swampy rivers in southern

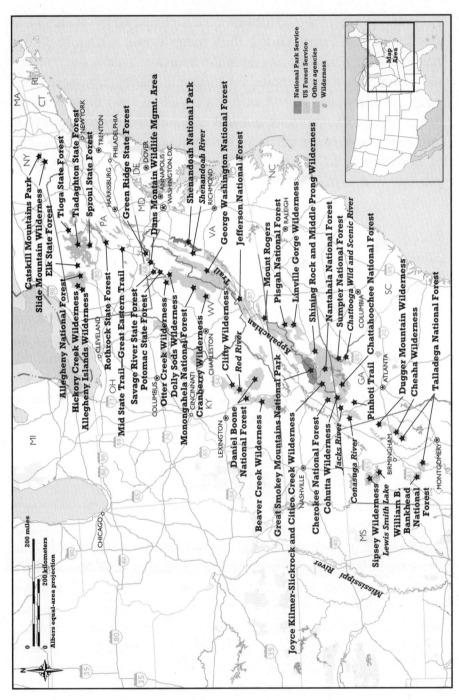

Bug-Out Locations of the Appalachian Mountain Corridor

Alabama detailed in Chapter Five, as it carves through wooded valleys and is often bounded by rocky shores and hills. Two sizeable national forests can also be found in this part of the state, encompassing some of the most and remote and rugged terrain in this southernmost part of Appalachia.

William B. Bankhead National Forest

At 181,230 acres, the William B. Bankhead National Forest is Alabama's second-largest national forest. Although it is located to the west of the main mountain ranges of Alabama, the land within its boundaries is rugged and heavily wooded, with mixed pine and hardwood forests riddled with deep gorges and a network of streams. Alabama's only National Wild and Scenic River, Sipsey Fork, winds through the forest before terminating in Lewis Smith Lake, a man-made reservoir with many arms reaching into wooded valleys, creating 500 miles of shore-line along its banks. The lake and the river make many areas of the Bankhead National Forest accessible by canoe or small boat, but even the most remote parts can be reached on the existing network of hiking trails or by bushwhacking cross-country.

The Sipsey Wilderness Area is a 25,906-acre designated wilderness within the national forest, and is popular with hikers and horse packers. But by getting off the trails it is possible to find seldom-visited hollows and hideaways in this nearly pristine natural area. Water is abundant throughout the wilderness and you will seldom be far from the sound of waterfalls or running creeks. The entire Bankhead National Forest area is prime wildlife habitat, and hunting for deer and smaller game will be productive for those who are prepared.

Nearest Cities: *Russellville, Decatur, Huntsville, Cullman*

Talladega National Forest

Alabama's largest national forest contains a total of 392,567 acres, part of it in the Oakmulgee district southwest of Birmingham, and the other part in the Shoal Creek and Talladega districts, east of Birmingham and taking in the best of the extreme southern reaches of the Appalachians. Much of the land within this national forest was clear-cut and eroded before the forest service purchased it and replanted it in second growth. The area is now once again a diverse ecosystem and is accessible by a number of hiking trails, including the 100-mile-long Pinhoti Trail, which was recently established and continues for 140 miles in Georgia as well. There are also designated ATV trails as well as various fire roads and forest service roads within the Talladega, offering more options besides bugging out on foot.

Two designated wilderness areas within the Talladega National Forest are situated in the most scenic and best-preserved parts of the mountain range here: the 7300-acre Cheaha Wilderness and the 9220-acre Dugger Mountain Wilderness. These roadless areas remained relatively intact because the steep terrain made logging so difficult. Even outside of such designated wilderness areas, the entire Talladega mountain range offers rarely visited gorges and ridges off the beaten track that could serve as bug-out locations in an emergency.

Nearest Cities: *Birmingham, Talladega, Anniston, Gadsden*

Georgia

Like Alabama, Georgia is another Deep South state with its northern portion reaching to the Appalachian Mountains. North Georgia is much more rugged than its western neighbor, however, with peaks reaching as high as 4784 feet and deep river gorges and canyons flowing with whitewater rivers. Due to this region's proximity to Atlanta, the mountains of northern Georgia are heavily visited in the most accessible areas, and the countryside is quite populated with vacation homes, cabins, and tourist attractions. Off the beaten track, however, out in the wilds of Georgia's national forests and designated wilderness areas, can be found some of the best hideaways in the southern Appalachians. These potential bug-out locations are truly wild and densely forested, with populations of black bear, deer, wild turkeys, and many species of small game animals.

Cohutta Wilderness

The 35,247-acre Cohutta Wilderness and parts of the surrounding national forest lands along the border of Georgia and Tennessee make up a 56,000-acre roadless area that is the largest in Georgia. The Cohutta Wilderness is a rugged slice of wild Appalachia containing the canyons of the Jacks and Conasuga Rivers, which feature many waterfalls and hidden gorges with stands of virgin forests. Travel deep into the Cohutta is possible only on foot. More than 87 miles of hiking trails penetrate into the roadless area, but many of them are so seldom used that you'll need a machete to cut a path through the dense rhododendron thickets that are ubiquitous in these mountain forests. It's not unusual to hike for days here without seeing another backpacker. In times of need, the Cohutta has much potential as a game-rich bug-out location, with easy access to water and rivers filled with trout and Coosa bass. Caves and rock overhangs that can provide hideouts and natural shelter are plentiful among the rocky ravines and cliffs. Getting there is not easy, however, and if you plan to bug out in the Cohutta, you'll need to be in good physical condition.

Nearest Cities: *Ellijay, Dalton, Gainesville, Atlanta*

Chattahoochee National Forest

The 749,689-acre Chattahoochee National Forest covers a large portion of northern Georgia's mountains, including the Cohutta Wilderness Area, mentioned above. Divided into six ranger districts, the Chattahoochee National Forest spreads over 18 counties and is traversed by 450 miles of trails and 1600 miles of roads. Many pockets of wilderness with great bug-out location potential can be found just a short walk from a major road.

Besides the Cohutta, there are nine other designated wilderness areas within the forest boundaries, as well as the Chattooga Wild and Scenic River, a remote whitewater river made famous in the 1970s movie *Deliverance*. Flowing out of the mountains of North Carolina, the Chattooga forms 40 miles of the border between northern Georgia and South Carolina. In this stretch it is a pristine wild river that drops a half-mile in elevation, creating raging Class Five and greater rapids. Despite the river's popularity with rafters and kayakers, the surrounding gorges and forested mountains are remote and infrequently visited, making this a bug-out location to rival the Cohutta.

On the South Carolina side of the Chattooga River, the 371,000-acre Sumpter National Forest offers additional options in similar terrain. Sumpter National Forest has both hiking and horse trails that link to the mountain wilderness areas of Georgia and North Carolina.

Nearest Cities: *Toccoa, Gainesville, Dalton, Atlanta (GA), Greenville (SC)*

Tennessee and North Carolina

I've grouped eastern Tennessee and North Carolina together here because of the huge overlaps of contiguous national forests, national parks, and wilderness areas, as well as the similarity of ecosystems in this southern region of the Appalachians. This part of Appalachia contains the highest mountains of the corridor, as well as the largest tracts of federal land, including America's most visited national park. This expansive complex of rugged public land offers excellent bug-out options to the residents of many sizable cities of the region, including Chattanooga, Knoxville, Asheville, Charlotte, and Winston-Salem.

The southern Appalachians here are incredibly diverse, due to the wide range of elevations and the generally warmer climate of these latitudes. In the lower valleys in summer, the weather can be hot and muggy, making the lush green deciduous forests seem positively jungle-like. In winter on the peaks and ridges, deep snowfall and even severe blizzards can make these mountains seem like the far north. Because of this wide range of weather and temperature patterns, both animal and plant life is more diverse here than anywhere else in the eastern U.S.

Great Smokey Mountains National Park (NC and TN)

Straddling the border between Tennessee and North Carolina, the Great Smokey Mountains National Park takes in over 500,000 acres of forested mountains, with elevations ranging from a low of 800 feet to a high point of 6643 feet. Some 900 miles of trails traverse the mountains and valleys within the park. High humidity and up to 85 inches of precipitation each year contribute to the steaming mists that rise off the forested slopes and give the Smokey Mountains their name.

This national park is immensely popular with tourists, ranging from those who see it from the windows of their cars on the park service roads to hard-core backcountry hikers. Over nine million people a year visit this park, but despite this, in a rugged mountain wilderness of this size, it is still possible to find seldom-visited valleys and ridges off the beaten paths. Being that it is a national park and an International Biosphere Reserve, strict rules are in place to protect the plant and animal life in the park. But in a bug-out situation, the wilder reaches of this park would be an excellent place to live, with large numbers of deer, elk, and other game species that have never been subjected to hunting pressure.

Nearest Cities: *Knoxville, Maryville (TN), Waynesville, Asheville (NC)*

Nantahala and Cherokee National Forests (NC and TN)

The Nantahala National Forest, the largest in North Carolina at 1,349,000 acres, and the Cherokee National Forest in both Tennessee and North Carolina, at 640,000 acres, take in an immense area of the southern Appalachians south of Great Smokey Mountains National Park. This vast national forest complex, although cut with numerous highways and interspersed with towns and private lands, offers many options for bug-out locations accessible by vehicles, bikes, ATVs, horses, pack animals, small boats, and foot travel. The best parts of these national forests can be reached on unpaved forest service roads, ATV and horse trails, and the hundreds of miles of hiking trails that weave through them. Within the greater national forests, there are also substantial designated wilderness areas that can only be accessed by hiking rugged and strenuous trails. Since many of these areas are little-known to the public compared to well-publicized areas like the Great Smokey Mountains National Park, they do not get nearly as many visitors, yet offer the same scenery and diversity of ecosystems with much more seclusion.

Nearest Cities: *Asheville, Franklin, Robbinsville (NC), Newport, Cleveland, Chattanooga (TN)*

Joyce Kilmer-Slickrock and Citico Creek Wilderness Areas (NC and TN)

The Joyce Kilmer-Slickrock Wilderness and Citico Creek Wilderness are among the best examples of pristine Appalachian wilderness to be found anywhere in the entire corridor covered in this chapter. Although popular with serious backpackers and some hunters and other locals of the region, these two adjacent wilderness areas that straddle the Unicoi Mountains in the Cherokee and Nantahala National Forests offer lots of possibilities for getting away on their lightly used trails. These combined wilderness areas total over 30,000 acres of roadless terrain than is much the same today as it was when it was home to the Cherokee. Many areas of virgin forest remain, especially in the Citico Creek area, where impossibly steep terrain has always limited human endeavors and left the wilderness largely intact.

Rhododendron thickets, aptly named "hells" by the early explorers who attempted to settle in these mountains, are a common feature in this area and can make off-trail travel extremely difficult, even with a sharp machete. But they also offer unparalleled hideout potential in the rugged gorges along the small, clear-running creeks that are plentiful here. Hunting is good, with plenty of deer, Russian boar, ruffed grouse, wild turkeys, and squirrels. Black bears are also plentiful, and can definitely be a threat here, as this is a favorite relocation zone for large problem individuals that have to be removed from the nearby Great Smokey Mountains National Park.

Nearest Cities: *Tellico Plains, Cleveland, Athens (TN), Robbinsville, Murphy (NC)*

Pisgah National Forest (NC)

Not far behind the Nantahala in size, the Pisgah National Forest in North Carolina covers 1,076,711 acres, much of it in the Blue Ridge and Great Balsam Mountains. Pisgah National Forest can be accessed by a number of roads, including the Blue Ridge Parkway, and offers hundreds of miles of hiking trails, including part of the Appalachian Trail, as well as various ATV, mountain bike, and horse trails.

There are several designated wilderness areas in Pisgah National Forest, including one of the nation's first such areas: the 18,500-acre Shining Rock Wilderness. The adjacent Middle Prong Wilderness adds 7900 acres. The rugged terrain in this area contains five peaks over 6000 feet, with high elevations forested in spruce and other species more typical of the north woods. Like other parts of southern Appalachia, these wilderness areas and the greater Pisgah National Forest contain numerous mountain streams, waterfalls, and hidden canyons.

One of the biggest of these is also one of the largest river gorges in the eastern United States, Linville Gorge. Within this gorge, which is often called the "Grand Canyon of North Carolina," Linville Gorge Wilderness covers an area of 11,786 acres, approximately 10,000 of which is old-growth hemlock and yellow poplar forests, including some virgin stands in the most inaccessible coves. The Linville River runs approximately 1400 feet below the rim of the gorge, making the trip in and out a rugged hike up and down steep slopes. It has been a favorite training ground for U.S. Army Rangers and other special forces, and like many areas within the Pisgah National Forest, it offers great potential as a bug-out location.

Nearest Cities: *Asheville, Morgantown, Boone, Hickory*

Kentucky, West Virginia, and Virginia

I've grouped Kentucky, West Virginia, and Virginia together because they straddle the Appalachian Mountain Corridor at approximately the same latitude, just to the north of the southernmost part of the system described in the previous sections. Much of the mountainous parts of these three states is rural, sparsely populated, and/or federally owned as part of various national forests and national parks. Man's influence in these mountains has been heavy-handed in the past, with many strip mines and clear-cuts that have in more recent years begun to heal as such activities have been curtailed.

The mountain regions of these three states have plenty of options for bug-out locations and parts of them are just as rugged and remote as the wilderness areas of Tennessee and North Carolina. Moving incrementally north along the mountain corridor, winters become longer and more severe, but these areas are still far enough south to suffer from heat and humidity in the summer, especially at the lower elevations. The range of weather conditions here contributes to a diversity of plant and animal life, so plenty of wild food resources are available.

Daniel Boone National Forest (KY)

Daniel Boone National Forest is Kentucky's only national forest, but it is a big one, totaling 2,100,000 acres. However, the national forest boundaries, which are shown as green patches in two large segments on the eastern part of most state road maps, are a bit misleading. The reality of this national forest is that it is highly fragmented into small holdings interspersed between tracts of private land. The boundaries between these private and federal holdings are often in dispute, but whether the land is public or private is of less concern in a bug-out situation. Most of it is equally suitable and there are plenty of uninhabited valleys and ridges within this national forest along the Cumberland Plateau.

Two wilderness areas within Daniel Boone National Forest are the Clifty Wilderness, 12,646 rugged acres in the Red River Gorge area, and the Beaver Creek Wilderness, a 4791-acre tract within an area of sandstone cliffs that contain many caves and rock shelters used by early Native Americans. Within the national forest boundaries, there are over 600 miles of hiking trails leading to places accessible only on foot. But with so much private land interspersed, Daniel Boone National Forest is also cut by many roads of varying condition, from pavement to ATV-only, offering bug-out potential for many modes of transportation.

Nearest Cities: Hazard, Williamsburg, London, Morehead, Lexington

Monongahela National Forest (WV)

West Virginia's largest tract of public land is the 919,000-acre Monongahela National Forest, spreading across ten counties along the eastern border of the state. Parts of this national forest resemble more northerly natural areas, with features such as blueberry thickets and highland bogs containing plants such as reindeer moss. Colder-climate mammals such as the snowshoe hare and fisher are also present here, and in addition to these north woods species, other wildlife common in most of the Appalachians is also abundant, including white-tail deer, black bear, gray squirrels, fox squirrels, and rabbits. The area receives an average of 60 inches of precipitation per year, and winter storms can bring as much as 12 to 18 inches of snow.

There are 825 miles of trails in the Monongahela National Forest, as well as 570 miles of roads, offering access from many angles and a variety of transportation options. The forest also contains eight designated wilderness areas, collectively totaling just over 118,000 acres. The largest of these, the Cranberry Wilderness, is located in the Yew Mountains, a sub-range of the Allegheny Mountains. Already substantial in size for an eastern U.S. wilderness area, the more than 35,000-acre Cranberry Wilderness was increased in 2009 by the addition of another 11,951 adjacent acres. Known as the Cranberry Backcountry, the designated wilderness area now totals 47,896 acres, but the greater roadless area is even more extensive, coming to 82,000 acres. Elevations range from 2300 feet to 4600 feet, with boreal forests in the higher areas.

Of the other seven wilderness areas within the Monongahela, five are less than 10,000 acres in size, while the Otter Creek Wilderness totals 21,438 acres and the acreage of the Dolly Sods Wilderness is 17,430.

***Nearest Cities:** Lewisburg, Beckley, Summersville, Elkins*

Shenandoah National Park (VA)
Shenandoah National Park is a long, narrow band of national park land straddling some of the most scenic Appalachian ridges in north-western Virginia, paralleling the Shenandoah River valley. The Skyline Drive section of the Blue Ridge Parkway winds for 105 miles through Shenandoah National Park, offering views into the surrounding valleys and numerous trailheads for stopping and getting out to hike into the backcountry. The Appalachian Trail also passes through this elongated park for 100 miles, connecting it to other wild lands along the mountain corridor both north and south.

Within the national park boundaries are 79,579 acres of designated wilderness that most visitors only see from the scenic overlooks or from the windows of their cars. Anyone traveling the Skyline Drive through Shenandoah National Park cannot help but notice the innumerable whitetail deer that cross this highway, unafraid of humans because they have long been protected from hunting pressure. In a bug-out situation, the hunting would be good anywhere with the park, and it would be relatively easy to step off the road most anywhere and disappear among these heavily forested slopes.

Nearest Cities: *Waynesboro, Harrisonburg, Front Royal, Charlottesville*

George Washington & Jefferson National Forests (VA)

In the Appalachians of Virginia, two national forests, the George Washington and the Jefferson, combine to form a complex totaling 1.8 million acres, over half of which is remote and undeveloped. Within these lands there are still some 230,000 acres of old-growth forests remaining, and approximately 140,000 acres that have been set aside as designated wilderness areas.

George Washington National Forest contains one million acres, and within these holdings are six designated wilderness areas. Nine hundred miles of trails and 2000 miles of roads crisscross these forest lands, including 200 miles of mountain bike trails and some designated ATV trails. A portion of the forest also borders the south fork of the Shenandoah River, making it possible to access some of this wilderness by canoe.

The Jefferson National Forest takes in much of Virginia's Appalachian country along the West Virginia border in the central and southwestern part of the state, including Mount Rogers, the highest point in the state. Eleven separate wilderness areas are designated within its 690,000 acres. In addition to 400 miles of hiking trails, this national forest also features 150 miles of horseback trails, including the Virginia Highlands Horse Trail.

Taken as a whole, the George Washington and Jefferson National Forest complex creates a vast labyrinth of potential bug-out locations among Virginia's mountain ranges on the western edge of the state. This area is a logical choice for most of the state's population living in the cities and densely populated countryside of the central lowlands.

Nearest Cities: *Marion, Wytheville, Blacksburg, Roanoke, Covington, Harrisonburg*

Maryland, Pennsylvania, and New York

The Appalachian Mountain Corridor in these three heavily populated states offers many of the last and best areas of uninhabited land accessible to millions who live in some of the country's largest urban and industrial centers. Among so much development, there is a surprising amount of wild country in this region, much of it protected in national and state forests and other parks and refuges.

This part of the Appalachians is subject to longer, colder winters than the mountains farther south, but the elevations are generally lower, averaging 3000 feet or less. These mountains are home to most of the same big game species found farther south, including black bear, whitetail deer, wild boar, and reintroduced elk. As in most parts of Appalachia, heavy forest cover and an abundance of water sources and plant and animal foods mean that a bug-out survival location does not have to be large to provide easy evasion and sufficient resources.

Maryland

The smallest of these three states, of course, is Maryland, and only a small corner of the western part of this state is within the Allegheny and Blue Ridge ranges of the Appalachians. Even so, there are several state forests and wildlife management areas here that protect 120,000 acres of backcountry, providing some possibilities for residents who wish to bug out in the mountains. The largest of these is the 54,000-acre Savage River State Forest, which can be accessed by hiking and mountain bike trails, as well as by canoe on the Savage River and Savage River Reservoir. Other options include the 46,000-acre Green Ridge State Forest, the 11,535-acre Potomac State Forest, and the 9504-acre Dans Mountain Wildlife Management Area. In a bug-out situation, of course, the small size of western Maryland need not be a concern, as state lines into the neighboring mountain areas of West Virginia and Pennsylvania can easily be crossed.

Nearest Cities: *Cumberland, Friendsville, Oak Park (MD), Keyser (WV)*

Pennsylvania

Pennsylvania's wild Appalachian lands are much larger and more diverse than those in Maryland. The state is known among deer hunters for the size of its big bucks, and hunting is probably more popular here than in any other state in this region of the eastern U.S. Public land in Pennsylvania consists of many state forests, state parks, and wildlife management areas, as well as one large national forest.

Allegheny National Forest

Located in the northwestern plateau part of the state, the Allegheny National Forest is west of the main mountain corridor that passes through Pennsylvania, but is nonetheless a rugged piece of public land containing many large tracts of virgin beech and hemlock forest. The total area of the national forest is 513,000 acres, and within it are two designated wilderness areas, the Allegheny Islands Wilderness and the 8663-acre Hickory Creek Trail and Wilderness Area. Parts of the Allegheny River are navigable by canoe and the man-made Allegheny Reservoir adds the possibility of access to this national forest by boat along its shoreline.

Nearest Cities: Erie, Warren, Bradford, Franklin, Clarion, Du Bois

Pennsylvania's State Forests

Most of the public land in Pennsylvania's Appalachian region can be found in an extensive network of state forests. Totaling over 2,000,000 acres, there are 20 individual state forests in this management system, four of which are larger than 200,000 acres. The 280,000-acre Sproul State Forest is one of the best examples, taking in some of the most remote and scenic wild land in the state. These forests are managed for hunting and fishing as well as other forms of outdoor recreation such as canoeing, camping, and hiking. Designated trails are available for ATVs, mountain bikes, horseback riding, and in winter, snowmobiling and cross-country skiing.

Pennsylvania's longest and wildest hiking trail is the 327-mile long Mid State Trail, which winds through several state forests in the state's Appalachian region from Maryland to New York. This trail runs west of the Appalachian Trail, which also traverses the state, and is part of the Great Eastern Trail project, with a goal of providing another long hiking route through the entire Appalachian Mountain Corridor.

Other large state forests in Pennsylvania's Appalachians include the Tiadaghton (215,000 acres), the Tioga (160,000 acres), the Rothrock (215,000 acres), and the Elk (200,000 acres).

Nearest Cities: *Altoona, State College, Harrisburg, Williamsport, Scranton*

New York

The state of New York contains significant tracts of wild land, despite the huge populations of New York City and other urban areas located there. Northern or "Upstate" New York, in particular, has true north woods wilderness in Adirondack Park, which will be described in the next chapter. The southern part of the state, adjoining the Appalachians of Pennsylvania, also has mountain areas that, while not large, could offer bug-out locations that would suffice at least temporarily, until travel to wilder areas is feasible. Some of these areas are simply rural wooded lands and farmlands among the ridges and valleys of the sub-ranges of the Appalachians found here, the Catskill Mountains and the Blackhead Mountains. Other areas are protected by the state in the form of parks or state wilderness areas. Eighty-eight miles of the Appalachian Trail cut across the southeast corner of the state, offering a wooded foot path through the hills just a short distance from the concrete jungles of the coast.

Catskill Mountains

Catskill Park is made up of a patchwork of public and private lands designated by the state in 1904 to be protected from further development. Management is under New York's Forest Preserve, as is the much larger Adirondack Park to the north. Under this system, the land is not all "wilderness" or even completely public in the way that many state and federal lands are, but areas included in the preserve are supposed to remain "forever wild" and cannot be transferred to new ownership that will endanger that status.

The land area within the boundaries of Catskill Park comes to about 700,000 acres, but public lands total only about 300,000 acres. Still, considering where it is located, it is a large area of mountain woodlands and is certainly the best bug-out option in this part of New York. The highest point in the park tops out at 4180 feet, but with more than 30 peaks above 3500 feet, the Catskills are sufficiently rugged to contain off-the-beaten-track backcountry for those willing to bushwhack on foot and off-trail.

Within the park, there is one fairly large state-designated wilderness area that is protected in much the same way as its federal counterparts in the national forest system. The Slide Mountain Wilderness Area of Catskill Park contains 47,500 acres, making it the largest wilderness in the state outside the Adirondacks. Other parts of the park can be accessed on easily followed hiking trails, bicycle trails, snowmobile and ski trails in winter, and roads.

The Catskill Mountains provide good wildlife habitat, and animals found there in abundance include whitetail deer, black bear, snowshoe hares, porcupines, gray squirrels, beaver, ruffed grouse, and wild turkeys. The streams within the range contain brook, brown, and rainbow trout. Hunting and fishing are allowed within the forest preserve lands.

*Nearest Cities: Kingston, Hudson, Binghamton, Newburgh,
New York City*

8

LAKES & BIG WOODS OF THE NORTH
MAINE, NEW HAMPSHIRE, VERMONT, NEW YORK, MICHIGAN, WISCONSIN, AND MINNESOTA

The northern borderlands of the eastern United States from the Atlantic coast of Maine west to Minnesota are a region of dense coniferous forests, thousands of lakes and rivers, and rocky granite outcrops and shorelines. Often called simply the "North Woods," the forests that begin in the states included in this chapter continue across the Canadian border and in many places still stretch mostly unbroken to the sub-arctic tundra. These northern forests are true wilderness, still home to big game and big predators such as moose and gray wolves. In many areas that have been preserved in a natural state, they are much the same as they were in the early days of frontier exploration when a thriving fur trade depended on the rivers and lakes as wilderness highways to move goods by birch bark canoe. Millions of acres of such wild north country are contained within various national and state parks and forests on the U.S. side of the border alone, not to mention the exponentially greater acreage in Canada. Interestingly, much of the North Woods country of the U.S. is actually wilder today than it was 100 years ago. Many abandoned dirt roads are fading back to nature and fields marked by stone walls have returned to forest again. In these great forests of evergreen and boundless water, you can see eagles fly, listen to the call of the loon, and occasionally hear the howl of a wolf.

All the essential resources needed for survival are easily obtained in these North Woods bug-out locations: abundant fresh water, plenty of fish and game, and the materials with which to make shelter from the elements. A prepared survivalist can do well in the north and will have vast expanses of potential locations to retreat to. But for the unprepared or unskilled, the north is a harsh and unforgiving environment, especially in winter. Simple mistakes can quickly lead to disaster and often result in death.

NORTH WOODS BUG-OUT ESSENTIALS

Weather and Climate

Cold defines this region, as is evident at a glance from the appearance of the natural wildlands here. The boreal forests are made up primarily of evergreen coniferous trees, such as pines, cedars, spruce, and fir, as well as a few hardy deciduous species, such as ash, birch, and maple. Strong arctic winds and heavy snow loads in winter limit the growth of other trees and bushes and contribute to dense groves of trees with lots of deadfall and undergrowth, which makes cross-country travel difficult. Winter temperatures stay well below freezing for extended periods of time, and can drop far below zero degrees on occasion. Annual precipitation in this northern part of the U.S. ranges from less than 30 inches to up to 50 inches in a few locations, with only about half of that in rain. Snow covers the ground in many areas up to five months of the year. Although summers are short here, they can be hot, with temperatures in the 90s and averages of around 77 degrees.

Land and Resources

A large portion of the northern border of the eastern United States is taken up by the five Great Lakes and many smaller lakes, rivers, and man-made canals. This part of the United States is within the southern limit of the Canadian Shield, a landscape typified by lakes, rivers, bogs, thin soil, and granite rock. Since so much of this land is not suited for agriculture and the many waterways were obstacles to road building, large tracts of wilderness remain, preserved today in vari-

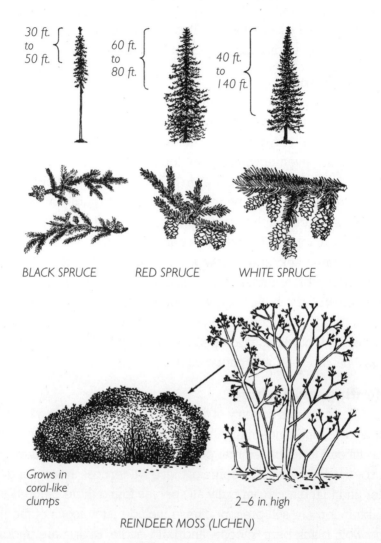

30 ft. to 50 ft.

60 ft. to 80 ft.

40 ft. to 140 ft.

BLACK SPRUCE   RED SPRUCE   WHITE SPRUCE

Grows in coral-like clumps

2–6 in. high

REINDEER MOSS (LICHEN)

Despite the conditions in the North Woods, edible plants, such as reindeer moss and the young shoots of spruce trees, can be found.

ous public lands. Suitable bug-out locations are plentiful in this region, and many are so large that a survivalist willing to work a bit to get off the beaten track will have complete isolation and solitude. Obtaining water is never a problem in the North Woods, and even many of the larger lakes and rivers appear crystal clear and unpolluted. Despite this, you should always treat any surface water just as you would in more populous regions to the south. In the winter your water source will be melted snow, which by itself is reason enough to carry at least one metal pot as discussed in Chapter Two.

Edible Plants

There are many varieties of edible plants in the North Woods, despite the cold and the short growing season. In the warmer months there is an abundance of berries and herbs that can be used for salads and greens, and even in winter plant food can be found if you know what to look for, sometimes in the form of berries and roots hidden beneath the snow. Lichens such as reindeer moss are readily available, as are the buds of trees such as basswood, poplar, and maple. The inner bark of willow, alder, birch, and pines can be eaten, as can young shoots of spruce, tamarack, and willow when boiled. Other plant foods in season include blueberries, currants, cranberries, strawberries, raspberries, crowberry, bunchberry, creeping snowberry, partridge berry, licorice-root, common wood-sorrel, northern mountain ash, wild rice, arrowhead, burdock, fiddlehead ferns, wild leeks, nettles, ground nut, hazel nut, bur oak, and choke cherry.

Hunting and Fishing

The North Woods country of the eastern U.S. is home to a large variety of wildlife, and since many of the largest tracts of protected areas are so difficult to reach, animal populations have thrived relatively undisturbed in these areas. In some of these wilderness areas along the border and to the north, virtually all species found there before European exploration are still present. These include such icons of the north as the wolf, black bear, moose, and bald eagle. Efforts are underway to reintroduce the woodland caribou to the Boundary Waters Canoe Area and Lake Superior area of northern Minnesota. The mountain lion has also apparently made a comeback, as sightings have occurred from Maine to Wisconsin and Michigan's Upper Peninsula. Common animals that can provide a food source in the North Woods region are the whitetail deer, snowshoe hare, cottontail rabbit, muskrat, opossum, porcupine, raccoon, beaver, rodents such as red squirrels and chipmunks, and wild turkey, ruffed grouse, ptarmigan, and waterfowl including wild geese and a variety of ducks. Other than the bear, the wolf, and the occasional mountain lion, predators that will be competing with you for animal food include the bobcat, lynx, gray fox, red fox, coyote, fisher, mink, and ermine.

Wildlife Hazards

In the North Woods, large mammals pose the greatest potential threat from wildlife. In this climate you do not have to worry about the threat of dangerous reptiles such as snakes, as the only snakes you will find in most places described in this chapter are harmless garter snakes. The most common dangerous animal is the black bear, which is found in greater densities here than in most other wild areas of the East. Incidences of black bear attacks are higher in the North Woods, on both sides of the border, than in other areas of North America, and most of them are for predatory reasons rather than in defense of cubs or because the animal was surprised. The gray wolf, or timber wolf, is also present in some of the areas described in this chapter. Although wolf attacks on humans are quite rare, the fact remains that these are large carnivores; they hunt in packs and have every advantage if they do decide to attack, unless you have a weapon capable of stopping them. As mentioned already, mountain lion sightings are on the increase in the North Woods. If they make a comeback in significant numbers, they could become a threat here just as they are in the West. Another dangerous animal in the North Woods is not a predator at all, but rather a huge herbivore. The moose, which can stand as tall as seven feet at the shoulder and weigh up to 1500 pounds, does charge humans on occasions with unpleasant results and should always be treated with respect and not approached too closely.

Recommended Equipment

Other than in winter, when many routes are frozen over, lakes and rivers offer some of the best travel options in the dense forests of the North Woods. The waterways will get you into the wildest areas of roadless wilderness, many of which are almost impossible to reach any other way. This is classic canoe country, and canoes are well suited to most of the waters here for a number of reasons, in particular their load-carrying capacity and ease of portaging over land between lakes. Sea kayaks and other boats can also be used; they will be more difficult to portage in places where this is required but will come into their own on the open, windswept waters of the Great Lakes, where seaworthiness is of prime importance. In the winter, snow and ice will make travel difficult unless you have a snowmobile, a dog sled, cross-country skis, or at the very least, snowshoes. Conventional vehicles, ATVs, and bikes can be used at other times of the year in many areas where there are roads or trails, and in these places backpacking is an option as well.

Clothing and shelter against the cold are, of course, top priorities in this region, and you should choose gear for both with the goal of staying dry and well-insulated in mind. It is equally important in the North Woods to have reliable means to start fires and cutting tools such as a large knife, machete, or axe to obtain quantities of dry wood. In a land where edible plants are harder to find, especially in winter, hunting becomes the primary means of obtaining food, and if you plan to bug out here you need to be prepared to take both small and large game and to catch fish. As in most places, the .22 rifle is a natural choice for smaller animals and birds, and if at all possible you should carry a larger-caliber rifle that can take deer or moose and provide protection against bears.

Voracious swarms of biting insects, especially black flies and mosquitoes, plague most parts of the North Woods in the warmer months. Mosquito netting and a good supply of strong insect repellent will be essential to keep from being driven insane by these pests when they are at their worst.

◆ ◆ ◆

The following sections, organized by state, will discuss the various regions of the North Woods in terms of their suitability as bug-out locations.

Maine

Located in the far northeastern corner of the United States, Maine is the least populated state east of the Mississippi River, with only 41.3 persons per square mile and 90 percent of its land area still forested. There are many expansive tracts of uninhabited North Woods in Maine, and in fact the northern part of the state, known as the Aroostook, is mostly uninhabited. Much of the uninhabited land is privately owned by paper companies, but even so, large tracts of this land are essentially wilderness. In addition to many rivers, countless lakes, and dense forests, the Appalachian Mountain Corridor, described in the previous chapter, extends through the state of Maine. This combination of rugged mountain country meeting with the Canadian Shield makes this an area of many superb bug-out locations where getting away from other people is easy.

If this were not enough, in addition to large areas of inland wilderness, Maine's rocky and fog-bound coast, which is 228 miles long, is so dense with bays, coves, and islands that there are almost 3500 miles of tidal shoreline in the state. This coast has a long and colorful maritime history and is popular with boaters of all types. For the properly prepared, it is a great place to bug out by boat, from cruisers right down to sea kayaks.

Aroostook County

Aroostook County is in the far northern tip of the state and is the largest county in any state east of the Mississippi River, with a total area of 6829 square miles and only 5.8 percent of the state's population. The northwest corner of the county, known as the Northwest Aroostook, is an unorganized territory of 2668 square miles and contains some of Maine's best wild North Woods, as well as the headwaters of the St. John River and much of the Allagash Wilderness Waterway. The Allagash River is a major tributary of the St. John, and the Allagash Wilderness Waterway is a 92-mile-long corridor of river and lake shore established to protect and preserve the wilderness quality of this isolated place. It is now part of the National Wild and Scenic River system. The waterway can be traveled by canoe with short portages in the summer months, and much of it can be accessed by snowmobile in winter.

Hunting and fishing in this region of the state is popular, and in a bug-out scenario, living off the land would be feasible for a skilled survivalist, with large populations of whitetail deer, moose, grouse, and waterfowl, as well as trout, bass, and land-locked salmon in the lakes and streams.

Nearest Cities: *Presque Isle, Caribou, Van Buren, Madawaska*

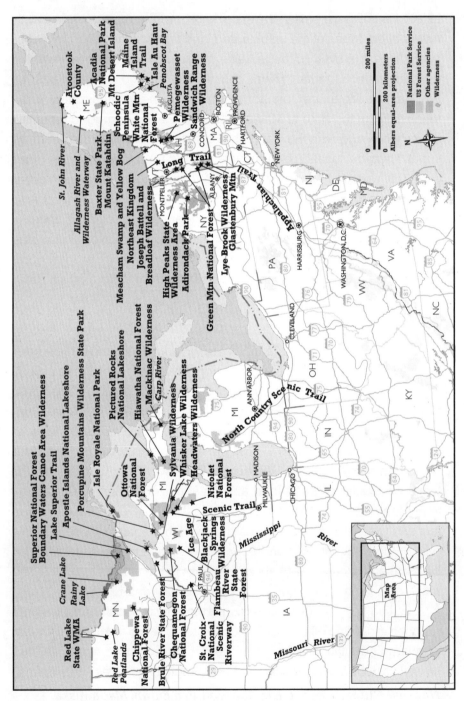

Bug-Out Locations of the Lakes & Big Woods of the North

Baxter State Park

Baxter State Park is the epitome of North Woods, with its lakes, streams, mountains, and boreal forests inhabited by bear, moose, and millions of black flies. It contains the highest point in Maine—5268-foot Mount Katahdin—which is also the northern terminus of the Appalachian Trail. The park contains a total of 209,501 acres but is surrounded by large tracts of private roadless lands to the east and north, adding tens of thousands of additional acreage to the area for those seeking a bug-out location in this part of Maine. Compared to national forest areas, access to Baxter State Park is highly regulated, but many activities are allowed with permits, including hiking, camping, and limited hunting, fishing, and snowmobiling. Located in Piscataquis County, just south of Aroostook, the park is close to the Allagash Wilderness Waterway and other lakes and rivers of northwestern Maine that provide a whole range of potential routes through this lightly populated region.

***Nearest Cities:** Millinocket, Houlton, Lincoln, Dover-Foxcroft*

The Maine Coast

The waters of Penobscot Bay and the many islands that make up Acadia National Park represent some of the most unspoiled areas of Maine's rocky and often fog-bound Atlantic coast. Acadia National Park was the first national park to be established east of the Mississippi and is primarily located on Mount Desert Island, where parklands total 30,300 acres, but also includes part of Isle Au Haut and the Schoodic Peninsula. Like much of the Maine coast, Mount Desert Island is rugged, heavily forested in spruce and fir, and home to bear, deer, moose, bobcats, beaver, porcupines, and red and gray squirrels.

There are countless smaller islands and stretches of uninhabited shoreline on the coast of Maine beyond this well-known national park, however. Many of them are protected in an array of smaller state parks that are found along the entire coast. Connecting the best of these small islands and isolated mainland beaches is the Maine Island Trail, a 325-mile water trail established to link together a series of campsites so that travelers by small boats such as sea kayaks can explore this wild coast. The trail is open to use by powerboats and other watercraft as well as kayaks, however, and those in larger cruising boats can find many remote places to anchor up and down the length of Maine's coast.

Nearest Cities: *Bar Harbor, Camden, Portland, Kennebunkport*

New Hampshire

Even though it is tiny in overall land area, ranking 44th in size of the 50 states, New Hampshire is the second most forested state in the U.S. after Maine in percentage of land covered by woods. Less than five percent of the state's population lives in the rugged northern third of New Hampshire, where most of the White Mountains and North Woods lakes and rivers are included in national and state forests. The highest point in New Hampshire is Mount Washington, which at 6288 feet is also the tallest mountain in the Northeast and among the tallest in the Appalachians. Mount Washington is noted for having the worst weather in North America, with a sub-arctic climate but unusually high precipitation for such climates, most of it in the form of snow. It is also the site of the world's highest recorded wind speed, at 231 miles per hour.

White Mountain National Forest

The White Mountain National Forest (a small portion of which is actually in Maine) is New England's largest national forest, totaling 784,505 acres and including five designated wilderness areas within its boundaries, as well as over 100 miles of the Appalachian Trail. The White Mountains include several sub-ranges, such as the Sandwich Range, where a large roadless area of 81,000 acres can be found, centered around the 25,000-acre designated Sandwich Range Wilderness Area. The largest wilderness area in White Mountain National Forest is the Pemegewasset Wilderness Area, which contains 45,000 acres of designated wilderness and is part of a larger roadless area totaling 125,000 acres. It is, in fact, the largest roadless area on national forest land in the Northeast, and includes two peaks over 5000 feet and 13 that exceed 4000 feet. These high points plunge to lower elevations of under 1000 feet, making this a rugged mountain wilderness that is popular with backpackers. Ecosystems in the Pemegewasset range from northern hardwood and spruce-fir forests in the valleys and on the slopes to sub-alpine vegetation and alpine tundra on the peaks.

Nearest Cities: *Berlin, Littleton, Plymouth, Lebanon, Laconia*

Vermont

Like neighboring New Hampshire, Vermont contains mountain ranges that are part of the northern end of the Appalachian Corridor, and also borders Canada on the north. These mountains in Vermont are called the Green Mountains and run from north to south through the state, where they contain a mix of national forest lands, state parks, and rural, lightly populated countryside. A variety of suitable bug-out locations can be found scattered throughout the state, mostly in the mountains but also along the rivers and lakeshores. Vermont is the only New England state that has no coastline on the Atlantic, but in the northwest it does border the 435-square mile Lake Champlain, which can be navigated to the St. Lawrence River to the north by way of the Richelieu River, and to the Hudson River to the south by way of the Champlain Canal.

Green Mountain National Forest

At just over 400,000 acres, Green Mountain National Forest makes up about half of Vermont's public lands and stretches across two-thirds of the state. The Green Mountain Range runs north and south for approximately 250 miles, right through the length of Vermont. The name comes from the dense boreal forests of evergreen conifers that keep the mountains green even in the harsh winters when everything is white with snow. Twenty-five percent of Green Mountain National Forest is designated wilderness, totaling 101,000 acres spread across eight separate wilderness areas.

One of the largest areas of roadless national forest land in Vermont is Glastenbury Mountain. In 2006 a new federal wilderness area, the Glastenbury Wilderness, was established to protect 22,425 acres of a 52,000-acre roadless area. Dominated by a massive ridgeline and cloaked in old-growth forest, Glastenbury Wilderness is densely populated with black bear and is ideal habitat for most North Woods game animals. Other significant wilderness areas in Green Mountain

National Forest are Breadloaf (25,237 acres), Lye Brook (17,718 acres), and Joseph Battell (12,333 acres).

Outside of these designated wilderness areas, many forest service roads provide access into relatively remote backcountry, making it possible to bug out by vehicle, ATV, or snowmobile, depending the season and current conditions. For those traveling on foot, in addition to numerous shorter hiking trails, the Appalachian Trail passes through the Green Mountains, and the 272-mile Long Trail winds through the range for the length of the state from Massachusetts to Canada.

***Nearest Cities:** Bennington, Rutland, Middlebury, Montpelier*

Northeast Kingdom

One of the largest spots on the map of Vermont that is devoid of large towns and many roads is the so-called Northeast Kingdom, especially the part north of Bloomfield and between the Connecticut River to the east and Highway 114 to the west. This area contains Bloomfield Ridge, Monadock Mountain, Sable Mountain, and Yellow Bog, which is the largest bog in Vermont. Meachum Swamp is a roadless area of around 50,000 acres in this area. This area is an important moose habitat in Vermont and is also home to many other North Woods species. Most of the land in this area is privately owned by timber companies and as such it is penetrated by numerous dirt roads. There was a proposal to establish a Northeast Kingdom National Park in the area, but regardless of land ownership, this remote corner of the Vermont North Woods offers many options for remote bug-out locations.

***Nearest Cities:** Bloomfield, Island Pond, Newport, St. Johnsbury*

New York

As already mentioned in the previous chapter, the Appalachian Mountains reach into New York in both the southeastern part of the state and the northern region known as "Upstate" New York. This northern region of New York, a land of quintessential North Woods forests, lakes, ponds, and wildlife, has more in common with the North Woods than the Appalachian Corridor in general, so I've included it in this chapter.

Adirondack Park

Adirondack Park is impressive by any standards. For one, it is the largest state park in the United States, and amazingly contains roughly as much land area as Yellowstone, Yosemite, Grand Canyon, Glacier, and Olympic National Parks combined—for a total of 6.1 million acres. Unlike these national parks, however, Adirondack is far from uninhabited, and the number of residents that live within the park boundaries is about 130,000. Land ownership in the park is a complex issue; some 3.7 million acres of the total area are privately owned, but still controlled to some degree by the park agency, which prohibits development, in much the same way as the smaller Catskill Park described in Chapter Seven. The lands within the park that are owned by the state fall into different categories, including wilderness, primitive, wild river, and wild forest. About one million acres of the park meet the definition of wilderness, despite the fact that there are almost 7000 miles of roads within the total park area.

The wilderness areas within Adirondack Park are protected in much the same way as national forest designated wilderness areas and remain largely pristine. The High Peaks State Wilderness Area, at 197,215 acres, is big indeed by eastern standards, and is only part of a total roadless area of 336,000 acres. The area is forested in a mix of spruce-fir and mixed beech, birch, maple, and hemlock.

Game animals found in the park include moose, whitetail deer, spruce grouse, rabbits, turkeys, and waterfowl. Sport hunting is popular here and hunters of black bear and deer consider it one of the best places in the eastern U.S. The fishing is also a large draw to the Adirondacks, and the rivers, ponds, and lakes are home to rainbow, brook, and brown trout; northern pike; walleye; yellow perch; landlocked salmon; and largemouth, smallmouth, and black bass.

Nearest Cities: *Platsburgh, Glen's Falls, Utica, Watertown, Syracuse*

Michigan

North of the largely urbanized southern part of the state, Michigan offers quite a few bug-out options in its interior forest lands and along the shores of Lake Michigan, Lake Huron, and Lake Superior. The best of these options are to be found on the Upper Peninsula—a world away from the rest of the state. This 320-mile-long by 125-mile-wide peninsula between Lakes Michigan and Huron to the south and Lake Superior to the north makes up a third of the state, and a third of the peninsula consists of public national forest lands. The Upper Peninsula is home to many North Woods animal species, including moose, black bear, gray wolf, martin, fisher, and snowshoe hare. The waters of the many lakes and rivers are home to northern pike, walleye, trout, salmon, and bass. There is a noticeable absence of large towns and cities in most of the Upper Peninsula.

There are also large tracts of wild land to be found in the northern half of Michigan's Lower Peninsula, specifically in the Huron National Forest and the Manistee National Forest, which under combined management total approximately one million acres. There are also a significant number of uninhabited small islands and stretches of undeveloped shoreline on both Lake Huron and Lake Michigan, some of which are managed as state parks and the larger Sleeping Dunes National Lakeshore. This part of the state has a lot to offer no matter what your preferred mode of transportation: boat, vehicle, ATV, or on foot. But the true North Woods of Michigan are found on the Upper Peninsula, especially in the rugged western half, which is part of the Canadian Shield.

Ottowa National Forest

Most of the western end of the Upper Peninsula is taken up by the nearly one million acres of federal land in the Ottowa National Forest, which stretches from the south shore of Lake Superior to the Wisconsin border. Over 50,000 acres of the Ottowa are designated wilderness. As much water as it is woods, Ottowa National Forest contains over 500 named lakes and 2000 miles of rivers and streams besides its shoreline on Lake Superior. The highest elevations in this part of the Upper Peninsula reach more than 1800 feet in the Sylvania Wilderness, which contains 18,327 acres of old-growth forests and pristine lakes.

Nearest Cities: *Houghton, Ishpeming, Iron River, Ramsay (MI), Ironwood (WI)*

Porcupine Mountains Wilderness State Park

Porcupine Mountains Wilderness State Park, bordering Ottowa National Forest to the south and Lake Superior to the north, totals 60,000 acres of lakes, streams, and a tract of 31,000 acres of virgin timber. The highest point in the Porcupine Mountains (or "Porkies") is 1958-foot Summit Peak. These modest-sized but unspoiled mountains are home to moose, black bear, gray wolf, fisher, martin, mink, lynx, and of course, their namesake North Woods animal, the porcupine. About 90 miles of hiking and cross-country ski trails wind their way through the park and offer access to the interior ridges. The Lake Superior Trail hugs the park's shoreline for about 16 miles, but this area can also be accessed by sea kayaks and other small boats in settled weather.

Nearest Cities: Silver City, White Pine, Ontonagon, Ramsay

Hiawatha National Forest

Other than the Ottowa National Forest, the two other largest tracts of public land on the Upper Peninsula are the east and west units of the Hiawatha National Forest, which combined contain 880,000 acres. Both units span the width of the peninsula, and they include a total of 100 miles of shoreline on Lake Superior and Lake Michigan. The east unit also has shoreline on Lake Huron. There are six designated wilderness areas in the Hiawatha, most of which are small, but the 12,230-acre Mackinac Wilderness area is part of a significant roadless area along the Carp River, which is also listed as a Wild and Scenic River. The Mackinac Wilderness is not only roadless, but also lacks trails, the only access being the Carp River and an adjacent road to one side. Other parts of the Hiawatha National Forest can be accessed from the bordering Great Lakes by sea kayaks or other boats. Many of the interior lakes are ideal for canoe travel, and foot trails, ski trails, and a variety of dirt and paved roads offer lots of options to get into the backcountry.

Nearest Cities: Mackinaw City, Sault Ste. Marie (east unit),
Escanaba, Marquette (west unit)

Pictured Rocks National Lakeshore

Adding another 42 miles of protected public land along the shore of Lake Superior to the sections included in the Hiawatha National Forest and Porcupine Mountains Wilderness State Park is the 73,236-acre Pictured Rocks National Lakeshore. This park is named for a 15-mile stretch of limestone cliffs that tower up to 200 feet above the lake and feature unusual formations and many caves. Although roads go through the park, over 20 miles of the lakeshore is roadless. Some of this area is accessible by hiking, and other parts can only be reached from the water. This is an ideal bug-out location for sea kayakers with the skills and equipment to negotiate the frigid waters of Lake Superior.

Nearest Cities: Marquette, Munising, Grand Marais

Isle Royale

Isle Royale, the largest island in Lake Superior, is over 45 miles long and up to 9 miles wide at its widest point. The island interior has a roadless area totaling 133,000 acres, protected as a wilderness area administered by the National Park Service. Isle Royale is quite inaccessible from the rest of Michigan, as it is 55 miles to the northwest across the lake from the Upper Peninsula and can only be reached by boat or sea plane. For those with a seaworthy vessel that can reach its shores, Isle Royale could serve as a remote island bug-out location, and a jumping-off point to the even wilder Canadian shores of Lake Superior.

Nearest Cities: Copper Harbor, Houghton (MI), Grand Portage (MN)

Wisconsin

Northern Wisconsin, especially along the shores of Lake Superior and the border with Michigan's Upper Peninsula, still has a few remnants of the North Woods wilderness that once covered this part of the state. Most of the old-growth forest was cut long ago, but there are several large tracts of public land in two national forests and some smaller state forests, as well as on the Apostle Islands. In addition, the St. Croix National Scenic Riverway winds through the northeastern part of Wisconsin to join the Mississippi River below Minneapolis-St.

Paul. The North Woods of Wisconsin are popular hunting and fishing grounds, with large numbers of whitetail deer, wild turkeys, and small game such as grouse and rabbits. The lakes and streams offer abundant trout, bass, and walleye. Other North Woods animals that were once wiped out have been reintroduced or are coming back on their own, including the gray wolf, elk, wolverine, martin, and lynx.

Nicolet National Forest

Named for the French explorer Jean Nicolet, Nicolet National Forest covers over 650,000 acres of woods and lakes in the northeastern part of Wisconsin. Within the Nicolet, there are 800 miles of hiking trails and 450 miles of snowmobile trails, as well as roads suitable for travel by vehicle and ATV. There are three designated wilderness areas: Blackjack Springs, Whisker Lake, and Headwaters. Headwaters Wilderness Area is the largest of these, at 20,000 acres, most of it forested swamp, bog lowlands, and muskeg. It contains the headwaters of the Pine River, a state-designated wild river.

Nearest Cities: Green Bay, Wausau, Rhinelander, Kingsford

Chequamegon National Forest

"Chequamegon" is an Objibwa name for "place of shallow water." Today the Chequamegon National Forest is comprised of three units totaling 865,825 acres. It contains lakes formed by ancient glaciers, bogs, muskeg, rivers, streams, and large expanses of North Woods forest. There is good road access in many areas and numerous hiking trails penetrate the wilder sections, including two National Scenic Trails, the North Country Scenic Trail and the Ice Age Scenic Trail. Much of the surrounding area outside the units of the Chequamegon National Forest is sparsely populated rural land. Three sizable Indian Reservations are also located nearby, as well as the 47,000-acre Brule River State Forest and the 90,147-acre Flambeau River State Forest.

Nearest Cities: Ashland, Drummond, Perkinstown, Eau Claire

Apostle Islands National Lakeshore

Just off the northernmost point in Wisconsin, scattered in the frigid waters of Lake Superior, lies an archipelago of 21 islands known as the Apostle

Islands. The islands and 12 miles of lakeshore on the mainland make up the 69,372-acre Apostle Island National Lakeshore. The Apostle Islands are a wonderland of sandstone bluffs, sea caves, and old-growth forests. Because of their relatively close proximity to each other, the Apostle Islands are a popular destination for sea kayakers, and in a bug-out situation sea kayaks or similar small, seaworthy boats that can land on rocky beaches would be ideal vehicles to reach them. There are many miles of hiking trails on the various islands, and the interior forests are home to whitetail deer and black bear, as well as typical North Woods small game such as the snowshoe hare. Stockton Island, which is a little over 10,000 acres, has one of the highest concentrations of black bears in the U.S. Some deer and bear hunting is allowed on some of the islands. In a bug-out situation, this island group could make a good hideaway and foraging ground for someone equipped to navigate it.

Nearest Cities: Red Cliff, Ashland, Superior, Ironwood

St. Croix National Scenic Riverway

Northern Wisconsin, like all of the Great Lakes states, offers many options for those who choose to bug out by canoe. This is traditional canoe country after all, and just as in the fur trade days, you can still launch a canoe in this region and embark on a journey of hundreds or even thousands of miles. One of the best wild river routes in Wisconsin is the 252-mile long St. Croix National Scenic Riverway. The protected status of the corridor along the St. Croix makes it a great river highway, with abundant game in the surrounding forests and plenty of secluded camping and hideout locations. Downstream, the St. Croix joins the Mississippi just below Hastings, Minnesota. This part of the upper Mississippi is a series of man-made lakes and slow-moving water created by a system of navigation locks and dams. In a real SHTF scenario, the locks may be shut down, but those traveling light in a canoe can simply portage around the dams to continue on downstream, all the way to the Gulf of Mexico, if desired.

Nearest Cities: Trego, St. Croix Falls, New Richmond, River Falls

Minnesota

Northern Minnesota's North Woods country is as wild and sparsely populated as most parts of the West and, in fact, is the only place in the lower 48 states where the timber wolf, an icon of true wilderness, held its own (without needing reintroduction) while being wiped out in the rest of the country. Although many people outside of the region may not realize it, Minnesota's Boundary Waters Canoe Area (combined with Canada's Quetico Provincial Park) is the third largest roadless area in the U.S. outside of Alaska. Northern Minnesota is, in fact, the epitome of North Woods wilderness, with an array of thousands of jewel-like, clear water lakes, beaver ponds, bogs, and marshes sprinkled among vast stands of virgin conifer and hardwood forests.

Boundary Waters–Superior National Forest

The Boundary Waters Canoe Area Wilderness, combined with Superior National Forest, Voyageurs National Park, and Canada's Quetico National Park just across the border, is an incomparable North Woods wilderness containing a roadless area of nearly three million acres. This area along the southern edge of the Canadian Shield contains thousands of lakes greater than ten acres in size, in addition to beaver ponds, bogs, marshes, and streams offering thousands of miles of potential canoe routes. This is certainly canoe country, as no other boat is as well-adapted to travel here, and except in winter when the lakes are frozen over, no other method of travel is really feasible.

Just as in the fur trade days, when the route between Montreal and the Northwest Territories passed this way, the Boundary Waters is still home to bears, moose, wolves, lynx, fishers, pine martins, bald eagles, and the ever-present loon, whose lonely calls echo across the still lakes. This area is so vast and the bug-out potential so great that you can choose just about any part of it according to your liking and be assured of finding seclusion—especially if you are willing to portage your canoe and gear overland to some of the smaller lakes that are off the beaten path. Since all of this area is essentially wilderness, there is no clear demarcation between the various parts. The Boundary Waters Canoe Area Wilderness comprises 972,537 acres, most of it in the 3,900,000-acre Superior National Forest. This vast national forest stretches from the shores of Lake Superior all the way west to Crane Lake, where the 218,000-acre Voyageurs National Park begins and takes in all the wilderness on the U.S. side of the border to Rainy Lake.

Depending on the type of bug-out situation that would make you head off into the Boundary Waters, it may or may not be feasible to cross the border into Canada. In normal times it is certainly not advisable to do so without proper clearance, and you will not be allowed to carry across any survival firearms. In a real bug-out situation, the reality is that most of the border here is so desolate and remote that no one will know if you've crossed it or not. Regardless of where you are in this wilderness, if you have the means to hunt and fish, and sufficient protection from the cold, living off the land here should be as good as it gets in the North Woods region.

Nearest Cities: *Duluth, Grand Portage, Ely, Crane Lake, International Falls*

Red Lake Peatlands

While the Boundary Waters–Superior National Forest may be largest and most obvious bug-out location in northern Minnesota, there are many more huge areas of North Woods country in the state, including the 1.6 million-acre Chippewa National Forest, several expansive but sparsely populated Indian reservations, and the unique Red Lake Peatlands, a 350,000-acre roadless wilderness made up of the Red Lake State Wildlife Management Area, Beltrami State Forest, and Red Lake Indian Reservation. The Red Lake Peatlands is a primitive landscape of raised peatlands, bogs, lakes, and conifer forests. It was the last stand of the woodland caribou in Minnesota, and is still home to wolves, black bear, and the highest concentration of moose in the lower 48. If you're looking for a large North Woods bug-out location that is less obvious to most outsiders who will gravitate to the Boundary Waters, this is the place.

Nearest Cities: *Bemidji, Baudette, Thief River Falls*

9

THE MIDWEST & HEARTLAND

OHIO, INDIANA, ILLINOIS, ARKANSAS, OKLAHOMA,
MISSOURI, IOWA, KANSAS, NEBRASKA, SOUTH DAKOTA,
AND NORTH DAKOTA

T
he Midwest and Heartland region of the United States covers a
large and diverse swath of North America, with many different
types of ecosystems and some crossovers and similarities to
neighboring regions. In this chapter I'll describe a variety of possible
bug-out locations in a region where big wilderness is not the norm, but
population densities are often low, creating many options for those who
know where to look. This region covers the Mississippi and Ohio River
Valleys, the southern parts of the North Woods states described in the
previous chapter, and the transition states west of the Mississippi but
east of the Rockies. Except for a few areas like the Ozarks, Quachitas,
Black Hills, and Badlands, this part of the country is devoid of rugged
mountains or spectacular landmarks. There are no vast roadless areas,
expansive swamps, or even seashores, but sprinkled throughout there
are pockets of natural areas preserved in federal and state parks and
forests, as well as many former agricultural areas that have been abandoned and are returning to a natural state.

Just as in the Gulf Coast and East Coast regions, some of the
best remaining wild areas are found along the courses of rivers and
streams. As the philosopher Lao Tzu stated long ago, it still holds true
that "water flows in places men reject." This region contains the largest
river valleys in the United States: the Ohio, the Missouri, and of course,

the Mississippi. And along these rivers and their many tributaries are countless forgotten pockets of uninhabited land that can serve as bug-out locations.

MIDWEST AND HEARTLAND BUG-OUT ESSENTIALS

Weather and Climate

The Midwest and Heartland region of the United States for the most part has four well-defined seasons, with hot summers and cold winters. Most of the region is squarely in the track of strong frontal systems that sweep across the continent, bringing icy arctic winds and occasional blizzards in the winters, which are especially harsh in the plains areas in the western and northern reaches. In warmer months, strong thunderstorms and tornados are common, along with heavy rainfall that sometimes causes flooding in the river valleys. West of the Mississippi, extended periods of drought can occur. Annual precipitation varies from 10 to 15 inches per year in some of the western parts of the region, like Kansas and the Dakotas, to 50 to 60 inches per year in the Ohio and lower Mississippi Valleys.

Land and Resources

Since the earliest days of European settlement, the Midwest and Heartland of the United States has traditionally been farm country. Most of it still is today, although small family farms have been largely replaced by huge mechanized operations. In many parts of the Midwest, farming has been abandoned as younger generations leave rural family lands behind for lives elsewhere. Some of this farm country has reverted back to natural grasslands and even some small towns have died out. There are public lands scattered through this region, but they are not as large or as numerous as in most other parts of the country. In the eastern parts of the region and in the mountains of Arkansas and Missouri, there are some sizeable national forests, but throughout much of the farm country of the upper Midwest, these are nonexistent.

There are a few national grasslands on the plains that are managed in much the same way as national forests, however. In this farm country, the rivers are vital corridors of semi-wild woodland that can offer bug-out locations in areas that are otherwise completely tamed and in agricultural use.

Edible Plants

A huge range of wild edible plant foods can be found in the region, with many species crossing over from adjacent regions in the South, East, North, and West. In many areas of the Heartland, the rich soil that was so attractive to farming settlers makes for an abundance of useful plants that can be harvested by a knowledgeable survivalist. Because the climate and soil conditions vary quite a bit across this large region, you won't find every edible plant listed in every potential bug-out location. Some are suited to shady riverside forests, others to marsh and lakeshore, and still others to open fields, plains, or rocky hill country, but you can be assured of finding some wild plant foods throughout this region. The most common include wild rice, common sunflower, dandelion, burdock, amaranth, arrowhead, cattail, wild onion, wild asparagus, sweet flag, pokeweed, chicory, Jerusalem artichoke, passion flower, prickly pear, paw paw, persimmon, red mulberry, black cherry, crabapple, elderberry, blackberry, dewberry, huckleberry, wild grape, acorn, walnut, and hickory nut.

Hunting and Fishing

Most of this region is inhabited by the same game animals that are indigenous to all of the eastern United States, including whitetail deer, wild turkey, rabbit, gray squirrel, fox squirrel, opossum, muskrat, beaver, raccoon, and waterfowl such as ducks and geese. Crossover species from the North Woods that can be found in some of the areas described in this chapter include moose, snowshoe hare, and porcupine. In the extreme western reaches of the Midwest, there are also species present that are more typical of the Rocky Mountains and high deserts of the West, including elk, bighorn sheep, and pronghorn antelope. The mule deer is also found in the western part of the region, from western

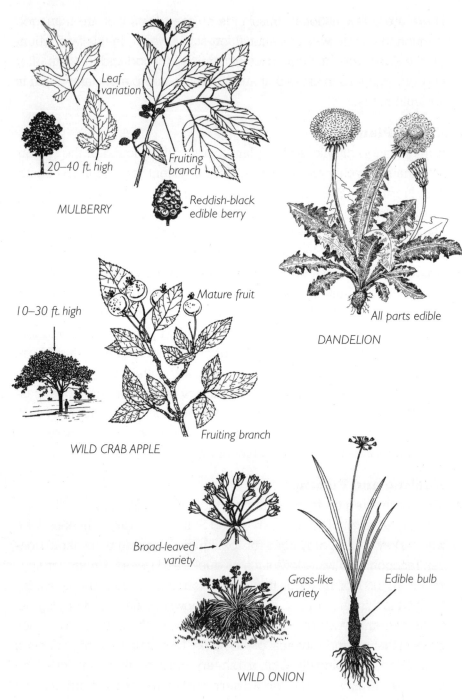

Leaf variation

20–40 ft. high

MULBERRY

Fruiting branch

Reddish-black edible berry

All parts edible

DANDELION

10–30 ft. high

Mature fruit

WILD CRAB APPLE

Fruiting branch

Broad-leaved variety

Grass-like variety

Edible bulb

WILD ONION

Some edible plants of the Midwest and Heartland.

Oklahoma and Kansas north through Nebraska and the Dakotas. The open plains and farmlands of the Midwest are also home to grassland species such as prairie dogs, quail, and pheasant.

Wildlife Hazards

Those who bug out into the wild in the Heartland and Midwest have little to fear from wildlife hazards compared to other regions of the U.S. There is a sizeable population of mountain lions in the Black Hills of South Dakota, and the big cats have been spotted or killed by traffic in other Midwest states such as Nebraska, Iowa, Missouri, Oklahoma, and Illinois, but they are rare and no attacks on humans have been recorded in this region in modern times. The only other large and potentially dangerous predator in some areas of this region is the black bear. But where bears are found here, their scarcity makes them shy and consequently they pose little threat to humans. The climate in this region is unsuitable to large reptiles like alligators, although rattlesnakes can be found throughout most of it and in the southernmost areas the cottonmouth and copperhead are present as well. Wasps and bees are also common in most parts of this region, so individuals who are allergic to their stings should be careful to avoid approaching too closely to their nests and hives.

Recommended Equipment

Since landscapes and ecosystems vary so much across the Midwest and Heartland, there is no one checklist of gear that is suitable for all parts of the region. A lot depends on whether your bug-out locations will be in the forested river valleys, the mountains of Oklahoma, Missouri, or Arkansas, or in the plains and badlands of the western reaches of the area. The best transportation options are also dependant upon this, as the rivers offer possibilities for boats the size of canoes all the way up to small cruisers. A variety of motor vehicles can serve well in this area, as there are many rural roads, both paved and unpaved. The more open country of the western half has some locations suitable for travel on horseback, and parts of the Ozarks and Ouachitas are best accessed on foot. The parts of this region that are open prairie and plains are exposed to severe weather, both in summer and winter. Portable shelter for protection from wind, rain, and snow is essential here. Firearms for hunting should include a .22 for small game and a rifle capable of longer-range shots in the open county where stalking close to game may not be an option. Most defensive needs for a weapon here will be for potential human aggressors and, far less likely, a bear or mountain lion.

◆ ◆ ◆

Since most of the individual states in this region do not have a large number of big tracts of public lands or other obvious bug-out locations, I've organized this chapter into groups of states with similar terrain and climate conditions rather than devote a separate section to each state.

Ohio, Indiana, and Illinois

I'm grouping these states of the northern and central portion of the Heartland together, as they have more of an eastern woodland ecosystem than the rest of this region, contain several national forests, and are interconnected via some of the nation's largest navigable river systems. Situated between the Great Lakes to the north, the Appalachians to the east, and the Mississippi River to the west, this area of the Heartland contains major cities as well as rural farmland, and in general, is much more densely populated than the other sections to be described in this chapter. Even so, there are bug-out locations to be found here, and the rivers offer the means to travel far to other regions of the country even in a major SHTF situation where travel by road would not be possible. From these river systems, it is possible to navigate to the Gulf of Mexico, the East Coast, or even the Arctic, if your boat is small enough to portage where necessary. In the following sections, we will look at the national forest lands in this three-state area, and then discuss the river systems.

Wayne National Forest (OH)

If you are looking for a bug-out location in the heavily urbanized state of Ohio, your best bet is in the southern part of that state, and better yet, the southeastern part, where you will find the 240,900-acre Wayne National Forest spread out across three separate units. This part of Ohio is a fairly rugged landscape of Appalachian foothills, covered in mixed forests of hardwoods and pine. Throughout the wooded hills of Wayne National Forest you will find an abundance of springs, streams, rivers, and small lakes. Over 300 miles of hiking trails can be found in the various units of this national forest, including a part of the North Country Scenic Trail, 43 miles of which winds through the Athens Ranger District and 41 miles through the Marietta Ranger District.

Wayne National Forest is also popular with ATV and off-road vehicle enthusiasts, as it offers many designated trails and roads for these pursuits. The major networks for these recreation trails are the Monday Creek, Hanging Rock, and Pine Creek systems. The mix of privately owned rural countryside adjacent to tracts of national forest land means that access points to Wayne National Forest are numerous and varied, opening up plenty of route options no matter what your chosen bug-out transportation, from motor vehicles on down to walking. In addition, several tracts of the forest border the Ohio River, and the Marietta District in particular offers good access to a long section of it at Willow Island Pool.

Nearest Cities: *Marietta, Cambridge, Lancaster, New Lexington, Athens, Gallipolis*

Hoosier National Forest (IN)

Like Ohio, Indiana's best semblance of "wild" land can be found in the southern portion of the state, where there are fewer cities and more woodland compared to the open farm country of the central and northern areas. Hoosier National Forest totals 201,047 acres in an area of hills, sandstone cliffs, and barrens of prairie more typical of the Great Plains. There are approximately 266 miles of trails within this national forest that are open to hikers, mountain bikers, and horseback riders. Within Hoosier National Forest, there is one wilderness area that has been designated in a previously settled area that has been uninhabited since the Great Depression. The 13,000-acre Charles C. Dearn Wilderness Area is popular with hikers and horseback riders for its unusual topography of karst landscape that contains many sinkholes and caves. It is adjacent to the man-made Lake Monroe, which also makes it accessible to a variety of small boats.

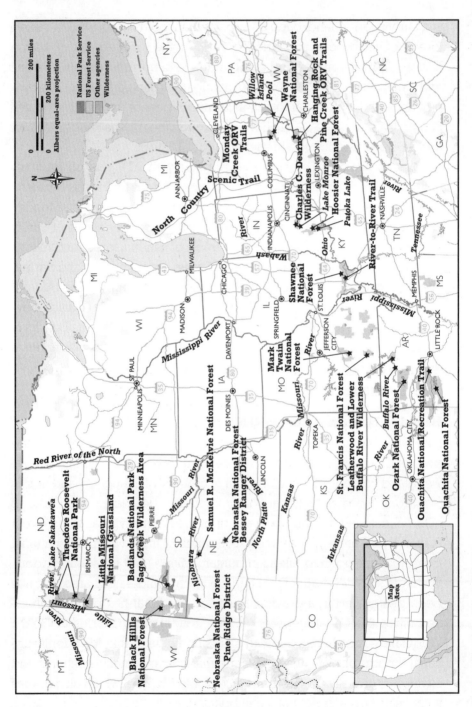

Bug-Out Locations of the Midwest & Heartland

The larger southern section of Hoosier National Forest reaches all the way to the Ohio River along the border with Kentucky and contains another sizable man-made lake within federal lands, Patoka Lake. Several smaller state recreation areas and state parks can also be found in this southern part of Indiana, so a variety of options exist here with the combination of state and federal lands and the waterway of the Ohio River.

Nearest Cities: *Bloomington, Bedford, Salem, Jasper, Tell City, New Albany*

Shawnee National Forest (IL)

The extreme southern end of Illinois has much to offer in the way of bug-out locations in a state that is otherwise quite heavily settled and developed. In this region near the confluence of the Ohio River and the Mississippi River, a large portion of the land falls within the holdings of the 270,000-acre Shawnee National Forest, as well as several state and federal wildlife refuges. These large tracts of public lands exist here because this is a surprisingly rugged area much different than the typical flat Heartland farm country found farther north in the state. Within Shawnee National Forest, there are many miles of hiking trails, including the excellent River-to-River Trail that runs 160 miles between the Ohio and Mississippi Rivers through some of the most scenic and remote sections of the forest.

Nearest Cities: *Metropolis, Carbondale, Marion, Harrisburg*

Ohio River

Forming the common southern border of all three of these states— Ohio, Indiana, and Illinois—the Ohio River is a major inland navigation waterway in the Heartland region that connects the Mississippi and Tennessee River Systems to the industrial and urban centers of Pennsylvania and northeastern Ohio. The river has been tamed in a series of locks and dams, creating a string of more than 20 lakes called "pools" that stretch 981 miles from Pittsburg, Pennsylvania, to Cairo, Illinois. But despite these man-made alterations and obstructions to its natural flow, as with all the major river routes described in this chapter, there are many isolated areas along the banks of the Ohio that can serve as bug-out locations. Some of these are best for short-term use while traveling up or down the river by boat, while others may be secluded enough for a more long-term camp. Many types of boats can be used on the Ohio, so long as the locks are operational and open to traffic. If they are ever shut down or closed, those traveling by canoe or kayak could portage around the dams.

Important tributaries that connect to the Ohio River and also provide long-distance travel options and potential bug-out locations are the Wabash and the Tennessee. The Wabash River forms much of the border between Indiana and Illinois, and provides a water route out of the northern part of Indiana. The Tennessee River enters the Ohio from the south near Paducah, Kentucky, and provides a route to the Ohio River from the Appalachian Mountains of eastern Tennessee and a connection to the Gulf of Mexico via the Tennessee-Tombigbee Waterway. The Ohio is itself a tributary of the mighty Mississippi, and from its mouth at Cairo, Illinois, one can go downstream to New Orleans and the Gulf, upstream to the north woods of Minnesota, or west via the Missouri River to the Rockies.

Nearest Cities: *Marietta, Cincinnati (OH), Louisville, Paducah (KY), Evansville (IN), Cairo (IL)*

Arkansas, Oklahoma, and Missouri

Arkansas, Oklahoma, and Missouri make up most of the lower section of the Midwest and are grouped together here because of the similarity of their terrain, in particular the low mountain ranges they share that are distinct from both the Appalachians to the east and the Rockies further west. This area of mountains in southern Missouri, eastern Oklahoma, and western and northwestern Arkansas offer some of the wildest tracts of land in the region covered in this chapter. These mountain ranges are friendlier in terms of resources and climate than other areas in the region, such as the open, windswept plains. A skilled survivalist could do well here by making use of the abundant game, diverse plant and forest communities, and plentiful water. Thick forests, deep canyons, heavily wooded ridges and valleys, and many caves and rock shelters throughout this area offer good, inaccessible hide-outs to those willing to bushwhack.

Ouachita Mountains (AR and OK)

The Ouachita Mountains are a rocky, rugged range stretching from west-central Arkansas into southeastern Oklahoma. They have a unique feel to them, situated as they are in an area where elements of both the Deep South and the West converge. These mixed pine- and hardwood-clad ridges combine the heat and humidity of the coastal plain to the south with rocky escarpments and vistas similar to the Ponderosa-forested slopes of the mountains in New Mexico and Arizona. Out in the wilder areas of the Ouachitas it's sometimes easy to forget just where you are. The name "Ouachita" is a French derivative of the Indian name for the region, which means "good hunting grounds." These mountains offer some first-rate bug-out locations with plenty of uninhabited public land.

The Ouachita National Forest is the largest national forest in the Midwest and Heartland region, taking in 1,784,457 acres, mostly in Arkansas but also reaching into parts of Oklahoma. Within these federal holdings, there are designated wilderness areas totaling 65,000 acres. Much of the forest land in Ouachita National Forest is old-growth forest, simply because it consists of stunted oak, hickory, and other species of little commercial value growing in the poor soil of steep slopes were logging was not worth the effort. An abundance of wild food such as acorns and hickory nuts on these slopes provides good forage for survivalists and many game animals like squirrels and deer.

A highlight of the Ouachitas is the 223-mile-long Ouachita National Recreation Trail, two-thirds of which is open to mountain biking, with the rest reserved for hiking only. This trail traverses some of the best wild country in the range, connecting central Arkansas with Pinnacle Mountain State Park in Oklahoma. Several man-made reservoirs within the Ouachitas offer many miles of uninhabited shoreline where one could operate out of a canoe. These include Lake Ouachita in Arkansas and Broken Bow Lake in Oklahoma.

Nearest Cities: *Hot Springs, Mena (AR), Poteau, McAlester (OK)*

Ozark Mountains (AR and MO)

The Ozark Mountains are the largest mountain range between the Appalachians and the Rockies, covering most of northwestern Arkansas and much of southern Missouri. Compared to those other major mountain ranges to the east and the west, the Ozarks may seem like foothills, with the highest elevation only reaching 2560 feet. But some sections of these small mountains are indeed rugged and steep, and traveling cross-country through them on foot can be more difficult than you would imagine. This is also a region of many first-rate white-water streams and rivers that are popular with canoeists and kayakers. The Buffalo River, in particular, is an outstanding clear-water mountain stream that flows through 600-foot-deep canyons and traverses some of the wildest parts of the Ozarks, dropping 2000 feet along its 135-mile length. Still free-flowing and unaltered by man, the Buffalo River was the first National River to be designated in the United States.

One of the wildest areas the Buffalo River flows through is the Leatherwood Wilderness, a 16,956-acre designated wilderness area of steep slopes, rocky cliffs, and dense oak-hickory forests that make travel away from river unfeasible for all but the most determined. The Leatherwood is a good bug-out location, as is the larger Lower Buffalo River Wilderness that totals 34,933 acres.

Large tracts of national forest land that offer everything from hiking trails to four-wheel-drive roads and large lakes and rivers make up much of the Ozark Mountain regions of Arkansas and Missouri. In Arkansas, Ozark National Forest totals a huge 1.2 million acres, and St. Francis National Forest adds another 22,600 acres. In Missouri, Mark Twain National Forest spreads over 1.5 million acres, mostly in the Ozarks, but also in parts of the gentler terrain of southeastern Missouri. Within Mark Twain National Forest, there are 78,000 acres of designated wilderness and scenic rivers.

Nearest Cities: *Jasper, Harrison, Mountain Home (AR), Springfield, Branson, West Plains (MO)*

Iowa, Kansas, and Nebraska

These three Midwestern states today are mostly in use as farm or ranch land, with comparatively few tracts of public land and little that could be called wilderness except for a few areas of western Nebraska. Despite the settled and tamed nature of most of the land here, there are nevertheless acceptable bug-out locations to be found. Rivers are once again the key to finding narrow slices of uninhabited terrain, and the rivers of this open farm country are more often than not bounded by a buffer zone of trees and other vegetation where there is a surprising abundance of wildlife to be found. Along many of the rivers of the upper Midwest, you will see large numbers of deer, rabbits, wild turkeys, and squirrels, as well as aquatic species such as beavers. The rivers also support plenty of edible fish and the mixed vegetation of the banks always includes some useful plant species. For the most part, these rivers are ignored by nearby farmers in normal times. In a bug-out scenario they would be the best options in most parts of these three states and also provide water routes to other regions, assuming you had a lightweight boat that could be portaged over dams.

Of these three states, only Nebraska has national forest land. Iowa and Kansas have little in the way of public lands, with the exception of Cimarron National Grassland in the southwestern corner of Kansas and scattered small state wildlife refuges, state parks, and state forests in both Kansas and Iowa. Iowa is bounded to the east and west by navigable rivers, the Mississippi and the Missouri, and the Missouri also defines the northeast corner of Kansas. The Kansas and the Arkansas are two other river systems that cross the state of Kansas and in the western grasslands area there are many smaller rivers and creeks.

Nebraska is bounded to the east and northeast by the Missouri River as well, and is crossed from west to east by another major western river, the Platte, and its tributary, the North Platte. One outstanding river in the northwestern part of this state that offers a first-rate canoe route and has hiking and horseback riding along its course is the Niobrara River, 76 miles of which have been designated as a National

Scenic River. This river winds through Nebraska's sand hills, where a mix of prairie grasslands and pine forests provide habitat for deer, elk, and other game species. The western half of Nebraska has several other significant areas of public land and preserves, as well as many large tracts of roadless land, both public and private. Among these are Crescent Lake National Wildlife Refuge, Valentine National Wildlife Refuge, Oglala National Grassland, and two national forests, Nebraska National Forest and Samuel R. McKelvie National Forest.

Samuel R. McKelvie National Forest (NE)

Samuel R. McKelvie National Forest in northern Nebraska is unique in that it is mostly man-made. Consisting of 115,703 acres, this national forest in Nebraska's sandhills grassland region is now an area of mixed prairie and Ponderosa pine "islands." These forest areas were planted by hand over 75 years ago, and include juniper and Scots pine as well. The whole area is good wildlife habitat and it is well populated with mule deer, whitetail deer, and pronghorn antelope, along with grouse, pheasants, and wild turkeys. A 61,000-acre tract of this national forest is roadless, and there are additional large areas of private roadless ranch lands outside the forest boundaries.

Nearest Cities: Valentine, Alliance, Broken Bow

Nebraska National Forest (NE)

The Nebraska National Forest is split into two units: the 90,000-acre Bessey Ranger District, which is located in the sandhill region of central Nebraska not far south of the Samuel R. McKelvie National Forest, and the 52,000-acre Pine Ridge District, located in the northwest corner of the state. The Pine Ridge District is an area of natural Ponderosa pine forest, while the Bessey Ranger District consists of man-made forests planted in 1902 as an experiment to see if the area could be used for timber production. A 20,000-acre tract of this forest is the largest man-made forest in the United States.

Nearest Cities: Chadron, Alliance, Dunning, Broken Bow, North Platte

South Dakota and North Dakota

The northern plains states are a mix of farm and ranch land, as well as sizable remnants of the wilderness that was once home to great herds of buffalo and the nomadic Native American cultures that hunted them. This part of the Midwest is defined by harsh winters and is a tough place to live outdoors, but the advantage that residents of these states have is that the population densities are low and refugees from big cities in other areas are not likely to come here looking for a bug-out location. Most of the wild country remaining in the Dakotas is to be found in the western halves, with more farmland and towns and cities concentrated in the east.

Rivers of the Dakotas

As in the other states discussed in this chapter, those areas of the Dakotas that are in agricultural use have little to offer as bug-out locations except along the river corridors. Fortunately for residents of the eastern parts of the Dakotas, there are many miles of such rivers that are part of major, long-distance river systems. The Red River of the North in North Dakota is one such river, sharing the eastern border of that state with the western border of Minnesota. The Red River of the North is a north-flowing river that drains to the Arctic and is navigable by canoe along its whole length, from south of Fargo to Lake Winnipeg in Manitoba, Canada. The banks of this river are for the most part clothed in a narrow belt of dense forest, concealing the river from the surrounding farms and providing good habitat for deer, moose, and many other game animals.

The biggest river system in the Dakotas is the Missouri River, which flows into western North Dakota from Montana's high plains country and winds through the center of that state as well as South Dakota before flowing southeast along the southern boundary to the extreme southeast corner of the region. All of the Missouri River in these two states can be navigated by canoe or any watercraft light enough to portage around dams. For much of its course, this upper part of the Missouri River flows through a lonely landscape with many pockets of uninhabited plains and badland country. In this kind of terrain, the river provides the best options for transportation, water, food, and shelter in small stands of woods along its banks.

Nearest Cities: *Grand Forks, Fargo, Williston, Bismarck (ND), Mobridge, Pierre, Yankton (SD)*

Badlands (SD)

Among the best-preserved remnants of the wild Great Plains are the Badlands of western South Dakota. Badlands National Park contains 244,000 acres in this area, with 64,250 acres within the park established as the Sage Creek Wilderness Area. The Badlands area got its name from early settlers who deemed this rugged country of rocky buttes, pinnacles, and spires "bad lands to travel across." Today, the Badlands are an oasis of wildlife-rich hideaways and could serve as a nearly ideal bug-out location. Bighorn sheep and bison have been reintroduced, mule deer and pronghorn antelope are common, and many smaller game animals and birds abound.

Nearest Cities: *Cactus Flat, Pine Ridge, Box Elder, Rapid City*

Black Hills National Forest (SD)

Another first-rate bug-out location in the far western end of South Dakota is the Black Hills National Forest. This mountainous area of the high plains that is disconnected from the Rockies farther west has a granite peak of over 7000 feet and 1.2 million acres of meadows, canyons, and the dark spruce forest that gives the range its name. The area covered by the Black Hills range is approximately 125 miles long by 70 miles wide. Elk, mule deer, whitetail deer, and pronghorn antelope are present throughout the range, and bighorn sheep and mountain goats are also in the area, as well as mountain lions.

Nearest Cities: *Rapid City, Hot Springs, Sturgis, Spearfish*

Little Missouri River Corridor (ND)

The western edge of North Dakota is drained by the Little Missouri River, which flows through some of the best examples of wild badlands and prairie remaining in the Great Plains region. The ecosystems here vary from shortgrass prairie and Ponderosa pine forests on the ridges to elm, elder, ash, and cottonwood in the canyons and ravines. Wildlife is abundant in this entire river corridor and includes mountain lions, lynx, elk, bighorn sheep, mule deer, pronghorn antelope, porcupines, and prairie dogs, as well as a herd of reintroduced buffalo. This area is preserved in the 1,000,000-acre Little Missouri River National Grassland and the 70,466-acre Theodore Roosevelt National Park. Depending on the water level, it may be possible to paddle the 274-mile long Little Missouri River, a state-designated scenic river, by canoe or kayak. Downstream, the Little Missouri can be navigated to the larger Missouri River, which in this part of North Dakota is dammed to create a vast man-made reservoir, Lake Sakakawea.

Nearest Cities: *Sentinel Bluff, Dickinson, Williston*

10

WILDERNESS STRONGHOLDS OF THE ROCKY MOUNTAINS

MONTANA, IDAHO, WYOMING, COLORADO, UTAH, ARIZONA AND NEW MEXICO

The Rocky Mountain Corridor, forming the Continental Divide that runs from Mexico all the way north to Canada, contains vast strongholds of quintessential North American wilderness—the kind of terrain most people think of when the term "wilderness" is mentioned. Parts of this great mountain range were some of the last areas of the lower 48 to be explored and settled, and many of the places described in this chapter are essentially as unspoiled today as they where when the first white fur trappers ventured into them in the "mountain man" heyday of the late 1700s and early 1800s. This is one of the best regions of the country to live in if you are interested in wilderness adventures, and it certainly offers some of the best potential bug-out locations to be found anywhere, so long as you are properly equipped to handle the terrain and climate conditions.

Unlike all the regions previously described, the Rocky Mountains contain so many diverse tracts of designated wilderness areas that it would be impossible to cover them all in this chapter. The wilderness areas alone make up millions of acres of public land in each of the states included here, in addition to the many greater areas of national forest surrounding them, which in many cases are just as remote and wild. Some of America's most spectacular national parks are found within this region and add several million more acres of wilderness options. The Bureau of Land Management (BLM) also has vast holdings of uninhabited land here, including entire sub-ranges of the Rockies, many of which are remote and seldom-visited.

Rocky Mountains Bug-Out Essentials

Weather and Climate

"Unpredictable" is the best word to describe the weather in the Rocky Mountains, particularly at the higher elevations. Summers in the Rockies are short, generally beginning in June and ending in mid-September, and while they can be mild or even hot—with many days of perfect weather—the highest parts of these mountains are subject to severe thunderstorms, heavy rainfall, high winds, and sudden blizzards at all times of the year. Winter temperatures can plummet to far below zero degrees Fahrenheit, and in higher elevations, cold can be the greatest danger in these mountains. Winter precipitation is also high, resulting in deep snow that remains on the ground for months—and on the peaks year-round. During periods of drought, frequent lightning strikes can start fires on the heavily timbered slopes, and fanned by high winds, they can spread rapidly and pose a serious danger to anyone caught in their path. Evidence of large-scale burns is found throughout the wilderness areas of the Rockies.

Land and Resources

Huge tracts of land in the Rocky Mountain region, including entire sub-ranges, are public lands owned by the federal government. Public land use in this region has long been at the center of heated debates between wilderness advocates who want it left in a pristine condition and those who engage in timber harvesting, mining and drilling, and livestock grazing. With so much land available, there is enough to support many uses and even the areas that do see more commercial use are in many cases sufficiently remote and wild to serve as good bug-out locations. In addition to all this private land, there are also expansive tracts of private and corporate-owned timber and ranch lands. Despite the harsh winters, much of the land in the Rocky Mountain region is inhabitable, though a few areas are more arid than average. The availability of water is often dependant upon elevation, and much of the mountain country in the middle elevations between 5000 and 9000 feet is forested and well watered with streams, rivers, and natural lakes.

Edible Plants

Plant species in the Rocky Mountain region vary dramatically with elevation and the amount of available of water. The diversity of plant life is, of course, limited at the higher elevations and in the more arid areas of the mountains. Some hardy species such as lichens and conifers have adapted to even those conditions, but you will find many more useful plants on the slopes at more moderate elevations and in the drainages and along rivers and streams. These include such widespread species as cattail,

The bracken fern is common in North America. In spring, it produces abundant edible young shoots and fiddleheads.

bracken fern, watercress, elderberry, burdock, nettles, wild rose, wild onion, wild dock, blackberries, dewberries, raspberries, blueberries, huckleberries, and wild strawberries. Other edible plants found in this region include high-bush cranberries, thimble berries, currants, chokecherries, serviceberries, Indian potatoes, lamb's quarters, fireweed, Mormon tea, waterleaf, and Pinon and Ponderosa pine, which bear edible nuts. In harsh winter conditions, when no other plant food is available, many of the trees that make up the forests here have edible inner bark or leaves that can be brewed into tea. These include spruce, Douglas fir, red cedar, aspen, balsam poplar, and white birch.

Hunting and Fishing

The Rocky Mountain region is the premier big-game hunting location in the United States, with a wide array of sought-after species, including moose, elk, mule deer, whitetail deer, mountain goat, bighorn sheep, and pronghorn antelope. Sport hunters also go after the abundant bears and mountain lions in the region, and with the comeback of the gray wolf, some hunting of them is now allowed to control the growing population. For a survivalist living off the land in these mountains, deer and elk are the most valuable big game, but an array

Small animals, such as ptarmigan, are readily available in the Rocky Mountain region.

of smaller animals that are candidates for the pot include wild turkeys, quail, sage grouse, forest grouse, chukar partridge, ptarmigan, ducks, geese, rabbits, snowshoe hares, and squirrels. Other common animals in the mountains that are not normally hunted but are certainly edible include beavers, porcupines, and rattlesnakes. The streams, rivers, and lakes of the Rocky Mountains provide good fishing, especially for trout, including native cutthroat and introduced species from other regions.

Wildlife Hazards

This is the one region in the lower 48 states where big, dangerous predators are the number-one wildlife hazard. A few locations in the Rockies are still home to the grizzly bear, which is generally considered much more dangerous than the more common black bear because of its larger size and its record of attacking humans. Grizzlies are most dangerous when surprised or when their cubs are approached too closely. Black bears are also found throughout the region, and just as in the North Woods and Appalachian regions, they too have been responsible for attacks on humans here. In addition, the Rockies are prime habitat for mountain lions, which are present in large numbers and have attacked humans with increasing regularity as they more frequently cross paths with people in the outdoors. Other big animals that can charge if you get too close or threaten their young are moose and elk, and the reintroduced bison have also been responsible for attacks in places like Yellowstone National Park. Rattlesnakes can be found in many parts of the Rockies, particularly at lower elevations and in open sunny areas.

Recommended Equipment

Since most of the bug-out locations described in this chapter are designated wilderness, getting into them means either walking with a backpack or pack animals or riding a horse or mule. Even in a SHTF scenario, when the rules prohibiting mechanized travel may not be enforced, foot or horseback travel will still be the only way to access the backcountry of most of these areas. But outside the wilderness areas, thousands of miles of forest service, BLM, and primitive private roads make four-wheel-drive vehicles viable, as well as travel by ATV, off-road motorcycle, or mountain bike. Snowmobiles are also an option in winter months, when foot travel will necessitate snowshoes or cross-country skis.

Firearms for this mountain region should include a hunting weapon capable of taking down deer, elk, and other large animals at reasonable ranges, as well as a .22 rifle for the abundance of small game such as grouse and rabbits. You will also need a suitable weapon for defense against the large predators mentioned above. If you are in areas known to be inhabited by grizzly bears, a hard-hitting rifle caliber such as the .45-70, .454 Casull, or 30.06 is best, and can be used for hunting as well. The .44 magnum should be considered a minimum caliber choice in either a handgun or a lever-action rifle.

◆ ◆ ◆

The following sections, organized by state, will discuss the various regions of the Rocky Mountains in terms of their suitability as bug-out locations.

Montana and Idaho

I'm grouping the two northernmost Rocky Mountain states together because of similarities in terrain and climate, as well as the fact that two of the largest and most remote wilderness areas in the lower 48 states overlap the border between these two states. Montana and Idaho are the northernmost states straddling the Rocky Mountain range, which continues on across the border into Canada, where there are even bigger areas of roadless wilderness. Montana is a land of huge, wide-open spaces, containing uninhabited land both in the Great Plains, in the eastern part of the state, and in the remote mountain ranges of the western third. And while Idaho may be known as the Potato State, it would be more accurate to describe it as the Wilderness State, as a larger percentage of its land is wilderness than any other state outside of Alaska. Idaho also contains the largest virgin forest remaining in the lower 48 states.

Because so many of the spectacular big tracts of wilderness in Idaho and Montana adjoin each other or are separated by only a road or other insignificant boundary, it's hard to separate one from another; taken as a whole, these connected lands form huge uninhabited areas that you can move between without realizing you've crossed from one to another. One such area is the Northern Continental Divide Ecosystem, a vast area of Montana that takes in Glacier National Park, the Bob Marshall Wilderness, Flathead National Forest, and Great Bear Wilderness, to name a few.

Glacier National Park (MT)

Glacier National Park, which extends north to the Canadian border to adjoin Alberta's Waterton Lakes National Park, has been designated an International Biosphere Reserve and the world's first International Peace Park. The U.S. part of the park contains 1.4 million acres of spectacular Rocky Mountain country preserved in a pristine state. The park is named for its glacier-carved mountains shaped in the last Ice Age and is full of U-shaped valleys and outflow lakes radiating from the highest peaks. Glacier National Park supports a nearly intact northern Rockies ecosystem inhabited by every species native to the region except the woodland caribou and the bison. There is a large population of grizzly bears in the park, and several fatal attacks on humans have occurred in recent years. Until recently National Park Service regulations prohibited carrying firearms for protection from these bears, but regardless of the status of these rules, they will not likely be enforced in situation warranting bugging out. Survival hunting would be good here, with 62 species of mammals present, including large herds of elk and deer.

Nearest Cities: *Kalispell, Colombia Falls, West Glacier, Essex, St. Mary*

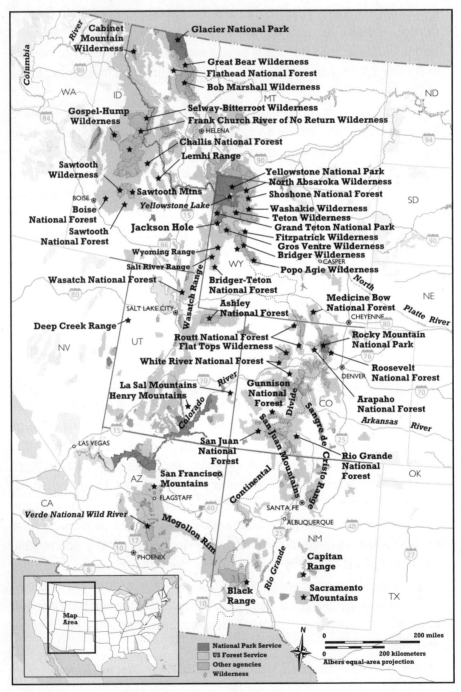

Bug-Out Locations of the Wilderness Strongholds of the Rocky Mountains

Flathead National Forest (MT)

Adjoining Glacier National Park to the west and south, Flathead National Forest adds 2.3 million acres of public land to this northern part of Montana, including a million acres of designated wilderness. There are no roads within the designated wilderness, so if you're bugging out by vehicle, you'll be limited to the other areas of the forest; and even there you'll need a rugged four-wheel-drive vehicle to get many places. The wilderness parts of the Flathead are best reached by horseback or on foot with pack animals. One of the best wilderness areas in the Rockies is found in the Flathead National Forest: the Bob Marshall Wilderness Area, which totals almost 1.1 million acres. The "Bob," as it is known locally, has it all when it comes to the Rockies: big river valleys, rugged, snow-capped peaks, alpine lakes, waterfalls, pristine mountain streams, a blanket of coniferous forest, and mountain meadows. Within the Bob, a grand escarpment called the Chinese Wall extends for 22 miles along the Great Divide, with an average height of over 1000 feet. Big game is plentiful here, with huge herds of elk, bighorn sheep, and mountain goats. The top predators, grizzly bear, mountain lion, and gray wolf, also have a stronghold in the Bob.

Another wilderness area within the Flathead National Forest is the Great Bear Wilderness, which contains almost 300,000 acres and borders the Bob on the north. The Great Bear Wilderness is prime bear habitat, not only for the grizzly that gives it its name, but also the more numerous black bears, which in this area are often cinnamon colored and are frequently mistaken for grizzlies.

Nearest Cities: *Eureka, Colombia Falls, Kalispell, Essex, Heart Butte*

Cabinet Mountains (MT)

The Cabinet Mountains of northwestern Montana, south of Libby but north of the Bitterroot Range, are unique in the Rockies in that they receive over 100 inches of precipitation a year, making them more similar to the forested mountains of the Pacific Northwest. This wet microclimate in the Cabinet Mountains is ideal for lush forests of Douglas fir, red cedar, western hemlock, and western white pine. Dozens of streams and high mountain lakes are found throughout the range. A greater roadless area of 187,000 acres remains in the Cabinet Mountains around the core designated the Cabinet Mountain Wilderness, which contains 94,272 acres. Elevations in the Cabinets range from 3000 feet to 8738 feet.

Nearest Cities: Libby, Trout Creek, Thompson Falls

Selway-Bitterroot Wilderness (MT and ID)

The Bitterroot Mountain Range forms a large part of the border between Montana and Idaho from just south of the Cabinet Mountains described above to the southwestern corner of Montana. Located midway along this range, the Selway-Bitterroot Wilderness, at 1.3 million acres, is the third-largest designated wilderness area in the lower 48 states, behind only California's Death Valley Wilderness and the River of No Return Wilderness described in the next section. This mountain wilderness contains more than 20 major drainages flowing from the Bitterroot Range, as well as the Selway River, an outstanding wilderness river. High elevations in the Selway-Bitterroot reach above 9000 feet, topping out on Trapper Peak at 10,157 feet. Many large slices of the Selway-Bitterroot Wilderness completely lack trails and are rarely visited by humans, but are a haven for big game such as elk and mule deer. Serious hunters do penetrate deep into the wilderness, though, mostly on an extensive network of trails suitable for both backpackers and horseback riders with pack trains. The farthest reaches of the backcountry here can be hard to reach on foot due to the limited amount of supplies that can be carried in a backpack, so this is one wilderness area that is as popular with horseback riders and others using pack animals as it is with hikers.

This is a well-watered and heavily forested wilderness area. With over 100 mountain lakes in the high country and the streams and rivers in the drainages, finding drinking water in the Selway-Bitterroot is seldom a problem. With the teeming big game available, the mountain lion, the area's top predator, is said to be present here in higher densities than anywhere else in the United States. Black bears are also common throughout the area and the U.S. Fish and Wildlife Service has been conducting controversial studies and considering proposals to reintroduce the grizzly bear to the Bitterroots.

Nearest Cities: Grangeville, Clearwater (ID), Hamilton, Missoula (MT)

Frank Church River of No Return Wilderness (ID)

Just a single dirt road separates the 1.3 million acres of the Selway-Bitterroot Wilderness from an immense wilderness to the south of it that is the largest unbroken tract of roadless land in the lower 48 States. The Frank Church River of No Return Wilderness area alone contains 2.3 million acres, and combined with the adjacent Gospel Hump Wilderness, the core of this sprawling roadless mountain stronghold totals 3.3 million acres. Named for the Middle Fork and main Salmon River that course through it in some of the most spectacular canyons in the world, the River of No Return Wilderness is vast and diverse, with ecosystems ranging from dry grasslands at 2000 feet to barren peaks over 10,000 feet. The biggest part of the wilderness, however, is covered in coniferous forest consisting of Douglas fir, lodgepole pine, spruce, and Ponderosa pine; the northern part of the area contains the largest tract of virgin forest remaining in the Rockies.

This primeval land of unspoiled mountain wilderness is home to elk, mule deer, whitetail deer, moose, bighorn sheep, mountain goats, black bears, coyotes, pine martins, bobcats, mountain lions, wolverines, lynx, and timberwolves, which now number in the hundreds after being reintroduced in 1995.

A network of trails totaling more than 2600 miles provides access to various parts of this roadless area by foot or on horseback. But despite all these miles of trails, over a million acres of the River of No Return Wilderness remain trail-free and can only be accessed by rugged bushwhacking. The main Salmon River and the Middle Fork River provide access as well, but only to boats that can negotiate serious whitewater, including kayaks, river dories, whitewater rafts, and jetboats.

Nearest Cities: Salmon, Warm Lake, Boise

Sawtooth Mountains (ID)

Located in central Idaho north of Ketchum, the Sawtooth Mountains are a rugged sub-range of the Rockies with elevations ranging from 4000 to almost 11,000 feet. There are 800,000 acres of roadless wilderness in the Sawtooths, 217,088 acres of which are in the designated Sawtooth Wilderness Area, with the balance in the surrounding areas of Boise, Sawtooth, and Challis National Forests. The Sawtooth Mountains are popular with hikers and other outdoors enthusiasts for their stunning alpine scenery, which includes expansive forests and jewel-like mountain lakes. Most recreational visitors focus on the designated wilderness area, however, leaving the surrounding roadless area mostly untouched. As is the case in many Rocky Mountain areas, the best bug-out locations are sometimes found outside of noted attractions like parks and designated wilderness. There are certainly many isolated drainages within the Sawtooths where one could disappear for an indefinite period of time if need be.

Nearest Cities: *Ketchum, Clayton, Stanley, Boise*

Lemhi Range (ID)

The Lemhi Range is an outstanding example of a remote and little-known swath of wild country in a region full of national parks, national forests, and designated wilderness, and it is far from the radar of most tourists and even many locals in the area. In fact, the Lemhi range may be the least known significant mountain range in the lower 48 states. The range is approximately 120 miles long and is for the most part rugged, roadless, and inaccessible. Much of the range is dry, especially in the South Lemhis, but the northern portions feature natural lakes and have sizable populations of deer, elk, antelope, bear, and mountain lion. Although not enjoying any special protection as wilderness (as of this writing, a wilderness area to be named the Sacagawea Wilderness has been proposed but not implemented), some roadless areas of the Lemhi are as large as 410,000 acres in the northern end of the range and 230,000 acres in the South Lemhis. Throughout the range there are abandoned mines and old dirt roads fading back to nature.

Nearest Cities: *Salmon, Rexburg, Idaho Falls*

Wyoming

With a population of just over half a million in a state of almost 100,000 square miles, Wyoming is the least populated state in the U.S., and has long maintained that status. The availability and natural beauty of the wide-open, uninhabited space in Wyoming is astounding, and the Rocky

Mountain wilderness areas of the state would make first-rate bug-out locations. Forty-eight percent of all the land in Wyoming is federally owned, amounting to more than 30 million acres, several million of which are designated as wilderness in both national forests and national parks.

Wyoming contains some of North America's best-known scenic attractions, including Grand Teton National Park, Yellowstone National Park, and Devil's Tower National Monument. But outside these popular tourist magnets, there are remote and much less visited mountain areas that rival any place in the Rockies. The highest elevation in the state is the 13,804-foot Gannet Peak in the Wind River Range, where there are 40 more peaks exceeding 13,000 feet. The Continental Divide winds through the heart of Wyoming, from the Medicine Bow Mountains in the south to an area in the northwest known as the Greater Yellowstone Ecosystem, which includes the Tetons and Absarokas.

Yellowstone National Park

The entire northwestern corner of Wyoming is a complex of big roadless tracts of land, including several national forest wilderness areas and large sections of Yellowstone National Park that are remote and far-removed from the popular tourist attractions of the park. Yellowstone National Park was the world's first such park, established in 1872, when it was still an intact, true wilderness unspoiled by human interference. The park is home to some 600 grizzly bears, one of the highest concentrations of elk in North America, and free-roaming bison that are remnants of the huge herds that once roamed the West. Today, the park is heavily visited, but as with all large national parks of this nature, there are remote areas of backcountry that are difficult to access and receive little attention from all but the most hard-core wilderness travelers. This is to be expected in a chunk of rugged Rocky Mountain terrain measuring 63 miles north to south by 54 miles east to west, and encompassing 2,219,789 acres. The park features many natural lakes, including Yellowstone Lake, which covers almost 90,000 acres and has 110 miles of shoreline.

With its large numbers of grizzlies, black bears, mountain lions, and wolves, Yellowstone National Park has significant wildlife hazards to unarmed backcountry hikers and campers, which was the way most recreational visitors traveled here until recent changes regarding fire-arms in national parks. Several bear and mountain lion attacks on humans have occurred in recent years. Outside of the park, in the national forest areas that are also a part of the Greater Yellowstone Ecosystem, you can legally carry firearms with fewer restrictions, and it would be wise to pack a rifle or large-caliber handgun that could stop a grizzly.

Nearest Cities: Jackson, Puhaska, Tower Junction, Cody, Gardiner (MT), West Yellowstone (ID)

North Absaroka Wilderness/Shoshone National Forest/ Washakie Wilderness

Just east of the Yellowstone National Park boundary, the North Absaroka Wilderness takes in 350,488 acres of roadless backcountry within the 2.5-million-acre Shoshone National Forest. This national forest land adds a huge buffer of wilderness to the park and includes alpine tundra, conifer forest, lakes, and semi-desert sagebrush hill country. The North Absaroka Wilderness is a key part of the Greater Yellowstone Ecosystem and, like the park itself, is a stronghold for species like grizzly bear and bison. Several peaks here exceed 10,000 feet, with the highest point in the wilderness reaching 12,216 feet. The 217 miles of trails in the North Absaroka are narrow, steep, and minimally marked. Travel between drainages and off-trail is extremely difficult due to the rough terrain, but some of the upper reaches of the small creeks could make for first-rate mountain bug-out locations where the chances of encountering other people would be slim.

In the southern part of the Absaroka Range and within Shoshone National Forest, another 704,529 acres of designated wilderness is found in the Washakie Wilderness Area, named for a chief of the Shoshone tribe. This part of the Absarokas is made up of deep, narrow valleys separated by broad, flat-topped mountains and plateaus. Trails in the Washakie are mostly built for horses, as they ford many rivers, including the Greybull River, the Elk Fork, and the South Fork of the Shoshone River. Visitors are few, except during hunting season, when big game hunters pack in on horseback.

Nearest Cities: Cody, Puhaska, Tower Junction, Dubois, Meeteetse

Teton Wilderness Area/Bridger-Teton National Forest/ Wind River Range

Directly south of Yellowstone National Park and surrounding Teton National Park is another large buffer of wilderness that contributes to the overall integrity and size of the Greater Yellowstone Ecosystem. The 3.4 million acres of Bridger-Teton National Forest comprise a huge swath of green covering the western side of Wyoming along the border with Idaho all the through the Teton Range, Salt River Range, Wyoming Range, and part of the Wind River Range. This makes the Bridger-Teton the second largest distinct national forest in the lower 48 after the Humboldt-Toiyabe National Forest in Nevada. Like the rest of the large tracts of land that make up the Greater Yellowstone Ecosystem, this national forest is home to grizzly bears, bison, wolves, mountain lions, bighorn sheep, elk, and mule deer. Over 2000 miles of trails within the greater national forest area and a limited number of primitive roads provide access to this expansive backcountry. Included in the national forest holdings are three designated wilderness areas: Teton Wilderness, Gros Ventre Wilderness, and Bridger Wilderness.

Within the 585,468-acre Teton Wilderness Area (Wyoming's second largest), you can find the farthest point from a road in all the lower 48 states. This point is near the Thorofare River and is 21 miles from the nearest road. Despite the lack of roads, there are trails, approximately 450 miles of them, used mainly by serious backcountry hunters and fishermen. Not far south of the Teton Wilderness, the Gros Ventre Wilderness adds 287,000 acres of roadless high country to the bug-out options in Bridger-Teton National Forest, and to the southeast, on the western slopes of the Wind River Range, Bridger Wilderness contains 428,169 acres.

It's hard to separate the vast expanses of Bridger-Teton National Forest from the Wind River Range, as there is so much overlap here, but taken as a separate area, this massive mountain range contains approximately 1,171,000 acres of roadless terrain. The Wind River Range is famous for its glaciers, as it contains over 60 of them, including the largest ones in the Rockies south of Canada. The Continental Divide follows the crest of the Wind Rivers, and it is here that Wyoming's highest peak tops out at 13,804 feet. As the southern extension of the Greater Yellowstone Ecosystem, the Wind River Range is teeming with big game and is home to the largest herd of bighorn sheep in the Rockies. On the eastern side of the range, the Shoshone National Forest adjoins Bridger-Teton and includes two other designated wilderness areas: the 198,525-acre Fitzpatrick Wilderness Area and the 101,991-acre Popo Agie Wilderness Area.

Nearest Cities: Jackson, Dubois, Pinedale, Lander

Grand Teton National Park

Grand Teton National Park is a 310,000-acre island of park service land surrounded by the greater Bridger-Teton National Forest. The park is, of course, known for its spectacular peaks, the tallest of which is Grand Teton at 13,770 feet. Within the park, Jackson Hole is a 55-mile long valley rimmed by high mountains that was used as a winter camp by Native Americans in prehistoric times and was a favorite rendezvous point for fur-trapping mountain men during the early 1800s. Today the park is popular with hikers and climbers, and as no hunting is allowed, it is a sanctuary for game animals along with the much larger Yellowstone National Park to the north.

Nearest Cities: Jackson, Teton Village, Jackson Lake Lodge

Medicine Bow–Routt National Forest (WY and CO)

South-central Wyoming's Medicine Bow National Forest and the adjacent Routt National Forest across the state line in northern Colorado combine to include 2,769,949 acres in the 100-mile long Medicine Bow Mountain Range. Separate from the Greater Yellowstone Ecosystem, Medicine Bow Range is not inhabited by species such as grizzly bear and bison, but nevertheless it is teeming with mule deer, elk, moose, black bear, and mountain lions. Peaks in this mountain range reach over 12,000 feet, with Medicine Bow Peak being the highest on the Wyoming side at 12,013 feet. Trout fishing in the many streams and lakes and hunting for deer and elk are popular activities in the Medicine Bow Mountains. But overall, because this somewhat isolated mountain range is far from the tourist attractions like Yellowstone and the more popular mountain areas of Colorado, the backcountry here could serve well as a bug-out location.

Nearest Cities: *Laramie, Ryan Park, Woods Landing, Walden (CO), Steamboat Springs (CO)*

Colorado and Utah

Colorado is the Rocky Mountain State and the first place that comes to mind when the range is mentioned in other parts of the country. The highest peaks in the entire Rocky Mountain Corridor are found in Colorado, a state with 53 summits reaching past 14,000 feet. Two-fifths of Colorado is covered by the Rocky Mountains, and the Continental Divide splits the state. The slopes of the Great Divide in Colorado contain the headwaters of major rivers such as the Colorado (which drains to the Pacific at the Sea of Cortez), the Rio Grande (which runs directly to the Gulf of Mexico), and the Arkansas (which empties into the Mississippi River). The Colorado Rockies are a big attraction to tourists and resident outdoor enthusiasts alike. Outdoor recreation is a huge industry here, and includes everything from mountaineering to skiing, snowmobiling, hunting, fishing, and ATV riding. As a result of its popularity, this state is more developed and heavily populated than the other states discussed in this chapter, and there are fewer tracts of big wilderness here compared to the other mountain states. This is not to say that there is not plenty of public land in Colorado, as more than a third of the state's area is federal or state-owned public land. Among all these mountains there are plenty of good bug-out locations to be found, and compared to most of the locations east of the Rockies, Colorado's wilderness areas are still immense, even if they are small compared to those of Montana, Idaho, and Wyoming.

Rocky Mountain National Park/Roosevelt National Forest/Arapaho National Forest (CO)

This part of the Colorado Rockies adjoins the southern end of the Medicine Bow Mountains described in the Wyoming section. Located northwest of Boulder and Denver, Rocky Mountain National Park forms the core of a big chunk of mostly wild land that spills over the park boundaries into the surrounding Roosevelt National Forest and Arapaho National Forest. One of Colorado's most visited and heavily used recreation areas, Rocky Mountain National Park contains 265,770 acres split through the middle by the Continental Divide. This national park is truly high country, with over a fourth of the area above the tree line and 60 peaks higher than 12,000 feet. Despite the popularity of the park and the paved roads that provide access to the most popular parts of it, there are many remote parts that can only be reached on foot. Elk, mule deer, and moose are common in the park and are unafraid of humans, as they have not been pressured by hunting. While no grizzly bears are found in this area, black bears and mountain lions are present.

For bug-out locations in this part of Colorado, it is probably best to look to the surrounding national forest land, of which there is plenty. Roosevelt and Arapaho National Forests combine to take in more than 1.5 million acres and include a bit of everything from remote wilderness areas to off-road vehicle trails where you can access the backcountry.

Nearest Cities: *Estes Park, Boulder, Fort Collins, Granby, Dillon*

Flat Tops Wilderness Area (CO)

Located in northwestern Colorado south of Craig, in the middle of the 2,285,970-acre White River National Forest, the Flat Tops Wilderness Area is part of a 346,000-acre tract of roadless backcountry far removed from the weekend recreational crowds that swarm the Rocky Mountain National Park area. Part of Routt National Forest, this is a heavily forested, high-elevation plateau area, ranging from 7500 feet to over 12,000 feet and including everything from open meadows to steep cliffs. Flat Tops is Colorado's second largest wilderness area. It differs from other Colorado mountain areas in that it is mostly a high escarpment planed level at the top, hence its name. Access is relatively limited, with only 160 miles of trails within the wilderness boundaries and limited road access to the edges. But with over 100 miles of streams and some 110 mountain lakes populated with trout, this is a remote wilderness area where food, water, and solitude can be found as long as one is prepared to deal with the cold that accompanies high elevations.

Nearest Cities: *Craig, Meeker, Rifle, Glenwood Springs*

Maroon Bells-Snowmass/Collegiate Peaks/ Raggeds Wilderness Areas (CO)

In south-central Colorado, south of the Flat Tops Wilderness Area and Interstate 70, another huge chunk of green on the map is taken up by units of the White River, Grand Mesa, Gunnison, and San Isabel National Forests. Within that area of green is one of Colorado's larger roadless areas, a total of 632,000 acres split between the Maroon Bells-Snowmass Wilderness, the Collegiate Peaks Wilderness, and the Raggeds Wilderness, along with some of the surrounding national forest lands. Outside of the roadless areas are hundreds of thousands more acres of only slightly less wild forests that can be accessed by a number of trails and primitive roads.

Nearest Cities: Carbondale, Aspen, Crested Butte, Gunnison

Weminuche Wilderness Area (CO)

The Weminuche Wilderness Area, at 459,172 acres, is by far Colorado's largest designated wilderness, and it forms the core of a greater area of roadless land totaling 806,000 acres in the surrounding San Juan, Rio Grande, and Gunnison National Forests. This area of southwestern Colorado in the San Juan Mountain Range is without doubt the wildest region of the state in terms of lack of development. It is here that the last grizzly bear known to live in the wild in Colorado was killed in 1979, although rumors and reported sightings of grizzlies persist in the region today.

Despite its size and rugged terrain, the Weminuche Wilderness Area gets a lot of traffic from backpackers and other recreational users. The Continental Divide Trail crosses 21 miles of the wilderness, and combined with other trails there are some 500 miles of pathways here. But wilderness survival in a bug-out situation would be feasible in the far reaches of the mountains, which are teeming with deer and elk and well watered with mountain streams and lakes containing plenty of trout.

Nearest Cities: Silverton, Durango, Pagosa Springs, South Fork

Sangre de Cristo Wilderness Area (CO)

One of Colorado's newest designated wilderness area is the 226,420-acre Sangre de Cristo Wilderness, an elongated corridor of rugged mountain country in the isolated Sangre de Cristo Mountains southeast of Salida. Additional national forest land in this range brings the total roadless acreage here up to 418,000 acres. Although the Sangre de Cristo Range is narrow, its peaks rise over 14,000 feet—about 7000 feet above the surrounding plains. As a result of the varying elevation, there is a great diversity of ecosystems in this mountain wilderness, ranging from alpine tundra to Ponderosa pine and Douglas fir evergreen forest, on down to sagebrush and desert. In the high country there are some 60 lakes and many streams. Most of the trails leading into the wilderness follow the drainages of these streams to the lakes at their headwaters, where the going ends against near-vertical walls. Access to the wilderness is also possible along two four-wheel-drive roads that cross the Sangre de Cristo Range at Medano Pass and Hayden Pass.

Nearest Cities: *Salida, Westcliffe, Alamosa*

High Unitas Wilderness Area (UT)

Utah's highest peaks are found in the Unitas Mountains, an extensive sub-range of the Rockies that runs east and west from eastern Colorado almost to Salt Lake City in north-central Utah. The state's highest point is found in the Unitas—13,528-foot King's Peak. Many peaks in this range exceed 13,000 feet and the crests average 11,000 feet. The 460,000-acre High Unitas Wilderness is the largest designated wilderness in

---

UTAH'S MOUNTAINS

While Colorado is synonymous with the Rocky Mountains, Utah is often thought of by outsiders as desert country, and while it is true that the state is famous for its canyons and slickrock, there are also a few high mountain strongholds in Utah to rival the best in this chapter. Peaks in the Unitas Mountains surpass 13,000 feet, and in the Wasatch and other smaller ranges there are peaks of over 12,000 feet. This mountain country is well watered and heavily forested and is a world apart from Utah's desert canyonlands described in the next chapter. Federal lands make up over half of Utah's total area and include five national parks and six national forests.

Utah, but is just a part of a greater roadless area totaling 843,000 acres in Ashley and Wasatch National Forests. Unlike much of Utah, which is arid, the High Unitas Wilderness is well watered, with over 250 lakes and many streams that drop into deep canyons and form the headwaters of many of Utah's rivers.

Most of the wilderness is heavily forested in spruce, fir, pine, or aspen, depending on elevation, with lush open meadows interspersed throughout. This is prime wildlife habitat and is home to the typical Rocky Mountain fauna, including elk, moose, mule deer, mountain goats, bighorn sheep, black bears, and mountain lions. Approximately 545 miles of trails wind through the designated High Unitas Wilderness, while the surrounding national forest lands in the range can be accessed by various forest service roads.

Nearest Cities: *Vernal, Roosevelt, Heber City, Salt Lake City*

Other Areas of Utah

Smaller areas of high Rocky Mountain backcountry can be found in several scattered parts of Utah, including parts of the Wasatch Range to the north of Salt Lake City and the Deep Creek Range along the western border with Nevada. Scattered throughout the south-central and southeastern part of the state are several other high ranges, including the La Sal Mountains, near Moab, and the remote Henry Mountains north of Glen Canyon. The Henry Mountains are in BLM land and are a good example of a little-known wilderness that is not promoted for recreational purposes and is largely overlooked. One of the last remaining herds of free-ranging bison lives there, totaling over 500 animals. With two million acres of infrequently visited BLM land in the range and surrounding desert, the Henry Mountains could make for a superb bugout location.

The Rocky Mountain Areas
of Arizona and New Mexico

At this point, before proceeding to the next chapter on the deserts, canyons, and mountains of the Southwest, I should point out that the

Rocky Mountain Corridor extends south of Utah and Colorado into Arizona and New Mexico. Some of the biggest and wildest wilderness areas of the Southwest include a mix of dry desert or canyon country in the lower elevations and alpine forests and snowcapped peaks at the higher elevations. Notable big tracts of Rocky Mountain ecosystems in these southwestern states include parts of the Blue Range in eastern Arizona; the San Francisco Mountains around Flagstaff, Arizona; the southern end of the San Juan Mountains and the Sangre de Cristo Range in northern New Mexico; some areas of the Black Range and Mogollon Mountains in southwestern New Mexico; and the Sacramento Mountains in the area of Cloudcroft-Ruisoso, New Mexico.

11

DESERTS, CANYONS, & MOUNTAINS OF THE SOUTHWEST

WEST TEXAS, NEW MEXICO, ARIZONA, SOUTHERN UTAH, NEVADA, AND SOUTHERN CALIFORNIA

L ike the Rocky Mountains, North America's Southwest is synonymous with wilderness and rugged independence. This region is the "West" of most people's imagination and the setting for countless movies, television shows, and novels about the difficulties faced there by early explorers, prospectors, cowboys, and other settlers. In reality, it has not been all that long since the Southwest was still truly wild and untamed, and even today huge areas of this region are uninhabited and roadless.

Some of the longest and most difficult Indian wars the U.S. Army ever fought during the settling of the West were waged here against the elusive Apaches, who were masters of survival in this tough environment. The Apaches and other Native American tribes in the region adapted to the conditions and were able find resources in places that seemed to European settlers to be unfit for human habitation. They knew where to find the isolated springs and water holes of their territories and moved between various "islands" of wooded mountains and canyons where living by hunting and gathering was possible. Even for people as resourceful and tough as them, the barren wastelands in between these islands could not sustain life for long.

Many parts of the Southwest are surprisingly well watered, however, and are teeming with wildlife and a diversity of plant and tree species. Most of these areas are in the various mountain ranges that are sub-ranges of the Rockies and the Sierra Madre, which extends north into this part of the U.S. from Mexico. Other areas that are lush oases of plant and animal life are found in the canyon country that this region is famous for. Several large rivers course through the Southwest, draining both to the Gulf of Mexico and to the Pacific Ocean at the Sea of Cortez. Among them are the Colorado and the Rio Grande, both of which flow through some of the most spectacular canyons on Earth.

Just as in the Rocky Mountains region covered in the previous chapter, there are far more bug-out locations in this region than I can begin to cover in this limited space, but I've picked out a cross-section of some of the Southwest's most outstanding wild areas to give you an idea of the possibilities. If you live in this region you are lucky to have so many great options to get far away from the crowds in times of trouble, as many of these places receive virtually no human traffic. But if you plan to bug out in the Southwest, you certainly need to be aware of the region's unique challenges and be prepared to deal with them.

SOUTHWEST BUG-OUT ESSENTIALS

Weather and Climate

The Southwest is a land of extremes, where an elevation change of a few thousand feet can take you through several ecosystems ranging from alpine tundra down through lush evergreen forests to hot sun-baked valley floors, all within sight of one another. Lack of rainfall in some areas of this region creates an environment that is extremely hostile to human, plant, and animal life, and any living thing that survives in these places is forced to adapt. Except in a few of the high mountain areas, average rainfall throughout this region is extremely low, for the most part less than 14 inches per year. Some desert areas of Arizona, California, and Nevada receive less than five inches annually. When rain does come to the Southwest, it frequently comes along with severe thunderstorms. Flash floods can turn dry arroyos and canyons into raging torrents in short order. Lightning often sets fires on the dry mountain slopes and just as in the Rockies, big forest fires can quickly spread across thousands of acres. Winter storms can bring frigid temperatures and blizzards, particularly in the mountains. Despite these extremes, however, the climate in many areas of the Southwest is relatively benign and suited to outdoor living, as you don't have to deal with high humidity, and clear sunny days are the norm rather than the exception.

Land and Resources

Large cities are fewer and farther between in this region than in most of the United States. National forest lands, BLM holdings, and national wildlife refuges account for much of the backcountry found here, but there are also huge private holdings in the form of ranches that can be just as wild and unspoiled as the federal lands. While some of the public parks and national forests are well-known and attract tourists and recreational visitors, there is probably more overlooked and little-known public land in the Southwest than in any other region of the lower 48. Here, you can find entire mountain ranges and valleys that seldom see a human footprint. Finding water can certainly present a challenge in many parts of the Southwest, but if you know where to look there are springs, rock pools where surface water can be found, and many arroyos and depressions where digging down a short distance will yield water.

Edible Plants

A wide variety of edible plants can be found throughout the Southwest, although species distribution varies tremendously depending on the ecosystem. In the forested mountain areas, most of the plant life that is found in the Rockies is also present. Canyons and river basins often contain a mix of species from throughout the West and Midwest, while the drier desert areas contain exotic, highly adapted species like the various cacti that can thrive with little water. Some plants in this region are actually tropical or subtropical species from Mexico and farther south, reaching the northern limit of their range here. Keeping in mind the above and that not all of these are found in all areas of the Southwest, here is a partial list of edible plants you might find in the region: prickly pear, yucca, cattail, reed, amaranth, thistle, dandelion, saltbrush, wild

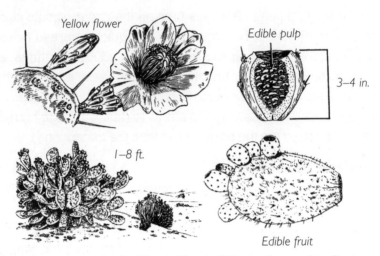

Yellow flower

Edible pulp

3–4 in.

1–8 ft.

Edible fruit

The prickly pear is one example of edible cacti found wild in the deserts of the Southwest.

rose, fireweed, sego lily, Indian ricegrass, wild rye, wheat grass, buffalo berry, chokecherry, serviceberry, elderberry, currant, wild grape, juniper (berries), manzanita (berries), pinon and Ponderosa pine (nuts), oak (acorns), and cottonwood and aspen (inner bark).

Hunting and Fishing

Wildlife is more abundant in the Southwest than most outsiders to the region would imagine. Much of the country that looks barren and lifeless from a distance is, in fact, teeming with life once you get up close. Plains and highlands of stunted juniper, sagebrush, cactus, and other plants adapted to this climate provide food and habitat for plenty of animals, including larger mammals such as mule deer, whitetail deer, pronghorn antelope, desert bighorn sheep, javelinas, black bear, mountain lions, and coyote. In the many mountain areas scattered throughout the region where dry canyon lands give way to forest of Ponderosa pine, elk are common as well. Small game animals common in the Southwest are rabbits (both cottontail and jack rabbits) and several varieties of squirrels, including gray squirrels and the tassel-eared squirrels such as the Albertson's squirrel and the Kaibob squirrel. Game birds include wild turkeys, several varieties of quail and doves, and waterfowl along the rivers and lakes. Fishing is also productive in mountain steams and lakes, which in most cases support good populations of trout.

In some of the harsher desert areas of the Southwest, it will be appropriate to shift your hunting focus away from big game and conventional small game, and consider instead the abundance of smaller animals not normally thought of as food that are found in this region. Snakes, lizards, small rodents, and small birds are the most abundant animals in these ecosystems and all of them can keep you alive in times of need. The best time to hunt in the desert is at night, when all wildlife there is most active.

Wildlife Hazards

Much of the mountain country of the Southwest was once home to the grizzly bear, but today the largest predators found in this region are black bears, which are quite common. Black bears are also found in places you wouldn't expect, such as in some of the canyon and semi-desert country. Mountain lions are also common in the Southwest and

Gila monster

are probably more likely than black bears to pose a threat to humans. Although elusive and rarely seen, another big cat that inhabits some of the southernmost parts of the Southwest and is likely increasing in numbers is the jaguar. Weighing in at up to 300 pounds, these spotted cats are capable predators but not as likely as mountain lions to attack humans. A rifle or handgun chambered for .357 magnum or greater will be sufficient to handle any large animal threat here. What you should worry about more than big predators are all the small biting and stinging things that are harder to see until it's too late. Most of this region is prime habitat for reptiles, arachnids, and insects.

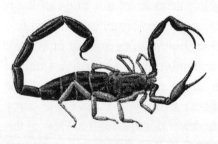

Scorpion

Poisonous snakes are especially prevalent and include the sinister sidewinder so often seen in Western movies, the western diamondback rattlesnake, the deadly Mohave rattlesnake, and the blacktail rattlesnake. Another extremely poisonous snake found in the region is the western coral snake, which is fortunately non-aggressive, just like its cousin in the Southeast. The Southwest is also home to a poisonous lizard—the Gila monster—which is also non-aggressive unless molested. Even harder to see than snakes are the thirty-odd species of scorpions that inhabit much of this area. The most dangerous of these is the Arizona bark scorpion, which has a sting that can be fatal in some cases. In places where scorpions are common, it is essential to check boots and other items of clothing that have been left on the ground before putting them on. Tarantulas and giant desert centipedes are also found in the region. Tarantulas look fierce and are somewhat poisonous, but rarely bite. The big centipedes have a nasty sting and should be avoided.

Like most warm areas of the U.S., the Southwest has its share of bees and wasps. It is also one of the first areas of the country to be invaded by migrating swarms of Africanized or "killer" bees, and on rare occasions, they have attacked humans here. The best way to avoid them is to never approach too closely to any large congregation of bees or sign of a hive.

Recommended Equipment

In the dry Southwest, an adequate supply of drinking water is a top survival priority. A reliable means to carry an adequate supply of water will be of utmost importance when choosing gear for bugging out in this region. As compared to other regions, you will need to carry more water at any given time while traveling in most of the bug-out locations described in this chapter, as resupply opportunities may be few and far between. I would suggest distributing your supply in several separate Nalgene bottles or other containers to decrease the risk of losing your entire supply if a single larger container is punctured or otherwise fails. When traveling in desert areas, you should also carry a means of collecting water from unconventional sources. One of the best such sources is early morning dew found on the blades of grasses and leaves of plants. Although this can be mopped up and squeezed out of a T-shirt or bandana, having a large sponge will make it an easier job. You should also carry some clear plastic and a tube for making a solar still, as well as a copy of a diagram and instructions on how to construct one if you are not familiar with the process. Equally important as your water supply is protection from the sun. A wide-brimmed hat, bandana, and long-sleeved shirt should always be in your bug-out bag here, and a tube of sunscreen is a good idea as well. It's also important not to overlook clothing and shelter to protect you from the cold, especially at high elevations, where weather can be just as severe as in the Rockies or North Woods.

In most parts of the Southwest, you will have more travel options than in any other region of the U.S. Wide-open deserts, often devoid of fences, make it possible to drive off-road even where there are no trails in sturdy four-wheel-drive vehicles or on ATVs or off-road motorcycles. Horses, mules, and donkeys are just as practical here today as they were 150 years ago, and mountain bikes can also serve well in many areas. In many parts of the mountains, though, foot travel may be the best option for truly getting to places where you will not easily be found.

Weapons here should include a .22 rifle for small game as well as a rifle for taking larger game at longer distances. Any caliber sufficient for black bears and mountain lions will suffice for protection. Be aware that some parts of this region, especially close to the Mexican border, have become extremely dangerous due to illegal human and drug trafficking, and you should use extreme caution to avoid being seen by the people carrying out these activities.

◆ ◆ ◆

The following sections, organized by state, will discuss the various regions of the Southwest in terms of their suitability as bug-out locations.

West Texas

Texas is the largest U.S. state other than Alaska, but has little public land compared to most states, especially most Western states. Relative to the national forest areas, national seashores, and national wildlife refuges in eastern Texas that I described in Chapter Five, the western part of the state has much more uninhabited land, but huge tracts that appear to be empty wilderness are, in fact, private ranch lands. Much of this ranch country is as wild as any designated wilderness area, and those with local knowledge could take advantage of some of these private holdings, many of which include entire mountain ranges. But be aware that trespassers are not welcome and take care to keep a low profile and stay out of sight. Private land ownership is highly revered in Texas and many ranch owners are opposed to the creation of federal and state reserves that take land out of production and open it up to the public.

But regardless of ownership, these west Texas areas of mountains, canyons, and deserts are in some cases almost as wild today as in the days of the Old West. No description of the Southwest would be complete without including the western part of Texas, especially the incredible canyon country through which the Rio Grande flows in the area of Big Bend National Park.

Canyons of the Rio Grande

The canyon country of the Rio Grande encompasses a huge expanse of roadless wilderness on both the Texas and Mexico sides of the Rio Grande, and the Texas part of this area contains by far the largest area of public land in the western part of the state.

The Rio Grande is a designated National Wild and Scenic River for 196 miles in this part of the 1000-mile-long boundary it forms between Texas and Mexico. In addition, the uninhabited mountain and canyon country north of the river is protected in several large public holdings, including Big Bend National Park, Big Bend Ranch State Park, and Black Gap State Wildlife Area. This amounts to several hundred thousand acres of roadless land north of the border, not to mention close to two million acres on the Mexican side of the river.

This part of Texas is remote and not particularly on the way to anywhere, and as a result, even Big Bend National Park sees relatively little use for its huge size. With a total of more than 800,000 acres of desert backcountry, Big Bend National Park's primary attraction is hiking and backpacking. As in all national parks, hunting is prohibited, but a testament to the remoteness of this area is the fact that it is a favorite smuggling area for both drugs and illegal immigrants, and the Park Service and Border Patrol have not been successful in stopping the flow across the border. In a bug-out situation, a savvy survivalist could elude detection as well. Hunting would be good, with plenty of mule deer, javelina, and small game such as rabbits. A few black bears and mountain lions are the only large animal threats, and of course one should always be wary of rattlesnakes in this kind of terrain.

West of the national park, Big Bend Ranch State Park is the largest state park in Texas, taking in over 300,000 acres of the Chichuahuan Desert, including two mountain ranges, extinct volcanoes such as Solitario Peak, and waterfalls as high as 100 feet. This is a newly acquired state park that was private ranch land until 1988. Many springs and a few perennial streams in these mountains make this harsh desert a viable bug-out location. The southern edge of the state park boundary is the Rio Grande most of the way between Presidio and Lajitas, just upstream of where the national park boundary begins. The park has 66 miles of trails, in addition to primitive roads, so parts of it can be accessed by vehicle, mountain bike, or horseback, as well as on foot, but hiking is still the only way to get to the most rugged sections.

Nearest Cities: *Presidio, Lajitas, Marfa, Boquillas, Alpine, Marathon, Fort Stockton*

Guadalupe Escarpment (also in New Mexico)

The Guadalupe Escarpment is an uplifted limestone reef rising above the Chichuahuan Desert from extreme western Texas north of Van Horn and extending into New Mexico. The mountains making up the Guadalupe Escarpment are laced with caves, including the well-known Carlsbad Caverns in New Mexico and many more remote and little-known caves. The highest point in the range is Guadalupe Peak, which at 8749 feet is also the highest point in Texas. Public lands in the Guadalupes total over 250,000 acres and are managed in several distinct units, including the 46,850-acre Guadalupe Mountains National Park Wilderness Area in Texas and the 33,125-acre Carlsbad Caverns

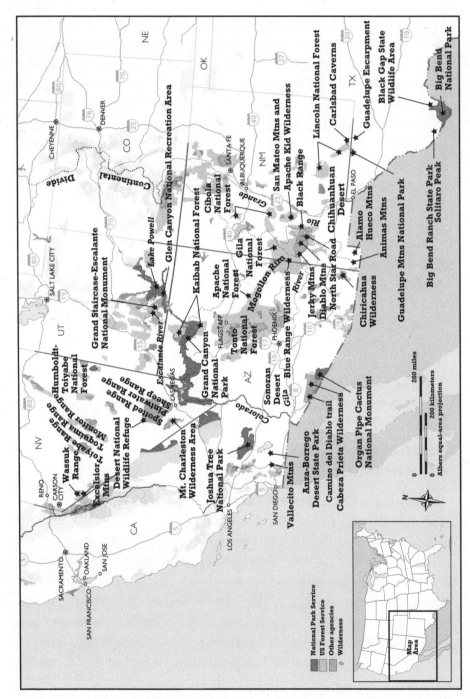

Bug-Out Locations of the Deserts, Canyons, & Mountains of the Southwest

National Park Wilderness Area in New Mexico. Other roadless parts of the Guadalupes are under BLM management or are part of the Lincoln National Forest in New Mexico. Wildlife includes elk, javelina, mule deer, black bear, mountain lions, and exotic Barbary sheep that have colonized much of the area after being released in the 1970s.

Nearest Cities: *Pine Springs, Van Horn, El Paso (TX), Carlsbad (NM)*

New Mexico

New Mexico is a state with an extreme diversity of ecosystems. Within its boundaries, the Great Plains meet the Rocky Mountains, and the Sierra Madres and the Chihauhuan Desert extend from the south in Mexico to meet the Colorado Plateau and the Great Basin in the northwest. New Mexico's bug-out locations include deserts, canyons, river basins, forested slopes, and alpine peaks, and although much of the land is privately owned agricultural or ranch land, the areas that are uninhabited federal lands are outstanding examples of Southwestern wilderness. Perhaps the wildest area of federally owned land in the state is within the huge (three million acre) White Sands Missile Range, which takes in much of the San Andres Mountains and is off-limits to the public. But aside from this, there are several sizable federal wilderness areas, including the first one designated in the United States, and larger tracts of national forest and BLM land.

Gila National Forest, Gila Wilderness Area, and Aldo Leopold Wilderness Area

Located in the lower western part of New Mexico north of Silver City, the Gila National Forest takes in 3.3 million acres in the Black Range and Mogollon Mountains, as well as smaller ranges, and contains two of the finest wilderness areas in the West. This mountain and canyon country is a virtual paradise for outdoor living, with a relatively mild climate and a huge diversity of plant and animal species in several ecosystem types ranging from desert to alpine forest. Human history here goes back to the Mogollon cliff dwellers and later bands of Apaches, including famous war chiefs such as Geronimo, Mangas Colorado, and Victorio. Throughout the remote canyons and slopes of this national forest land, evidence of the Native Americans and early white prospectors and miners can still be seen. Today many parts of the forest can be accessed by hiking and horseback trails, mountain bike trails, off-road vehicle trails, and unpaved forest service roads. But the best parts of the Gila National Forest are the wilderness areas that are closed to mechanized travel.

The Gila Wilderness, established in 1924, is the oldest federally designated wilderness in the United States. It takes in the rugged canyons of the headwaters of the Gila River, as well as the Mogollon, Jerky, and Diablo Mountain Ranges, encompassing a total area of 569,600 acres and making it one of the largest roadless areas in New Mexico. The Gila Wilderness is a supreme bug-out location with a great variety of game animals in abundance, diverse plant and forest communities, and plentiful streams and springs. It was the favorite hideout and hunting ground of modern-day mountain man Martin Price, as described in Chapter One.

If not for a single dirt road, the 127-mile-long North Star Road that runs north and south just east of the Gila Wilderness, the roadless acreage in this area would total over a million acres with the addition of the Aldo Leopold Wilderness that lies on the eastern side of the road. But even with this road's existence, there is little to diminish the wild quality of this part of the Gila National Forest. Driving the North Star Road is an adventure in itself and requires a dependable four-wheel-drive vehicle, as there are creeks to ford, rocks to negotiate, and steep, winding switchbacks. Bugging out anywhere along this road would be feasible, either by camping out of a vehicle or by striking off into wilder territory on foot.

Nearest Cities: Glenwood, Silver City, Mimbres, Truth or Consequences

Apache Kid Wilderness Area

Located in the San Mateo Mountains to the northeast of the Aldo Leopold Wilderness Area, the Apache Kid Wilderness Area was named for a notorious outlaw said to be the last Apache warrior to conduct raids on ranchers and settlers of the region well after the surrender of Geronimo.

Though historians do not all agree, according to the legend he was gunned down in this area of the Cibola National Forest by a posse of cowboys in 1909. The wilderness area named for him would be a good hideout for an outlaw or a modern-day survivalist, as it lies in a rugged area of canyons, steep cliffs, and ridges and ranges in elevation from 6000 feet to 10,325 feet. Water is somewhat limited in the area, with only a few reliable surface locations, but despite this, the mountains support Ponderosa pine forests in the middle elevations and spruce, fir, and aspen forests in the high country. Lower elevations and canyons are wooded with Pinon pine, juniper, cottonwood, live oak, and Arizona alder. Mule deer, elk, wild turkeys, and small game such as rabbits and squirrels are plentiful here. The designated wilderness area itself is relatively small by western standards, at 44,650 acres, but surrounding Cibola National Forest lands bring the core roadless area up to 131,000 acres.

***Nearest Cities:** Datil, Socorro, Truth or Consequences*

Animas Mountains

Located in the extreme southwestern tip or "boot heel" of New Mexico, south of Silver City, the Gila National Forest, and even Interstate 10, the Animas Mountains are within the vast Chihuahuan Desert that extends into this part of the state from Mexico and are also part of the Sierra Madre cordillera. The Animas range is one of the Chihuahuan Desert mountain ranges called "sky islands." These mountain "islands" rising above the surrounding flat desert floor receive more rain than the surrounding area and create a range of micro-habitats that would not be possible here if not for the elevation differences. In this particular range, the highest point is the 8531-foot Animas Peak.

The Animas Mountains are also the southernmost range along the Continental Divide in the United States, which runs right through the center of the range to the Mexican border. Land ownership in the Animas Mountains is a mix of BLM land, state land, and 321,703 acres of private ranch land owned by the Nature Conservancy. Because of their location and the fact that they are contiguous with the Sierra Madre in Mexico, the Animas Mountains are home to several exotic species of birds as well as the occasional transient Mexican wolf and jaguar.

This remote and seldom-visited range does not see much recreational use and, with its diversity of habitats and availability of water and game, could serve as a good bug-out location. Just to the east of the Animas Mountains, and east of Highway 81, another remote range called the Alamo Hueco Mountains makes up the center of a roadless tract of BLM land containing over 200,000 acres. The high point of this range is Big Hatchet Peak, at 8366 feet, and the BLM has proposed a wilderness designation for the area surrounding it. In either of these remote borderlands mountains, you should take precautions to keep a low profile to avoid running into smugglers and other outlaws crossing in from Mexico.

Nearest Cities: *Antelope Wells, Animas, Lordsburg, Deming*

Arizona

Like New Mexico to the east, Arizona is in a region of convergence between several major zones of the North American West: the Sierra Madre and Chichuahuan Desert to the south, the Sonoran and Mojave Deserts to the west, and the Colorado Plateau, Rocky Mountains, and Great Basin to the north. It is a land of red rock deserts, vast Ponderosa pine forests, and some of the most awesome canyons on Earth. Just as Colorado is synonymous to most people with the Rocky Mountains, Arizona, with its deserts of saguaro cactus and red rock buttes, is the first place that comes to mind when the American Southwest is mentioned. Most of the state lives up to the image, with annual rainfall averaging just 12.7 inches, but due to significant elevation differences, ecosystems can vary tremendously within a relatively small area.

While Arizona has huge tourist attractions like the Grand Canyon, which is one of the Seven Natural Wonders of the world, there also vast and little-known wilderness areas hardly anyone visits, such as the desolate Cabeza Prieta National Wildlife Refuge on the southern border and the wild Blue Range Mountains in the east.

Blue Range Wilderness and Primitive Area

The Blue Range Wilderness and Primitive Area is not far west of New Mexico's outstanding Gila Wilderness and is similar in many ways in topography and habitat. But the Blue Range is not as well-known to outsiders as the Gila and receives far fewer visitors in its rugged backcountry. With a roadless area of a half-million acres, the wilderness of the Blue Range is managed under the Apache National Forest in Arizona and the Gila National Forest in New Mexico. The designated "primitive area" is 180,139 acres and is managed essentially the same as national forest wilderness areas.

The Blue Range Wilderness and Primitive Area would be a first-rate bug-out location, with everything to offer from rocky canyon country up to mountain meadows and spruce-fir forest. It is teeming with elk, mule deer, and the largest herd of bighorn sheep in the Southwest. It is also home to a large population of mountain lions, so take care to avoid being surprised by one, especially if traveling alone.

Nearest Cities: *Clifton, Alpine (AZ), Glenwood (NM)*

Chiricahua Wilderness/Coronado National Forest

Located in the extreme southeastern corner of Arizona, south of Interstate 10 and north of the border town of Douglas, one of the large units of the fragmented Coronado National Forest takes in the Chiricahua Mountains. Like the nearby Animas Mountains in New Mexico, this "sky island" range is a northern extension of the Sierra Madre. The Chiricahua Mountains have been a wilderness bug-out location since the days of the Apache wars, when the Chiricahua tribe for which they are named used this mountain stronghold as hideout and base for raids on settlers and attacks on U.S. Army troops.

Today the designated Chiricahua Wilderness is only 87,700 acres, but combined with the additional roadless acreage of the surrounding Coronado National Forest, an area of 300,000 acres of backcountry exists here. Plant and animal life is diverse in the Chiricahuas, and includes many species normally seen much farther south in Mexico. Mountain lions and black bears are common, and a jaguar was killed in the area in 1987. Water is available in most of the canyons and in scattered springs. The few trails that penetrate deep into the Chiricahua Wilderness are rugged and rough.

Nearest Cities: *Douglas, Bisbee, Benson, Wilcox*

Mazatzal Wilderness Area

The designated Mazatzal Wilderness Area, located in central Arizona not far north of Phoenix, is a 251,912-acre protected area within a much larger area of national forest land, including the three-million-acre Tonto National Forest. The Mazatzal Wilderness is a land of brush and Ponderosa pine–covered hills broken by deep canyons and areas of mesas, buttes, and flatlands. The high point of the wilderness is at 7903 feet, on Mazatzal Peak. In the lower elevations, which range as low as 1600 feet, vegetation is typical of the Sonoran Desert, with saguaro cactus, palo verde, and mesquite. In this lower country, the Verde National Wild River cuts through a portion of the desert area of the wilderness, offering one of the few opportunities to access this sort of backcountry by canoe, kayak, or raft. For a distance of about 28 miles, the Verde Trail follows the river as well; this is part of a greater network of about 240 miles of trails in varying degrees of maintenance. Hunting should be good throughout the Mazatzal and beyond in the rest of Tonto National Forest. Most game animals of the Southwest can be found here, especially mule deer and javelina. Mountain lions and black bear are also common, as well as rattlesnakes.

Nearest Cities: Payson, Camp Verde, Cave Creek, Phoenix

Cabeza Prieta Wilderness Area

The Cabeza Prieta Wilderness Area is part of a huge expanse of un-inhabited Sonoran Desert along the Mexican border in southwestern Arizona. The designated wilderness alone protects 803,418 acres of this pristine area, making it the state's largest, but the greater roadless backcountry totals more than 1.6 million acres and includes the Organ Pipe Cactus National Monument to the east. Much of this area is uninhabited for good reason, as it is extremely arid, with 2 to 12 inches of rainfall each year and daytime temperatures of over 100 degrees. But despite the conditions, wildlife adapted to the environment thrives in this remote desert, including desert bighorn sheep, pronghorn antelope, javelina, jack rabbits, and a large variety of lizards, snakes, and birds.

The Cabeza Prieta is a harsh place to bug out to, but part of it can be accessed by four-wheel-drive trails, including what's left of the Camino del Diablo trail that claimed the lives of many frontier-era travelers. This is not a place to go unless you have a means of carrying plenty of water or possess truly expert-level desert survival skills. One viable option for foot travel here would be traveling with goats, the way Jim Corbett, the author of *Goatwalking*, advocates as mentioned in Chapter One of this book. Despite the risk of dying of thirst, this huge, waterless desert provides many tempting routes for illegal border crossings into the U.S. from Mexico.

Nearest Cities: *Lukeville, Ajo, Gila Bend, Aztec, Yuma*

Kaibab National Forest/Grand Canyon National Park

The other largest roadless area in the state of Arizona is at the opposite end, in the far north-central region where the Colorado River carves its way through some of the most spectacular canyons on earth. This area includes Grand Canyon National Park, Kaibab National Forest, and BLM and Indian reservation land for a total of 2.7 million acres of roadless backcountry, much of it extremely remote and difficult to access. Despite the popularity of Grand Canyon National Park with tourists who come for the views and to go whitewater rafting through the canyon, hundreds of thousands of acres both in the park and in the surrounding national forests are rarely visited and range from places that can only be reached by technical climbing to miles of little used forest-service roads. Habitats range from mesquite and cactus in the low elevations, to sagebrush plains and pine-covered hills in the middle elevations, all the way to forests of spruce, fir, and aspen on the canyon's North Rim. Throughout the area surrounding the canyon and away from the developed tourist areas there are excellent possibilities for bug-out locations with ample game and water and little chance of being discovered.

Nearest Cities: *Jacob Lake, Page, Desert View, Grand Canyon, Williams, Flagstaff*

Southern Utah

The canyon country of the Colorado Plateau extends across the border from Arizona into the southern part of Utah, where some of the most interesting landscapes in the Southwest can be found, including isolated buttes, pinnacles, mesas, natural bridges and arches, slot canyons, and grottoes carved into the limestone slickrock. Parts of southern Utah are so remote that they were the last unexplored region in the lower 48 states, and today this area of the Southwest still has much to offer someone looking for an inaccessible wilderness bug-out location. Some of the obscure canyons in this area are hidden away from the outside world, yet offer water, shelter, and plant and animal food in abundance despite the surrounding inhospitable desert. This canyon country is vast and under varied ownership, from national park lands to Indian reservation lands. Two of the biggest tracts of public roadless areas are discussed in the following sections.

Grand Staircase–Escalante National Monument

Grand Staircase–Escalante National Monument is a huge tract of land managed mostly as wilderness by the BLM and was created fairly recently, in 1996, despite much local opposition. The total acreage within Escalante comes to 1.9 million acres in three distinct areas: the Grand Staircase, the Kaiparowits, and the Canyons of the Escalante. Throughout this huge area there are many different types of habitat ranging from sagebrush and grassland to forests of stunted pine and juniper, and riparian forests of cottonwood and willow along the Escalante River. Other areas within the monument are waterless desert and slickrock. Wildlife includes most Southwest inhabitants, such as mule deer, pronghorn antelope, elk, desert bighorn sheep, and mountain lions.

It would be hard to find a more remote hideout location than some of the seldom-visited parts of the Grand Staircase–Escalante National Monument. Solitude can be had here in abundance, and because of that the area does attract hard-core hikers, but with all the options and room to roam, you won't find crowds here. Some of the lands within the national monument that are not managed as wilderness do have off-road vehicle access, so hiking is not the only means of bugging out here, unless you are heading to the most remote canyons.

Nearest Cities: *Escalante, Tropic, Kanab, Big Water, Cedar City*

Glen Canyon National Recreation Area

Glen Canyon National Recreation Area takes in 1.2 million acres of canyon country and lakeshore around the huge, man-made Lake Powell, an impoundment of the Colorado River. With over 1900 miles of shoreline created by the lake in the unlikely setting of a desert canyonland, this national recreation area offers unique bug-out opportunities by boat. An array of coves and bays were created when these canyons were filled, and today they offer miles of winding and branching waterways, allowing you transport more gear and supplies afloat than you could possibly carry into this remote desert country on foot. In good weather, recreational boaters use the lake in large numbers, exploring it in everything from houseboats to kayaks. But there are always shallow areas up in the ends of some of the canyons where a light vessel like a kayak or canoe can be paddled, then pulled from sight into the rocks or over a ridge. Hiking trails also lead into the backcountry of the park away from the lake.

Fishing is popular in Lake Powell, which is stocked with such species as striped bass, walleye, bream, and trout, and the lakeshore environment creates a habitat for many species of reptiles, amphibians, shorebirds, and waterfowl. The surrounding lands are home to rabbits, prairie dogs, mule deer, pronghorn antelope, and desert bighorn sheep.

Nearest Cities: *Hite Marina, Bullfrog Marina, Hall's Crossing Marina (UT), Wahweap Marina, Page (AZ)*

Nevada

Although Nevada is not particularly known for its wilderness and outdoor recreation opportunities, except for the Lake Tahoe area it shares with California, it does in fact contain large uninhabited areas—most of which are desolate landscapes of barren mountains, sagebrush plains, and empty desert. Much of Nevada is part of the Great Basin Desert created by the rain shadow of the Sierra Nevada and the Cascades that blocks clouds from the Pacific and captures moisture so that it never reaches these empty expanses that lie between those West Coast mountain ranges and the Rockies. Southern Nevada is part of the extremely hot Mojave Desert that extends into California. Isolated mountain ranges in this desert region rise to elevations high enough to support diverse forests, much like the Sky Islands of the Chiricahua Desert in southern Arizona and New Mexico.

Desert National Wildlife Refuge

Just to the northwest of the glitz of Las Vegas, several outstanding areas of roadless Nevada wilderness can be found in a series of these Mojave Desert mountain ranges, particularly within the Desert National Wildlife Refuge, which at 1.6 million acres is the biggest national wildlife refuge in the lower 48 states. And huge as it is, it is only a part of a greater complex of federal lands, including smaller wildlife refuges and military test and training sites. Habitats here range from desert shrub, yucca, Joshua tree, and various cacti in the lower elevations to juniper, pine, and sagebrush in the mid-elevations and coniferous forests above 7000 feet. Around 10,000 feet, the bristlecone pine is the dominant species. The refuge was primarily designated to provide protection for the desert bighorn sheep, as the largest population of them in North America can be found here, but many areas in the mountains also offer good habitat for mule deer, pronghorn antelope, mountain lions, and a variety of smaller animals and birds.

Individual ranges within this area include the Sheep Range, with elevations from 2500 to 9750 feet and a single roadless area of 468,000 acres, the Desert-Pintwater Range, which includes 467,000 roadless acres and elevations from 3200 feet to 6400 feet, and the Spotted Range, which also runs from 3200 feet to 6300 feet and contains 354,000 acres of roadless wilderness.

Nearest Cities: *Las Vegas, Indian Springs, Rachel, Alamo*

Toiyabe National Forest

Toiyabe National Forest is managed jointly with the Humboldt National Forest to create a single Toiyabe-Humboldt National Forest totaling 6.3 million acres. Over half of that acreage is in the Toiyabe, which is spread across several separate units in central and southern Nevada. The southernmost unit lies just west of Las Vegas and south of the

Desert National Wildlife Refuge, in the Spring Mountains. In this area the Mt. Charleston Wilderness Area takes in a large roadless area surrounding Charleston Peak, which towers 11,919 feet above the Mojave Desert. The designated wilderness area totals 43,000 acres, but is part of a greater roadless area of 200,000 acres, separated by only a dirt road from another 180,000 acres of roadless wilderness surrounding Mt. Stirling.

Other units of the Toiyabe National Forest are located in central Nevada in the Monitor Range, the Toquima Range, and the Toiyabe Range. Another unit borders California in the area of the Excelsior Mountains and the Wassuk Range southeast of Carson City. Many of these isolated units of national forest land contain primitive roads as well as trails, and remote parts of them can be accessed in a variety of vehicles, or on horseback or on foot.

Nearest Cities: *Las Vegas, Tonopah, Austin, Hawthorne, Carson City*

California

The high mountain country and rugged coastal areas of California will be the subject of much of the next chapter. But California is an incredibly diverse state in terms of geography, and while the northern regions have areas of rain-soaked forest, giant virgin timber, and snowy alpine peaks, much of California has more in common with the desert Southwest. In fact, the driest, hottest, and most barren desert in the United States can be found in California. A huge part of eastern and southeastern California, from the Great Basin south to the Mojave and Colorado Deserts, is a sparsely populated wasteland hardly fit for human habitation. Because of this, many large military training grounds and firing ranges are found there. But sprinkled throughout this harsh environment are a few wild places on public lands that could support a knowledgeable survivalist in a desperate situation, at least for the short term. In this kind of desert where water is so scarce, long-term living off the land will be difficult. For shorter periods of bug-out emergencies, getting out to one of these desert areas by four-wheel-drive or other means that will allow you to carry an adequate a supply of water would be a feasible option. The next sections will cover just a couple of big roadless areas in this part of California to give you an idea of what's available.

Joshua Tree National Park

Joshua Tree National Park contains almost 800,000 acres, with 429,690 acres of that designated as wilderness. The remote parts of the wilderness area can only be reached by hiking or on horseback, but outside the wilderness area there is a network of off-road vehicle routes. There are a few naturally occurring oases in the park where surface water can be found, and of course, wildlife is concentrated in these areas. Desert bighorn sheep are especially abundant here. Other wildlife includes coyotes, jackrabbits, and such desert reptiles as the sidewinder. Much of the park is barren rock and desert with forests of Joshua trees, for which it is named. Where water occurs there are isolated plant species such as the desert fan palm.

Nearest Cities: Twentynine Palms, Eagle Mountain, Indio, Palm Springs

Vallecito Mountains/Anza-Borrego Desert State Park

This mountain range located within the Anza-Borrego Desert State Park east of San Diego contains over 200,000 acres of roadless wilderness at its core, including several designated wilderness areas. The entire park contains 600,000 acres, making it the largest state park in California. Outside the wilderness areas, 500 miles of dirt roads and over 100 miles of trails provide access to the backcountry in the park. This mountain wilderness, while still harsh and dry, would likely be more conducive to living off the land in a bug-out situation than most of the barren areas of southern California, such as the above-mentioned Joshua Tree National Park. The Vallecito Mountains contain elevations from sea level to 5300 feet, and though water is scarce, wildlife includes bighorn sheep and mule deer, as well as desert reptiles such as rattlesnakes and lizards and small mammals and birds.

Nearest Cities: Borrego Springs, Julian, Descanso, San Diego

12

PACIFIC CREST MOUNTAINS & THE WEST COAST
CALIFORNIA, OREGON, AND WASHINGTON

Just as in the Appalachian Corridor and East Coast Regions, the wilderness areas of the Pacific Crest and West Coast are not far from some of the largest population centers in the nation. Seattle, Portland, San Francisco, and Los Angeles are all within easy reach of a complex of coastal and interior mountains connecting Canada to Mexico. In addition, many parts of the rocky Pacific coast in California, Oregon, and Washington have been protected from human development by their inaccessibility and by inclusion in federal and state-owned parks and forests.

As in the Rocky Mountains, the natural areas of the West Coast states offer stunning natural beauty on a grand scale, drawing throngs of people out of the cities to engage in outdoor pursuits. Wilderness adventure is popular here, and just as in the Appalachians, there is a long-distance trail, the Pacific Crest Trail, which traverses the entire length of the region from Mexico to Canada, passing through some of the most scenic spots in the nation on its 2650-mile route. Some popular areas here are overcrowded, as is to be expected, but despite this, the wild lands of the West Coast region are so vast that there would be little difficulty finding a suitably remote place to disappear intentionally if need be.

This part of North America is more diverse in terms of geography and ecosystems than any of the other regions described in this book. It is a land of contrasts, with everything from the lowest point in the lower

48 states to the highest peak, as well as volcanoes and expansive ranges
of jagged, snow-capped mountains. Here, you will find the largest trees
on the planet and vast tracts of temperate rainforest, but also the some
of the driest and most desolate deserts in North America. Combine this
with 1293 miles of ocean coastline and 7863 miles of tidal shoreline, including offshore and estuarine islands, and it's easy to see that bugging
out in this West Coast region can mean a lot of different things.

Pacific Coast Bug-Out Essentials

Weather and Climate

Overall, nature in this region is relatively benign, which is a big part of
the reason the human population is so large here. The parts of California
with a mild, Mediterranean climate and the parts of the Northwest with
good harbors and mild winters were the first places European settlers
built towns and cities, finding out what the Native Americans already
knew about how the living could be easy here. But today, the uninhabited parts of this region are mostly in the difficult areas of rugged
mountains, scorching deserts, and frigid alpine slopes. Along the coast
and in the coastal mountains, some significant tracts of temperate rainforest remain; temperatures are mild in these areas, but the rain, fog,
and perpetual dampness can take some getting used to. In the mountain areas, the weather is usually similar to that of the Rocky Mountain
region, which is to say it is quite changeable and good clothing and
gear will be required. In the drier parts of this region, desert conditions similar to those of the Southwest prevail, and protection from the
sun and an adequate water supply will be top priorities.

Like the Rocky Mountain region and the Southwest, parts of the
West Coast region where the mountains are dry and often windswept
are subject to large and furious wildfires, both natural in origin and
caused by man. Other potential disasters in this region are earth-
quakes, volcano eruptions, and along the Pacific Coast, tsunamis.

Land and Resources

In most parts of this region, the largest cities and densest human populations are along the coastline. But unlike the East and Gulf coasts of the

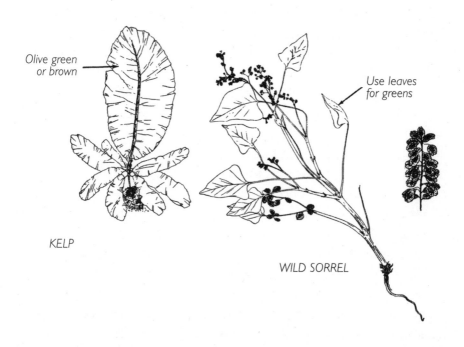

Olive green or brown

Use leaves for greens

KELP

WILD SORREL

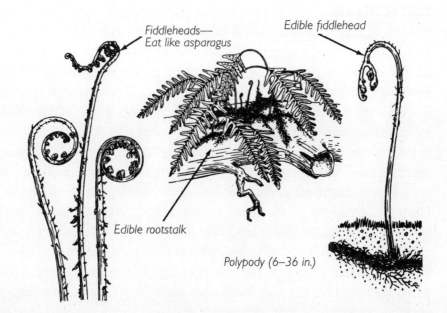

Fiddleheads— Eat like asparagus

Edible fiddlehead

Edible rootstalk

Polypody (6–36 in.)

EDIBLE FERNS

United States, with their broad expanses of flat coastal plains, the West Coast has a rugged topography that extends in many places right to the beaches of the Pacific. Many of the coastal cities that are built in valleys are within sight of substantial roadless areas of uninhabited wilderness in the nearby mountains. Some of these mountains are largely desert and open grasslands, while others, especially in the northern part of the region, are densely forested with evergreens. Just as in the Appalachians, the lush forests of the Coast Range are so thick in many areas that a large tract of land is not necessary for one to simply disappear, whether on purpose or by accident. For years, small planes have crashed in remote parts of the Cascades and the Sierra Nevada, never to be found, and the legendary skyjacker D.B. Cooper bailed out of a 727 airliner over the Oregon wilderness with a bag full of money and was never seen again, despite massive searches on the ground for his body or a trace of his parachute. In fact, the forests here, are so mysterious that legends persist to this day of unknown species—particularly the hairy, man-like primate known as Sasquatch, or "Bigfoot."

Edible Plants

The West Coast region is one of the most diverse in North America in terms of habitat and plant species. Many crossover species common to other regions can be found here, but others unique to the shores of the Pacific add to the forager's options in this region. The seashores, coastal forests, high mountain areas, and deserts all have their unique offerings, and as always, further study of specific species likely to be found in your nearest bug-out location is recommended. A partial list of what you might be able to forage for here includes kelp and dulce (from the sea), beach strawberry, Hottentot fig (a now-wild import from Africa), Oregon crab apple, black walnut, hazelnut, acorns (from several varieties of oaks), sierra plum, mountain ash (berries), hackberry, manzanita (fruits), madrone (berries), jojoba (nuts), gooseberry, huckleberry, crow berry, wild grapes, silver buffalo berry, blackberry, hawthorn (berries), pinon and Ponderosa pine (nuts), bush chinquapin (nuts), sunflower, Indian potato, miner's lettuce, Indian rice, grass (seeds), crowfoot grass (seeds), palo verde (seeds), quackgrass (seeds), amaranth, wild onion, balsam root, winter cress, black mustard, shepard's purse, squaw root, mountain sorrel, redwood sorrel, fern fiddleheads, prickly pear, cattail, and dandelion.

Hunting and Fishing

Wildlife is plentiful and diverse in the West Coast region, both in the backcountry and in surprisingly tame areas where the suburbs are encroaching farther and farther into good habitat. Big game animals in

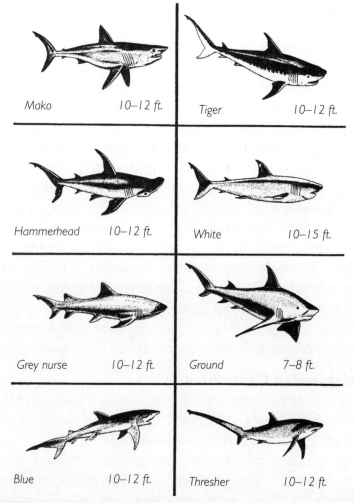

Mako	10–12 ft.	Tiger	10–12 ft.
Hammerhead	10–12 ft.	White	10–15 ft.
Grey nurse	10–12 ft.	Ground	7–8 ft.
Blue	10–12 ft.	Thresher	10–12 ft.

Several species of sharks, including the dangerous great white, can sometimes be found along the Pacific Coast.

this region include whitetail deer, blacktail deer, mule deer, elk, moose, mountain goats, bighorn sheep, and wild pigs descended from domestic stock. Small game includes cottontail rabbits, jackrabbits, snowshoe hare, beavers, muskrats, wild turkeys, sage grouse, and many varieties of waterfowl. The Pacific Coast ecosystem adds a tremendous variety of fish and aquatic animals to the possibilities for living off the land here. The sounds, estuaries, and coastal waters abound with saltwater fish, shellfish, crustaceans, and marine mammals.

Wildlife Hazards

Potential wildlife hazards in the mountains of the Pacific Crest and the coastal regions of the West Coast are much the same as in most of the Rockies and the Southwest. Black bears and mountain lions are the most common large predators, as grizzly bears are no longer found in this region. A few wolves are also making a comeback in Oregon and Washington. Because of increasing contact with humans, there have been mountain lion and black bear attacks in all three of the West Coast states in recent years. Mountain lions in particular have become bold in regard to humans and more attacks have occurred here than in other regions; however, they do not like prey that fights back, so attacks are generally not fatal. Other than big predators, dangerous wildlife here includes rattlesnakes, which are present in all three of these states, especially at lower elevations and in the desert regions. In Southern California, other small, dangerous creatures common to the Southwest can be found, including scorpions. In the coastal waters of the Pacific, sharks occasionally attack humans, and the most dangerous of them all, the great white, can sometimes be found close to shore along this coast.

Recommended Equipment

In a region so diverse, the appropriate gear for traveling outdoors can vary a lot depending on the specific location. In the major mountain areas such the Sierras and the Cascades, conditions will be much the same as in the high country of the Rockies, which means you will have to be prepared for frigid temperatures, high winds, snow, and blizzard conditions. Travel in the wilderness here will mostly be on foot or horseback, though some areas can be reached by various vehicles along forest service and other roads. In the soggy rainforests of the coastal mountains in the northwest part of the region, staying dry will be a primary concern, so shelter and clothing should be selected accordingly. It will also be important here to have the skills and tools to enable you to reliably build a fire in wet conditions.

The coastal areas, sounds, and islands of this area are ideal for bugging out by boat, and some of the best areas cannot be reached any other way. Sea kayaks are popular here, and with good reason, as they can land on surfbound, rocky beaches other boats cannot safely approach. Other parts of the West Coast region have hot, dry climates with desert conditions that mirror the Southwest. Some of the big desert areas can be reached by off-road vehicle. With a variety of small game and birds available to hunt, a .22 rifle is ideal for survival hunting here. A larger-caliber rifle would be a good addition for deer and for defense against black bears or mountain lions, or you could choose an adequate handgun for all defensive purposes, including two-legged aggressors. Be advised that California has more restrictions on handguns than most states. It's especially critical here to know the state and local-level firearms laws, and be aware that they are always subject to change.

◆ ◆ ◆

California may have the largest human population of any state, but it still has vast areas of undeveloped and uninhabited land, including six million acres of designated wilderness. California is such a large and diverse state that it is impractical to lump together all the potential bug-out locations in one place. For the purposes of this chapter, I will divide California into three sections: the coast, the Sierra Nevada Range, and the far northern section that includes the northern Coast Ranges and south end of the Cascades. A fourth major area of California is the Mojave Desert region mentioned in the previous chapter on the Southwest. While not every area of the state fits neatly into these arbitrary divisions, these sections do include most of the largest and most remote areas that could serve as potential bug-out locations.

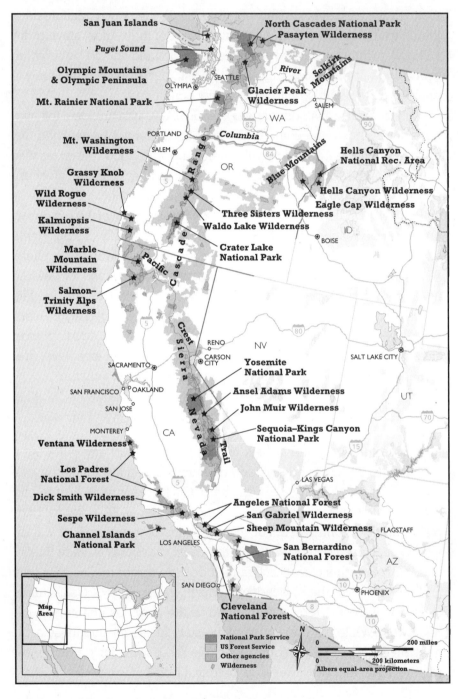

Bug-Out Locations of the Pacific Crest Mountains & the West Coast

Central and Southern Coastal California

The areas discussed in this section are located along the California coast from as far north as Monterey all the way down to the border with Mexico in the south.

Los Padres, Angeles, San Bernardino, and Cleveland National Forests

A glance at a map of California shows a long swath of green that represents national forest land stretching along much of the coastal mountain ranges from near Monterey to San Diego. The various units of these four national forests collectively total more the three and half million acres of public lands near some of the largest population centers in the state. While certainly not as wild and remote as the big wilderness areas of the Sierra Nevada to the north or the deserts to the east, these national forest lands offer a variety of mountainous hideaways that can be quickly reached from the teeming cities of the coast. Despite the proximity to so many people, they are home to lots of wildlife, including deer, black bears, and mountain lions. Within these national forests are several designated wilderness areas totaling 876,012 acres. They include the 41,883-acre Sheep Mountain Wilderness, the 36,118-acre San Gabriel Wilderness, the 64,800-acre Dick Smith Wilderness, the 219,700-acre Sespe Wilderness, and the 240,026-acre Ventana Wilderness described below.

Nearest Cities: San Diego, San Bernardino, Los Angeles, Oxnard, Santa Barbara, San Luis Obispo

Ventana Wilderness

Located in a separate ranger district of the Los Padres National Forest to the north of the swath of public lands described above, the 240,026-acre Ventana Wilderness is situated in the coastal Santa Lucia Mountains south of Monterey, in California's Big Sur region. It is unique in its size and proximity to the ocean, as it begins just east of Highway 1, the boundary in some places coming within a quarter-mile of the coast. The Ventana Wilderness is a rugged area of chaparral, oak woodlands, and stands of redwood and Ponderosa pine and fir. This coastal wilderness receives up to 100 inches of rain annually in some areas, and supports large communities of wildlife, including mule deer, wild boars, and a dense population of the mountain lions that hunt them.

Approximately 260 miles of hiking trails wind through the Ventana Wilderness, but the going is tough in this steep terrain. Few hikers venture off-trail here, so doing so would enable you to find good hideaways in the precipitous V-shaped valleys. Elevations range from 600 feet along the Big Sur Wild and Scenic River to 5862 feet at the highest peak in the range.

Nearest Cities: Big Sur, Monterey, Soledad, Cambria

Channel Islands National Park

Anacapa Island, the easternmost of a chain of islands making up Channel Islands National Park, is approximately 12 miles offshore across Santa Barbara Channel from the closest point on the crowded Southern California coast. Channel Island National Park totals 249,354 acres of isolated mountain and seashore habitat on several islands stretching west from Anacapa. This chain of undeveloped and lightly visited islands could offer a refuge a world apart from the congested mainland for those who have boats that can make the crossing. Most of the island land in this park was privately owned and used as hunting and ranch lands prior to the establishment of the national park in 1980. Today, the park service is working on designating a large part of the national park as wilderness areas. This will mean eliminating old roads or converting them back to trails, making the rugged backcountry of grasslands, chaparral, and pine forests of the islands even more inaccessible. Whether you want to explore the interior of the islands or remain along the coast, Channel Islands National Park offers isolated places to anchor a larger vessel or beach small boats like sea kayaks. Fishing, coastal foraging, and hunting in the interior would all be viable means of survival on these islands in a real SHTF scenario.

Nearest Cities: Santa Barbara, Ventura, Oxnard, Los Angeles

The Sierra Nevada Range

The Sierra Nevada range, which covers most of the eastern part of California north of the Mojave Desert, contains vast areas of uninhabited land as well as numerous national parks and wilderness areas.

Yosemite National Park

Located in the heart of California's Sierra Nevada Range, Yosemite National Park is the northern end of the largest contiguous roadless area in California. This area of the High Sierra totals almost three million acres of roadless wilderness from Yosemite south to Sequoia–King's Canyon National Park, second in size in the lower 48 only to the Frank Church River of No Return Wilderness described in Chapter Ten. It is here, from where Highway 120 crosses Yosemite at Tioga Pass, that the longest straight-line distance between roads in the lower 48 states can be found: 150 miles south from Tioga Pass to Bald Mountain.

Yosemite is certainly one of America's most popular and most visited national parks, but the vast majority of park visitors flock to Yosemite Valley for the spectacular scenery. Within the park boundaries, there are approximately 400,000 acres of less-traveled wilderness area to the north and about 300,000 acres to the south. There are still approximately 225,000 acres of old-growth forest in these areas. Yosemite is also surrounded by a buffer zone of national forest lands, including several national forest wilderness areas—especially to the south, where they continue as a roadless corridor, as described below.

Nearest Cities: Yosemite Village, Lee Vining, Merced, Modesto

Ansel Adams Wilderness Area/John Muir Wilderness Area

The 231,533-acre Ansel Adams Wilderness Area adjoins the southeastern boundary of Yosemite National Park along the crest of the Sierra Nevada. Much of the Ansel Adams Wilderness is high country, above the tree line, with open meadows and glacial lakes. This area gets a lot of recreational use because of the scenery and the fact that the Pacific Crest Trail and John Muir Trail pass through along the high mountain ridges, but many of the lower-elevation areas are heavily forested and largely neglected. As always in popular wilderness areas, these off-trail drainages and slopes will be the best way to get away from other wilderness travelers.

Where the Ansel Adams Wilderness boundary ends, the much larger John Muir Wilderness picks up, taking in a 100-mile stretch of the Sierras and adding another designated tract of 584,000 acres to this vast complex of pristine mountain country. Elevations in the John Muir Wilderness range from 4000 feet to a high point of 14,505 on Mt. Whitney—the highest point in the lower 48 states. This range of elevations makes this a diverse area of habitats, changing from ice and rock down to forests of lodgepole pine, fir, and cedar. Like the Ansel Adams Wilderness and Yosemite National Park, the John Muir Wilderness is popular and the main trails, such as the John Muir Trail, receive heavy traffic from hikers. (As a result, there are more regulations here than in most national forest wilderness areas; backcountry permits, similar to those issued in national parks, are required.) Still, you can be assured that in an area of this much acreage, there are many potential bug-out locations where no one will bother looking for you. Getting off-trail into some of the lower country, especially in the national forest lands outside the arbitrary "wilderness" boundary, is the way to avoid people. As in most of the High Sierra, bighorn sheep, deer, mountain lions, and black bear are common here, and the mountain lakes abound with trout.

Nearest Cities: *Mammoth Lakes, Mono Hot Springs, Bishop, Fresno*

Sequoia–Kings Canyon National Park

Located in the southern part of the long stretch of roadless lands straddling the Sierra Nevada, Sequoia–Kings Canyon National Park adds 866,952 acres of national park land to the wilderness complex. The eastern boundary of these two adjoining parks lies adjacent to the western border of the elongated John Muir Wilderness Area described above. The western slopes of Mt. Whitney fall within this park boundary. Also found in this park are natural wonders such as the great sequoia trees, including the single tree that is said to be the largest on the planet, and Kings Canyon, which some claim is the deepest canyon in

North America. (Others say that Kings Canyon is actually a river gorge, formed by faulting, unlike Oregon and Idaho's Hells Canyon, which was formed by water erosion. At any rate, both of these are deeper than 8000 feet, and far surpass the Grand Canyon for depth.)

Like Yosemite to the north, Sequoia-Kings Canyon is an old park and is popular with tourists. Even so, there are huge areas within the park boundaries that lack even foot trails, and even some areas that do have trails receive little foot traffic. There are many opportunities for off-trail bushwhacking in the various drainages. The Disappearing Creek Canyon, known as Enchanted Gorge, is said to be perhaps the most remote drainage in all the Sierra Nevada.

Nearest Cities: *Giant Forest Village, Hume, Three Rivers, Fresno, Bakersfield*

Northern California
Coast Range and Cascades

In northwestern California, two major ranges, the Cascades and the parallel Coast Range, contain many tracts of remote wilderness lands that stretch north through Oregon to Washington. Several expansive national forests cover much of these mountain ranges in California, including the 2.2-million-acre Shasta-Trinity National Forest (California's largest) and the 1.7-million-acre Klamath National Forest. Aside from these two first-rate wilderness areas discussed below, keep in mind that the huge complex of national forest lands outside wilderness area boundaries offers many more options for bug-out locations in areas that receive little use. Some of the backcountry here can be reached with various motor vehicles, ATVs, or mountain bikes. Other large areas of public land in Northern California can be found east of the Cascades, especially in the 1.6-million-acre Modoc National Forest.

Salmon–Trinity Alps Wilderness Area

At 517,000 acres, the Trinity Alps Wilderness Area is the second-largest designated wilderness in California, but is part of a greater roadless area in the Klamath Mountains totaling 620,000 acres.

The Trinity Alps Wilderness has a lot of diversity of ecosystems, with high peaks of over 9000 feet and low elevations of just 1360 feet. The lower-elevation areas of the western part of the wilderness, called the "Green Trinities," are where you are likely to find the best bug-out locations and have the best chance of avoiding recreational hikers. This area of heavy coniferous forest will also have milder temperatures and more game. Black bear and deer are common in these forest areas, most of the lakes within the wilderness have been stocked with trout, and the rivers and streams contain steelhead and some Chinook salmon.

Nearest Cities: *Willow Creek, Weaverville, Eureka, Redding*

Marble Mountain Wilderness Area

Marble Mountain Wilderness Area is a 241,744-acre roadless area north of the Trinity Alps in the Klamath Mountains. Much of the forest is old-growth conifers, with 21 distinct species of firs, pines, hemlocks, and spruce. Thirty-two miles of the Pacific Crest Trail traverse the Marble Mountain Wilderness, but a huge area of the southwestern part of the wilderness is devoid of trails and could be the wildest place in all of Northern California. These dark, rainy evergreen forests in the deep valleys are mysterious places, and it is little wonder that the legend of Bigfoot persists in the big Pacific Northwest wilderness areas even today. Whether there are unknown creatures or not, there is certainly plenty of wildlife, including elk, blacktail deer, and one of the densest populations of black bear in California. Eighty-nine lakes dot the Marble Mountain Wilderness Area; most are well stocked with trout. The larger streams also contain steelhead and salmon.

Nearest Cities: *Somes Bar, Sawyers Bar, Etna, Yreka*

Oregon

Oregon is split north and south by two major mountain ranges, the Cascades and the Coast Range, which run the length of the state from California to Washington and define the climate between the lush temperate rainforests of the western part of the state and the dry basins and deserts of the east. The awesome coastal rainforests of

Oregon and Washington once totaled more than 19 million acres of giant trees up to 300 feet tall and 1000 years old. Soaked by rain and fog from the Pacific Ocean, these cathedral forests were like no place on Earth, with their lush understories of fungus and moss. Today only a few scattered remnants remain, some protected as wilderness areas or in national parks. For all its diversity of geography and ecosystems, Oregon has comparatively few large roadless areas for a western state, but some of the uninhabited areas that do remain could make excellent bug-out locations.

Kalmiopsis Wilderness Area/Rogue River– Siskiyou National Forest

In the southwestern corner of Oregon and the northwest corner of California, the Siskiyou Mountains connect the Coast Range with the Cascades. This is the richest area of the Northwest in terms of botanical diversity, and the forests here are second only to those in parts of the Appalachians as the most diverse in the United States. Twenty-eight species of conifers make up these old-growth forests, which receive 100 inches of rain per year. Within Oregon's expansive Rogue River– Siskiyou National Forest complex, which totals 1.8 million acres, the 179,755-acre Kalmiopsis Wilderness Area is part of a greater roadless area of 408,000 acres. Elevations in the Kalmiopsis range from under 300 feet to more than 5000. The wilderness area contains the headwaters of several rivers, which begin here as rushing streams flowing through rugged canyons. In 2002, the largest forest fire in Oregon's recorded history burned through virtually all of the Kalmiopsis Wilderness, but in the larger scheme of things, such fires are part of the natural cycle, and though different in appearance today, the wilderness remains wild and regeneration began almost immediately.

Several other wilderness areas are scattered through the Rogue River–Siskiyou National Forest, including the 35,818-acre Wild Rogue Wilderness, which was designated to protect much of the 84-mile Wild and Scenic River section of the Rogue River. It lies north of the Kalmiopsis Wilderness and contains much of the same diverse coastal forest habitat. Closer to the coast, the 17,200-acre Grassy Knob

Wilderness takes in an area of old-growth Port Orford cedar and Douglas fir, and includes the watershed of the Elk River, which is rich in salmon and cutthroat trout.

***Nearest Cities:** Brookings, Gold Beach, Port Orford, Agness, Grants Pass*

Oregon's Cascade Range

Much of the Cascade Range that parallels Oregon's coast inland of the Coast Range is contained within several separate national forests and thus comprises a huge region of public lands with varying degrees of accessibility, ranging from roadless wilderness to areas of highly contested logging operations.

At the southern end of Oregon's Cascades, a separate unit of the Rogue River–Siskiyou National Forest discussed above includes a significant wilderness area, the 113,590-acre Sky Lakes Wilderness, which lies south of Crater Lake National Park. This wilderness area contains more than 200 lakes and small ponds in a forested mountain setting ranging from 3800 feet to 9495 feet. It is home to herds of elk and plenty of mountain lions and black bears.

Crater Lake National Park is best known, of course, for its centerpiece, the six-mile-wide Crater Lake. This is the deepest lake in the United States, its exceptionally clear water filling the collapsed cone of an extinct volcano. But aside from the lake itself, the park lands surrounding the lake totals 180,000 acres, 90 percent of which is maintained as wilderness. The Pacific Crest Trail passes through the park, and all the lands surrounding its borders are part of the national forest network that covers the Cascades.

Farther north in the central part of the range, the Three Sisters Wilderness Area, at 285,202 acres, is the second-largest designated wilderness area in Oregon, and part of a greater roadless area totaling 424,000 acres in Deschutes National Forest and Willamette National Forest. Named for the volcano peaks called the Three Sisters, this wilderness is located along the crest of the Cascade Mountains and is traversed by 40 miles of the Pacific Crest Trail. It is rugged and steep, with elevations from 2000 to over 10,000 feet in a relatively small area. The largest tract of old-growth virgin forest in Oregon is located in the western half of the Three Sisters Wilderness. This western side of the range is wet and mostly forested in Douglas fir. It is home to elk, mule deer, blacktail deer, and black bear. The eastern side of the wilderness, on the drier side of the Cascade Range, is mainly forested in Ponderosa pine. This side of the wilderness area also adjoins the 39,202-acre Waldo Lake Wilderness area that surrounds most of Waldo Lake, one of the purest natural lakes in the world, and the second-largest in Oregon.

Only State Highway 242 separates the Three Sisters Wilderness Area from another roadless tract to the north—the 52,516-acre Mount Washington Wilderness, which is also along the route of the Pacific Crest Trail. This is also an area of high, volcanic cones, alpine lakes, and evergreen forests. Continuing north through the Cascades to the Washington state line, there are several more areas of designated wilderness as well as millions of acres of national forest lands and Indian reservation lands.

Nearest Cities: *Medford, Fort Klamath, Oakridge, Bend, Sweet Home*

Eagle Cap Wilderness Area

Oregon's largest designated wilderness is not found in either the Coast Range or the Cascades, but rather in the northeastern part of the state in the Wallowa Mountains. The Eagle Cap Wilderness Area encompasses 361,446 acres of high meadows, alpine lakes, and heavily forested valleys. Beyond the wilderness area boundaries, the total roadless area comes to 450,000 acres, including parts of the surrounding Wallowa-Whitman National Forest. The lakes and streams of the area are full of trout, and four wild and scenic rivers originate in the Eagle Cap.

This mountain ecosystem with elevations from 2800 feet to just under 10,000 feet has more in common with the Rocky Mountains than the Coast Range. Once home to the Nez Perce Indians, it is now populated with bighorn sheep, mountain goats, elk, mule deer, black bear, wolverines, fishers, and other species that thrive in cold conditions. It is popular with backpackers and horseback riders for its high meadows, alpine lakes, and sweeping vistas, but many of the lower-elevation drainages are off the beaten path, and some of them have no paths at all. In this sort of wilderness area, most recreational visitors flock to the areas of the most spectacular beauty, leaving the enclosing forests that cloak the valleys and offer no panoramic views to the wildlife and those who are purposefully seeking places no one else cares about.

Nearest Cities: Joseph, Halfway, Medical Springs, La Grande, Baker City

Hells Canyon Wilderness/Hells Canyon National Recreation Area

Not far to the northeast of Eagle Cap Wilderness, another outstanding area of roadless lands can be found in the Hells Canyon region, in the far corner of the state along the border with Idaho. The largest roadless section here is 563,000 acres, consisting of a mix of designated wilderness area, National Recreation Area land, BLM land, and Wild and Scenic River corridor land. The entire Hells Canyon National Recreation Area totals 652,488 acres.

Hells Canyon, which is over 8000 feet deep in some places, vies with California's Kings Canyon as the deepest canyon in North America. (As mentioned in the section on California earlier in this chapter, there is some dispute as to whether Kings Canyon or Hells Canyon is truly the deepest canyon, but by measurement from the lowest to the highest points, Kings Canyon is deeper by almost 200 feet.) Deepest in North America or not, Hells Canyon is one impressive gorge. The Snake River twists through the bottom of it in a series of raging rapids at elevations as low as 800 feet, while nearby high points along the rim tower over 9000 feet.

These huge elevation changes in a compact area make this one of the most diverse areas in the Northwest in terms of plant and animal species. Big game includes elk, mountain goats, bighorn sheep, moose, and mule deer. Black bear and mountain lions are common, and there have been reports of grizzly sightings, though the last grizzly recorded killed in the area was in 1937. Hunting for small game, from rabbits to grouse, waterfowl, and other birds, should also be productive, as there are some species to be found in each type of habitat in the area. With a network of some 900 miles of trails in the Hells Canyon National Recreation Area, there are plenty of routes to remote parts of this wild canyon country.

Nearest Cities: *Imnaha, Joseph, Halfway, La Grande (OR), Grangeville (ID)*

Washington

The state of Washington is a paradise for outdoor recreation, with first-class backcountry areas for everything from backpacking and mountaineering to skiing, sailing, and wilderness sea kayaking. Washington has outstanding old-growth forests, 3026 miles of tidal shoreline, and some of the steepest, most rugged mountains in North America. As in Oregon to the south, the coastal region of Washington, despite its latitude, is a relatively warm and very wet area due to the effects of the Pacific Ocean and the high Cascade Range that divides it from the drier eastern part of the state.

Unlike Oregon, Washington has many expansive tracts of roadless land to rival the largest such areas in the West. Washington has the highest percentage of its land in designated wilderness protection and national parks in the lower 48 states, and three of the wilderness areas completely within its borders are larger than one million acres. Like Oregon and California, Washington has its share of rugged, rockbound Pacific Ocean coast, but unlike those states, it also has a huge network of protected estuarine waterways and islands that offer many opportunities for travel by water and are navigable by practically every type of watercraft.

Olympic Mountains/Olympic Peninsula

One of the largest roadless areas in Washington is located in the middle of the Olympic Peninsula in an isolated coastal range called the Olympic Mountains. This roadless area, which includes 860,000 acres of designated wilderness within the boundaries of Olympic National Park, comes to over a million acres when the surrounding backcountry of Olympic National Forest is included. The western parts of this

┌───┐
│ **CENTRAL AND EASTERN WASHINGTON**
│ The first-rate bug-out areas described in this chapter are all in northern Wash-
│ ington, but there are also promising locations and smaller areas of pristine wilder-
│ ness in other parts of the state. The entire Cascade Range all the way south to
│ the Columbia River at the state line with Oregon is a series of national forests and
│ parks, including Mt. Rainier National Park. The Columbia River itself is the largest riv-
│ er in the Pacific Northwest, and with its tributaries and man-made reservoirs offers
│ thousands of miles of waterways. Eastern Washington has additional areas of wil-
│ derness ranging from deserts to mountain forests, including the Selkirk Mountains
│ in the northeast corner of the state and the Blue Mountains in the southeast.
└───┘

area receive up to 140 inches of rainfall per year and support magnifi-
cent temperate rain forests with giant trees over 8 feet in diameter and
nearly 300 feet tall. The understory of these cathedral forests of Western
red cedars, Sitka spruce, Douglas fir, Western hemlock, and others is a
rich mat of moisture-loving plants such as ferns and mosses. Wildlife in
this area includes large numbers of Roosevelt elk, blacktail deer, black
bear, mountain goats, and isolated species such as the Olympic mar-
mot and the Olympic giant salamander. Approximately 366,000 acres
within the park boundaries are old-growth forest. None of the roads
that enter Olympic National Park penetrate far into the interior mountains. The only way to reach much of this area is on foot or horseback
on a network of trails, but there are still many areas with no trails that
are even more remote.

Another part of Olympic National Park that is separate from the interior mountain region of the peninsula is a long stretch of wilderness
coast that is unique in the United States. It the longest stretch of mainland coastline in the lower 48 states that is totally undeveloped and
can only be traveled by hiking on foot or, when sea conditions permit,
traveling alongshore in boats such as sea kayaks. This part of the park
takes in 73 miles of shoreline, with a narrow band of designated wilderness parkland along most of the way, offering numerous opportunities for bugging out to secluded pocket beaches hidden at the base of
the rugged coastal cliffs. There several access points to various parts

of this coast, but most recreational hikers do not venture to the most remote locales. Good hideouts could be found here, with access to the ocean and all the resources it contains, but it is an area with a large tidal range, and beach campers must be careful to avoid getting trapped at the base of a cliff by a rising tide.

Nearest Cities: *Ozette, Queets, Port Angeles, Port Townsend, Shelton, Seattle*

Puget Sound and San Juan Islands

Northwestern Washington's network of protected yet navigable inland waterways and the islands within them are one of the outstanding features of the West Coast, and are just the beginning of the great Inside Passage that continues northward behind a chain of islands all the way into southeastern Alaska. This is a boater's paradise of deep channels, hidden coves, and forested island shores with countless hideaways only reachable by boat. What makes this area so special is the intricacy of the myriad routes here, especially for small boats that can operate near shore. Clear, clean water, abundant marine life, and many protected and undeveloped areas of shoreline combine to offer an impressive array of options for bugging out by boat in this part of Washington. Some of these areas are not far from the urban areas of Seattle and Tacoma, and long fingers of the Puget Sound reach far to the south of the entrance to the estuary, offering many route options away from the cities. North of the sound, where the more open waters of the Strait of Juan de Fuca meet the Strait of Georgia, the San Juan Islands offer even more options for those bugging out on the water.

The San Juan Islands Archipelago straddles the U.S. and Canadian border with some 175 islands large enough to have names and hundreds more smaller islets and rocks visible at low tide. Of these islands, only about 30 are inhabited year-round, by some 15,000 residents. Despite the popularity of tourism among the best parts of the San Juan Islands, and ever-increasing numbers of posted signs on private property, anyone operating out of a small cruising boat or vessel such as a kayak with the flexibility to stay on the move will find good foraging and good hideouts here in times of crisis. An added bonus is the option to continue north into Canada and the gateway to one of the wildest and biggest coastal wildernesses in the world—the Inside Passage to Alaska.

Nearest Cities: *Tacoma, Seattle, Port Townsend, Anacortes, Bellingham*

North Cascades/Glacier Peak Wilderness Area

East of Puget Sound and the corridor of urban development that runs from Tacoma through Seattle and most of the way to Vancouver, British Colombia, the topography quickly changes to the knife-edge ridges and sharp, snow-capped peaks of the Cascade Range. Two roadless areas exceeding 1.5 million acres and many others of several hundred thousand acres in extent can be found in this most rugged part of Washington. These huge tracts of mountain wilderness are made up of both national forest and national park lands, including the Mt. Baker–Snoqualmie National Forest, the Okanogan National Forest, and North Cascades National Park. Outside of designated wilderness areas, there are many more expansive tracts of roadless forests that have long been at the center of controversy between wilderness advocates and proponents of Forest Service timber harvesting operations.

Typical of the wildest parts of the North Cascades ecosystem is the 576,600-acre Glacier Peak Wilderness Area. Centered around the 10,541-foot volcanic cone of Glacier Peak, this wilderness area contains both high ice and deep old-growth evergreen forests of firs, hemlocks, spruces, and cedars. It is home to a large variety of big mammals, such as blacktail deer, mountain goats, wolverines, gray wolves, black bears, and even a few grizzly bears.

The 684,000-acre North Cascades National Park is another large expanse of public lands in this part of Washington's Cascades. Despite the fact that it is managed as a national park with the usual restrictions that implies, it is a huge area with 93 percent of its acreage designated as wilderness, making it a viable bug-out option in this northernmost part of the range on the U.S. side of the border. As in other parts of the North Cascades, these mountains are home to wolves and grizzly bears that have crossed over from Canada and reestablished breeding populations here. Much of this border is so remote and impossible to patrol that a survivalist on the move could cross it with as much impunity as the wolf or bear.

Nearest Cities: *Darrington, Rockport, Diablo, Everett, Bellingham*

Pasayten Wilderness Area

Located to the east of North Cascades National Park, on the drier side of the range and also bordering Canada, is another great roadless area of nearly 1.2 million acres in Okanogan National Forest. The centerpiece of this area is the designated Pasayten Wilderness, which takes in 529,607 acres. This wilderness area includes 50 miles of the Canadian border and contains everything from sheer-walled canyons to peaks of rocks and ice and lower-elevation evergreen forests. It is home to deer, mountain goats, bighorn sheep, moose, grizzly bears, and wolves. The Pacific Crest Trail reaches the north end of its route at the border here, after winding for 32 miles through the Pasayten. Two Canadian provincial parks extend the area of roadless, protected wilderness well into the wilds of British Colombia. South of the wilderness boundaries, many areas of the Okanogan National Forest offer potential bug-out locations in places that can be reached by primitive roads and ATV trails.

Nearest Cities: *Nighthawk, Winthrop, Okanogan, Ellisford, Wenatchee*

APPENDIX A:
BUG-OUT BAG CHECKLISTS

This checklist includes the items I would take in a bug-out situation in which I had to head out into the wilds of the lower 48 states *on foot*. This list will need to be adjusted for high elevations or northern winters. Using a vehicle, boat, or other means of carrying gear would allow much more flexibility.

BUG-OUT BAG AND CLOTHING

- ❏ Kelty internal frame backpack
- ❏ Jansport fanny pack (for critical survival items)
- ❏ Lightweight mesh bag (for wild food gathering and carrying)
- ❏ Leather and Gore-Tex waterproof hiking boots (will be wearing)
- ❏ Neoprene river shoes with heavy-duty hiking soles
- ❏ Moisture-wicking inner socks (2 pair; will be wearing additional pair)
- ❏ Wool outer socks (2 pair; will be wearing additional pair)
- ❏ Wool watch cap
- ❏ Boonie hat or Tilley sun hat (will be wearing)
- ❏ Bandanas (3)
- ❏ Ripstop BDU pants (2 pair; will be wearing one pair)
- ❏ Synthetic long underwear (2 pair)
- ❏ Gore-Tex rain pants
- ❏ Heavy-duty belt
- ❏ T-shirts (2; will be wearing one under outer shirt)
- ❏ Long underwear shirt (1)
- ❏ Polar fleece long-sleeve (1)
- ❏ Cotton-canvas long-sleeve (2; will be wearing one)

- ❐ Gore-Tex parka
- ❐ Gloves or mittens (depending on climate and season)
- ❐ Camouflage poncho (doubles as small tarp, and useful to hide unattended gear)

SHELTER AND FIRE

- ❐ Hennessey camping hammock
- ❐ 550 paracord (100 feet)
- ❐ Synthetic sleeping bag rated for the climate and season
- ❐ Bic disposable butane lighters (6 or more)
- ❐ FireSteel Scout (2)
- ❐ Fire sticks (12-pack)
- ❐ Small pack of cotton balls soaked in Vaseline (tinder)

FOOD AND WATER

- ❐ 3-day supply of Mainstay or Datrex lifeboat rations, or MREs
- ❐ 1-gallon Ziploc bag of high-energy trail mix (dried fruits, nuts, and seeds)
- ❐ Power Bars or other high-protein bar food (6)
- ❐ Beef jerky (several small packages)
- ❐ 1-gallon Ziploc bag of whole-grain oatmeal
- ❐ Small quantity of Zatarains or Tony's Cajun seasoning (renders anything edible)
- ❐ 1-quart Nalgene bottles, pre-filled with drinking water (2 minimum)
- ❐ Polar Pure Water Disinfectant (2 bottles)
- ❐ Aquamira Frontier filter straw (1)

HUNTING AND FISHING

- ❐ Take-down .22 rifle
- ❐ .22 ammo (200 rounds minimum)
- ❐ Ruger GP 100 .357 magnum revolver (4-inch barrel)
- ❐ Holster for revolver to carry in accessible location
- ❐ Speed loaders for revolver
- ❐ Winchester Trapper .357 magnum carbine (optional, depending on situation)

- ❐ .357 magnum ammo (100 rounds)
- ❐ Selection of assorted fishhooks for bream up to large catfish
- ❐ Spool of monofilament line
- ❐ Spool of trot line for drop hooks
- ❐ Pre-made wire snares for small game

TOOLS

- ❐ Quality 18- to 24-inch machete with sheath
- ❐ Cold Steel XL Voyager (5-inch folding Bowie)
- ❐ Leatherman Wave multitool
- ❐ Small mill file
- ❐ Diamond sharpener
- ❐ Hand-bearing compass
- ❐ Casio Pathfinder PAW 1500 watch with electronic compass
- ❐ Topo-map-enabled GPS receiver
- ❐ Stainless-steel 4-quart cooking pot (with lid, handle removed)
- ❐ Stainless-steel spoon
- ❐ Sewing needles

MISCELLANEOUS

- ❐ Map of bug-out location and alternatives, laminated or sealed in Ziploc bag
- ❐ Insect repellant with DEET
- ❐ Small tube of SPF 50 sunblock
- ❐ Sunglasses with retainer and case (if traveling by water or open country)
- ❐ Heavy-duty Dacron sailmaker's thread (for sewing repairs)
- ❐ Basic first aid supplies, bandages, and antibiotic ointment
- ❐ Extractor Snakebite Kit
- ❐ Cortisone cream (for poison ivy, etc.)
- ❐ Benadryl (for bee and wasp stings)
- ❐ Epipen (for severe allergic reactions to stings)
- ❐ Imodium (anti-diarrheal)
- ❐ Ibuprofen pain capsules
- ❐ Field guide to edible plants (region-specific)
- ❐ Passport/driver's license

- ❐ Cash, plus gold or silver coins
- ❐ Toothbrush
- ❐ Small bottle of concentrated antibacterial soap
- ❐ Small amount of tightly packed toilet paper
- ❐ Comb
- ❐ LED version of the Mini Maglight, with extra AA batteries (or small LED headlamp that runs on AA or AAA batteries)
- ❐ Small quantity of duct tape
- ❐ Small bottle of gun oil or multipurpose oil
- ❐ Boresnake gun-cleaning tool of appropriate caliber(s)

This completes what I consider the bare minimum bug-out bag checklist. What follows are sub-lists of additional items if you have the means to carry more stuff or if you utilize caching techniques described in Chapter Three. The quantities of these items can be adjusted depending on the type of transportation you are using. Many of them add to your margin of safety and increase your comfort level in a difficult situation.

OPTIONAL CLOTHING
- ❐ Extra boots, plus camp shoes or moccasins
- ❐ Extra socks
- ❐ Extra long underwear
- ❐ Extra shirts and pants
- ❐ Camo pants and shirt or jacket for more effective hunting once you're out of town
- ❐ Additional winter clothing, wool sweaters, insulated parkas, etc.

OPTIONAL SHELTER AND FIRE
- ❐ Self-inflating sleeping pad (like a Therm-a-Rest)
- ❐ Inflatable pillow
- ❐ Larger tarp or additional small tarps
- ❐ Expedition-grade tent (depending on climate and season)
- ❐ Larger quantity and variety of fire-starting devices
- ❐ Larger quantity of pre-made tinder or fire-starter sticks

OPTIONAL FOOD AND WATER

❑ Larger supply of pure water in jerry cans, gallon jugs, or sealed bottles

❑ Water purification filter with spare filters and maintenance parts

❑ Reverse-osmosis desalinator (if operating in saltwater areas)

❑ Supply of dry provisions such as rice, pasta, beans, and cornmeal

❑ Pancake mix, granola, oatmeal, dried fruits, nuts, and seeds

❑ Larger supply of beef jerky

❑ Canned tuna, corned beef, and other high-protein canned goods

❑ Salt, pepper, and other seasonings

❑ Honey, powdered milk, coffee, tea, hot chocolate (great for morale)

❑ Backpacking stove (multi-fuel, propane, or alcohol)

❑ Stove fuel

OPTIONAL HUNTING AND FISHING GEAR

❑ Rifle for large game (if not already carrying the carbine mentioned in the basic list)

❑ Larger supply of ammo for all hunting weapons

❑ Take-down recurve hunting bow (if already proficient in archery)

❑ Spare bowstring

❑ Supply of arrows

❑ Bow fishing reel and fishing arrows

❑ Tools and supplies to repair and make more arrows

❑ Larger selection of snares, for small game up to deer-sized game

❑ Larger selection of fish hooks, line and other tackle

❑ Take-down rod and reel

❑ Bait traps, nets

OPTIONAL SELF-DEFENSE

❐ Magazine-fed semi-automatic rifle (AK-47, AR-15, FAL, etc.)
❐ Spare magazines for above, fully-loaded (4 or more, plus additional ammo)
❐ Optional high-capacity semi-automatic pistol (Glock, etc.)
❐ Spare magazines and ammo for pistol
❐ Additional firearm cleaning tools and supplies
❐ Critical spare parts
❐ Large canister of pepper spray in belt holster (bear-repellant variety)

OPTIONAL TOOLS

❐ Full-sized axe
❐ Folding saw
❐ Larger mill file for sharpening
❐ Larger assortment of various sizes of rope and cordage
❐ Extra cookware, especially a skillet, and coffee or tea pot
❐ Additional utensils and drinking cups
❐ Fillet knife
❐ Additional sewing and leatherworking tools and supplies

MISCELLANEOUS NICE THINGS TO HAVE

❐ Quality pair of binoculars
❐ Small, flexible solar panel with adaptors for charging different devices
❐ Rechargeable batteries for flashlights, radios, GPS, etc.
❐ Shortwave radio receiver
❐ High-intensity 3-cell lithium flashlight (Surefire or similar)
❐ Additional LED flashlights, headlamps, or area lights
❐ Reading material (field guides, survival manuals, etc.)
❐ Portable entertainment (Ipod, or similar with e-books, music, etc., if carrying an adaptor for solar charging)
❐ Supply of emergency candles
❐ Supply of one-gallon Ziploc bags
❐ Additional duct tape
❐ Extra sun screen

- ❏ Extra insect repellent
- ❏ Extra first-aid supplies
- ❏ Extra antibacterial soap
- ❏ Extra personal items (toothpaste, razors, mirror, nail clippers, etc.)
- ❏ Toilet paper
- ❏ Towel

ESSENTIAL EXTRAS IF BUGGING OUT BY BOAT:

- ❏ PFD (personal flotation device) for every person on board
- ❏ Foul-weather jacket and bib overalls (if traveling offshore)
- ❏ Dry bags or waterproof boxes for critical gear
- ❏ Handheld or fixed-mount VHF two-way radio (depending on type of vessel)
- ❏ Shortwave or SSB radio for receiving weather forecasts
- ❏ Chart-enabled GPS with pre-loaded nautical charts of the region
- ❏ Marine binoculars with bearing compass
- ❏ Flares and other Coast Guard–required signaling devices
- ❏ Fire extinguishers (2 or more on vessels with electrical systems and/or engine or stove fuel)
- ❏ Spare paddle or oars for canoes, kayaks, and other small boats
- ❏ Ground tackle (anchors and rodes) of adequate size and number for the vessel
- ❏ Mooring lines, bow painters, or other lines for securing the vessel to shore
- ❏ Bailer, bucket, or bilge pump for removing water
- ❏ Marine grade sealant, epoxy, and other hull-repair supplies and materials
- ❏ Spare parts and tools to maintain and repair engine, if any
- ❏ Spare parts and tools to maintain and repair sails and rigging, if any
- ❏ Large supply of fuel for stove if the boat is a self-contained live-aboard
- ❏ Additional fishing gear, trolling hooks, lures, etc.
- ❏ Mask, fins, snorkel, and spearfishing gear if in coastal waters

APPENDIX B:
SOURCES FOR MAPS &
RECOMMENDED EQUIPMENT

DeLorme *(state topographical atlases, digital maps)*
Two DeLorme Drive
P.O. Box 298
Yarmouth, ME 04096
800-561-5105
www.delorme.com

United States Geological Survey (USGS)
USGS National Center
12201 Sunrise Valley Drive
Reston, VA 20192
888-275-8747
www.usgs.gov

USGS Earth Explorer
edcn.sl7.cr.usgs.gov/EarthExplorer

Digital Data Services, Inc. *(direct source for USGS quad maps)*
10920 West Alameda
Suite 200
Lakewood, CO 80226
866-337-7226
www.usgsquads.com

NOAA Nautical Charts *(electronic and print-on-demand navigation charts)*
www.nauticalcharts.noaa.gov/staff/charts.htm

Google Maps
maps.google.com

Google Earth
earth.google.com

Bing Maps *(different imagery from Google Maps)*
bing.com/maps

NASA World Wind *(similar to Google Earth)*
worldwind.arc.nasa.gov/download.html

MapQuest
mapquest.com

Garmin *(GPS receivers, electronic nautical charts, and topographical maps)*
800-800-1020
www.garmin.com

Casio Pathfinder
800-836-8580
pathfinder.casio.com

Kelty Backpacks
6235 Lookout Road
Boulder, CO 80301
866-349-7225
www.kelty.com

JanSport Backpacks
2011 Farallon Drive
San Leandro, CA 94577
510-614-4000
www.jansport.com

Hennessey Hammocks
637 Southwind Road
Galiano Island, BC V0N 1P0
Canada
888-539-2930
hennessyhammock.com

FireSteel
firesteel.com

Polar Pure Water Disinfectant
408-867-4576
www.polarequipment.com

Aquamira Frontier Filter
Aquamira Technologies, Inc.
1411 Meador Avenue
Bellingham, WA 98229
360-306-5586
www.aquamira.com

Nalgene Water Bottles
Nalge Nunc International Corporation
Outdoor Products Division
75 Panorama Creek Drive
Rochester, NY 14625
800-625-4327
www.nalgene-outdoor.com

Sturm, Ruger & Co., Inc. *(firearms)*
411 Sunapee Street
Newport, NH 03773
603-865-2442
www.ruger.com

Marlin Firearms
100 Kenna Drive
North Haven, CT 06473
203-239-5621
www.marlinfirearms.com

Henry Repeating Arms Company
59 East 1st Street
Bayonne, NJ 07002
201-858-4400
www.henryrepeating.com

Winchester Repeating Arms
275 Winchester Avenue
Morgan, UT 84050
www.winchesterguns.com

Glock, Inc.
6000 Highlands Parkway
Smyrna, GA 30082
770-432-1202
www.glock.com

Cold Steel, Inc. *(knives)*
3036-A Seaborg Ave.
Ventura, CA 93003
800-225-4716
www.coldsteel.com

Leatherman Tool Group, Inc.
12106 NE Ainsworth Circle
Portland, OR 97220-9001
800-847-8665
www.leatherman.com

BIBLIOGRAPHY/
RECOMMENDED READING

WILDERNESS SURVIVAL

Alloway, David. *Desert Survival Skills*. University of Texas Press, 2000.

Benson, Ragner. *Survival Poaching*. Paladin Press, 1980.

Brockman, C. Frank. *Trees of North America*. Golden Press, 1986.

Brown, Tom. *Tom Brown's Guide to Edible and Medicinal Plants*. Berkley Books, 1985.

Brown, Tom. *Tom Brown's Guide to Living with the Earth*. Berkley Books, 1986.

Brown, Tom. *Tom Brown's Guide to Wilderness Survival*. Berkley Books, 1987.

Craighead, Frank C. *How to Survive on Land and Sea*. United States Naval Institute, 1984.

Forgey, William. *Wilderness Medicine, Beyond First Aid*, 5th Edition. Globe Pequot, 1999.

Gibbons, Euell. *Euell Gibbons' Beachcomber's Handbook*. David McKay Co., 1967.

Gibbons, Euell. *Stalking the Wild Asparagus*. Alan C. Hood & Co., 1962.

McCann, John D. *Build the Perfect Survival Kit*. Krause Publications, 2005.

McNab, Chris. *Special Forces Survival Guide: Wilderness Survival Skills from the World's Most Elite Military Units*. Ulysses Press, 2008.

McPherson, John and Geri McPherson. *Ultimate Guide to Wilderness Living: Surviving with Nothing But Your Bare Hands and What You Find in the Woods*. Ulysses Press, 2008.

Nestor, Tony. *Desert Survival Tips, Tricks, & Skills*. Diamond Creek Press, 2003.

Nestor, Tony. *The Modern Hunter-Gatherer: A Practical Guide to Living off the Land*. Diamond Creek Press, 2009.

Olsen, Larry Dean. *Outdoor Survival Skills*. Brigham Young University Press, 1976.

Peterson, Lee Allen. *Edible Wild Plants: The Peterson Field Guide Series, No. 23*. Houghton Mifflin Company, 1977.

Thayer, Samuel. *The Forager's Harvest: A Guide to Identifying, Harvesting, and Preparing Edible Wild Plants*. Forager's Harvest Press, 2006.

URBAN AND DISASTER SURVIVAL

Layton, Peggy. *Emergency Food Storage & Survival Handbook: Everything You Need to Know to Keep Your Family Safe in a Crisis*. Three Rivers Press, 2002.

Lundin, Cody. *When All Hell Breaks Loose: Stuff You Need to Survive When Disaster Strikes*. Gibbs Smith, 2007.

Maxwell, Jane, Carol Thuman, and David Werner. *Where There Is No Doctor: A Village Health Care Handbook*. Hesperian Foundation, 1992.

Rawles, James Wesley. *How to Survive the End of the World as We Know It: Tactics, Techniques, and Technologies for Uncertain Times*. Plume, 2009.

Stein, Matthew. *When Technology Fails (Revised & Expanded): A Manual for Self-Reliance, Sustainability, and Surviving the Long Emergency*. Chelsea Green Publishing, 2008.

BUG-OUT VEHICLES AND BOATS

Adams, Carl. *The Essential Guide to Dual Sport Motorcycling: Everything You Need to Buy, Ride, and Enjoy the World's Most Versatile Motorcycles*. Whitehorse Press, 2008.

Allen, Jim. *Four-Wheeler's Bible: 2nd Edition*. Motorbooks, 2009.

Alvord, Douglas. *Beachcruising*. International Marine Publishing, 1992.

Burch, David. *Fundamentals of Kayak Navigation*. Pacific Search Press, 1987.

Cardwell, J. D. *Sailing Big on a Small Sailboat.* Sheridan House, 1997.

Casper, Steve. *ATVs: Everything You Need to Know.* Motorbooks, 2006.

Casey, Don. *Sensible Cruising: The Thoreau Approach.* International Marine/Ragged Mountain Press, 1990.

Delong, Brad. *4-Wheel Freedom: The Art of Off-Road Driving.* Paladin Press, 1997.

Donaldson, Doug. *Bicycling Magazine's Guide to Bike Touring: Everything You Need to Know to Travel Anywhere on a Bike.* Rodale Books, 2005.

Dowd, John. *Sea Kayaking: A Manual for Long-Distance Touring.* Douglas and McIntyre LTD., 1986.

Gray, Michael E. and Linda E. Gray. *Auto Upkeep: Basic Car Care, Maintenance, and Repair.* Rolling Hills Publishing, 2007.

Hutchinson, Derek C. *Derek C. Hutchinson's Expedition Kayaking.* Globe Pequot Press, 1999.

Jacobson, Cliff. *Expedition Canoeing, 20th Anniversary Edition: A Guide to Canoeing Wild Rivers in North America.* Falcon, 2005.

Little, Ida and Michael Walsh. *Beachcruising and Coastal Camping.* Wescott Cove Publishing Company, 1992.

Lovett, Richard. *The Essential Touring Cyclist: A Complete Guide for the Bicycle Traveler, Second Edition.* International Marine/Ragged Mountain Press, 2000.

Mason, Bill. *Song of the Paddle: An Illustrated Guide to Wilderness Camping.* Firefly Books, 2004.

McKnew, Ed. *The Boat Buyer's Guide to Trailerable Fishing Boats: Pictures, Floorplans, Specifications, Reviews, and Prices for More Than 600 Boats, 18 to 27 Feet Long.* International Marine/Ragged Mountain Press, 2006.

Vigor, John. *Twenty Small Sailboats to Take You Anywhere.* Paradise Cay Publications, 1999.

Wicks, Robert. *Adventure Riding Techniques: The Essential Guide to All the Skills You Need for Off-Road Adventure Riding.* Haynes Publishing, 2009.

WILDERNESS TRAVEL

Back, Joe. *Horses, Hitches and Rocky Trails.* Johnson Books, 1994.

Burns, Bob. *Wilderness Navigation: Finding Your Way Using Map, Compass, Altimeter & GPS.* Mountaineers Books, 2004.

Chesbro, Michael. *Wilderness Evasion.* Paladin Press, 2002.

Curtis, Rick. *The Backpacker's Field Manual: A Comprehensive Guide to Mastering Backcountry Skills.* Three Rivers Press, 1998.

Daugherty, Stanlynn. *Packing With Llamas.* Juniper Ridge Press, 1999.

Elser, Smoke. *Packin' in on Mules and Horses.* Mountain Press Publishing Company, 1987.

Fletcher, Colin. *The Complete Walker.* Knopf, 2002.

Hinch, Stephen W. *Outdoor Navigation With GPS: Hiking, Geocaching, Canoeing, Kayaking, Fishing, Outdoor Photography, Backpacking, Mountain Biking.* Wilderness Press, 2007.

Johnson, Mark. *The Ultimate Desert Handbook: A Manual for Desert Hikers, Campers and Travelers.* International Marine/Ragged Mountain Press, 2003.

Kesselheim, Alan. *Trail Food: Drying and Cooking Food for Backpacking and Paddling.* International Marine/Ragged Mountain Press, 1998.

Mueser, Roland. *Long-Distance Hiking: Lessons from the Appalachian Trail.* International Marine/Ragged Mountain Press, 1997.

Rutstrum, Calvin. *The New Way of the Wilderness.* Collier Books, 1973.

FIREARMS

Boatman, Robert H. *Living with Glocks: The Complete Guide to the New Standard in Combat Handguns.* Paladin Press, 2002.

House, James E. *The Gun Digest Book of .22 Rimfire: Rifles, Pistols, Ammunition.* Gun Digest Books, 2005.

Rementer, Stephen R. *Essential Guide to Handguns: Firearm Instruction for Personal Defense and Protection.* Looseleaf Law Publications, 2005.

Shideler, Dan. *Gun Digest 2010.* Krause Publications, 2009.

Simpson, Layne. *Rifles and Cartridges for Large Game: From Deer to Bear—Advice on the Choice of a Rifle.* Safari Press, 2003.

Tappan, Mel. *Survival Guns.* Janus Press, 1977.

White, Mark. *Ultimate Ruger 10/22 Manual and User's Guide.* Paladin Press, 2000.

REGIONAL GUIDES AND BUG-OUT LOCATIONS

Churchill, James. *Paddling the Boundary Waters and Voyageurs National Park.* Falcon, 2003.

Clifford, Frank. *The Backbone of the World: A Portrait of the Vanishing West Along the Continental Divide.* Broadway, 2003.

Crowder, David A. *Google Earth For Dummies.* For Dummies, 2007.

Estes, Chuck, Elizabeth Carter, and Byron Almquist. *Canoe Trails of the Deep South.* Menasha Ridge Press, 1991.

Evans, Mari-Lynn, Robert Santelli, and Holly George-Warren. *The Appalachians: America's First and Last Frontier.* Random House, 2004.

Foreman, Dave, and Howie Wolke. *The Big Outside: A Descriptive Inventory of the Big Wilderness Areas of the United States,* Revised Edition. Harmony Books, 1992.

Go, Benedict. *Pacific Crest Trail Data Book: Mileages, Landmarks, Facilities, Resupply Data, and Essential Trail Information for the Entire Pacific Crest Trail, from Mexico to Canada.* Wilderness Press, 2005.

Hansen, Gunnar. *Islands at the Edge of Time: A Journey to America's Barrier Islands.* Island Press, 1993.

Herndon, Ernest. *Canoeing Louisiana.* University Press of Mississippi, 2003.

Herndon, Ernest. *Canoeing Mississippi.* University Press of Mississippi, 2001

Hinchman, Sandra. *Hiking the Southwest's Canyon Country.* Mountaineers Books, 2004.

Howorth, Peter. *Foraging Along the California Coast: The Complete Illustrated Handbook.* Capra Press, 1986.

Jenkins, Peter. *Along the Edge of America.* Mariner Books, 1997.

Kettlewell, John J. and Leslie Kettlewell. *Intracoastal Waterway Chartbook: Norfolk, Virginia, to Miami, Florida*. International Marine/Ragged Mountain Press, 2002.

Laine, Barbara. *Little Known Southwest: Outdoor Destinations Beyond the Parks*. Mountaineers Books, 2001.

Marchand, Peter. *North Woods: An Inside Look at the Nature of Forests in the Northeast*. Appalachian Mountain Club Books, 1994.

Mass, Leslie. *Appalachian Trail Thru-Hikers' Companion*. Appalachian Trail Conservancy, 2009.

Mohlenbrock, Robert H. *This Land: A Guide to Central National Forests*. University of California Press, 2006.

Mohlenbrock, Robert H. *This Land: A Guide to Eastern National Forests*. University of California Press, 2006.

Mohlenbrock, Robert H. *This Land: A Guide to Western National Forests*. University of California Press, 2006.

Molloy, Johnny. *A Canoeing & Kayaking Guide to Florida*. Menasha Ridge Press, 2007.

Molloy, Johnny. *50 Hikes in the Ozarks: Walks, Hikes and Backpacks in the Mountains, Wildernesses and Geological Wonders of Arkansas and Missouri*. Countryman, 2008.

Morton, Julia F. *Wild Plants for Survival in South Florida*. Fairchild Tropical Garden, 1982.

National Audubon Society. *National Audubon Society Field Guide to North American Wildflowers: Eastern Region*. Knopf, 2001.

National Audubon Society, *National Audubon Society Field Guide to North American Wildflowers: Western Region*. Knopf, 2001.

Parr, Barry. *Hiking the Sierra Nevada*. Falcon, 2005.

Rogers, Hiram. *Exploring the Black Hills and Badlands: A Guide for Hikers, Cross-Country Skiers, & Mountain Bikers*. Johnson Books, 1999.

Scherer, Migael. *A Cruising Guide to Puget Sound and the San Juan Islands: Olympia to Port Angeles*, International Marine/Ragged Mountain Press. 2004

Schueler, Donald G. *Adventuring Along the Gulf of Mexico: The Sierra Club Travel Guide to the Gulf Coast of the United States and Mexico from the Florida Keys to the Yucatan.* Sierra Club Books, 1986.

Young, Claiborne S. *Cruising Guide to the Northern Gulf Coast: Florida, Alabama, Mississippi, Louisiana.* Pelican Publishing Company, 1998.

GENERAL RELATED INTERESTS

Cook, Langdon. *Fat of the Land: Adventures of a 21st Century Forager.* Skipstone Press, 2009.

Corbett, Jim. *Goatwalking: A Guide to Wildland Living.* Penguin Books, 1991.

Forstchen, William R. *One Second After.* Forge Books, 2009.

Gonzales, Laurence, *Deep Survival: Who Lives, Who Dies, and Why.* W. W. Norton, 2004.

Horne, Jed. *Breach of Faith: Hurricane Katrina and the Near Death of a Great American City.* Random House Trade Paperbacks, 2008.

Krakauer, Jon. *Into the Wild.* Anchor Books, 1996.

Lee, Richard B. *The Cambridge Encyclopedia of Hunters and Gatherers.* Cambridge University Press, 2004.

McCarthy, Cormac. *The Road.* Vintage, 2006.

Miniter, Frank. *The Ultimate Man's Survival Guide: Rediscovering the Lost Art of Manhood.* Regnery Press, 2009.

North, Dick. *The Mad Trapper of Rat River: A True Story of Canada's Biggest Manhunt.* The Lyons Press, 2005.

Rawicz, Slavomir. *The Long Walk: The True Story of a Trek to Freedom.* The Lyons Press, 2006.

Rawles, James Wesley. *Patriots: A Novel of Survival in the Coming Collapse.* Ulysses Press, 2009.

Schuster, Henry. *Hunting Eric Rudolph.* Berkley, 2005.

INDEX

PHOTO CREDITS

ABOUT THE AUTHOR

Scott B. Williams has been exploring wild places and working on perfecting his wilderness skills for most of his life, beginning with hunting and fishing while growing up in Mississippi. His adventures have included thousands of miles of solo long-distance sea kayaking journeys both in the U.S. and abroad, as well as extended wilderness canoeing and backpacking trips in every region of the U.S. He has written about his experiences in many articles and four previous books. His other interests include boat building, sailing, and photography. He maintains several blogs related to these subjects, as well as *Bug Out Survival* (www.bugoutsurvival.com). More information can be found on his main website, www.scottbwilliams.com.